KU-570-668

Heavenly Serbia

Heavenly Serbia

From Myth to Genocide

Branimir Anzulovic

HURST & COMPANY
London

Published in the United Kingdom by
C. Hurst & Co. (Publishers) Ltd.,
38 King Street, London WC2E 8JZ

© 1999 by Branimir Anzulovic
All rights reserved

Printed in the U.S.A.
ISBN 1-85065-342-9

To the memory of my mother

It is not yet common practice today to link the current social and national habitus of a nation to its so-called "history," and especially to the state-formation process it has experienced. Many people seem to have the unspoken opinion that "What happened in the twelfth, fifteenth or eighteenth centuries is past—what has it got to do with me?" In reality, though, the contemporary problems of a group are crucially influenced by their earlier fortunes. . . . Perhaps it may have a cathartic effect if the relationship between past and present is seen in this way, and people may, through understanding their social development, find a new understanding of themselves.

—*Norbert Elias*

Contents

Acknowledgments

I wish to recognize the benefit I derived from discussions with Alan F. D. Potter, as well as with E. Wayles Browne, Philip J. Cohen, Daniele Conversi, Roy Gutman, Nenad Moačanin, Ivo Rendić-Miočević, Katherine J. Rosich, James J. Sadkovich, Ivan Slamnig, and Aleksandar Štulhofer. I also thank other friends and colleagues whose advice, though less extensive, was also valuable.

I also want to express my gratitude to the Library of Congress in Washington, D.C., the Library of the University of Illinois at Urbana-Champaign, and their staffs.

Thanks to the Tošo Dabac Archive (Zagreb) for permission to use the picture of Saint Merkourios from the Gračanica Monastery in Kosovo.

Thanks to the Cambridge University Press for permission to quote from D. H. Low (trans.), *The Ballads of Marko Kraljević.*

xi

A Note on Pronunciation, Transliteration, and Translation

In Serbian and Croatian,

c	is pronounced like	'ts' in *cats*
č		'ch' in *chop*
ć		't' in *future*
đ		'j' in *jeans*, but softer
dž		'j' in *jeans*, but harder
j		'y' in *yes*
lj		'll' in *million*
nj		'ny' in *canyon*
š		'sh' in *shop*
ž		's' in *pleasure*

In a few cases, where most readers are already familiar with the transliteration, the latter is followed. Thus *Djilas instead of Đilas,* and *Tudjman* instead of *Tuđman.*

In direct quotations, the original spellings are preserved.

Translations of texts from non-English publications are mine, unless noted otherwise.

Introduction

An event from medieval Serbian history permeates present-day Serbian culture and politics. The 1389 battle with the Ottoman Turks on the Field of Kosovo still exerts a powerful influence on the Serbs, who see it as the pivotal moment of their plunge from a prosperous, sovereign medieval Balkan state to a stateless community within the Ottoman Empire, a condition that lasted until the nineteenth century. Even after Serbia became sovereign in 1878 and formed the core of the Yugoslav union in 1918, the memory of the 1389 battle remained vivid to the Serbs. Many observers have noticed the intensity of the memory of that distant battle; an anthropologist described its commemoration five and a half centuries later:

> In the hinterland of Dalmatia, especially in the Knin area, one can hear a kind of a moaning song, a primitive archaic intonation, consisting of the well-known doleful modulations of the sounds *o-oy*. . . . A few peasants, usually in a tavern, put their heads together and let their sorrowful modulations sound for hours, which constitutes a very grotesque sight for a European. And if they are asked why they sing like this, they give the answer: the lament for Kosovo![1]

The Swiss sociologist Norbert Elias points out that significant loss of power is always a traumatic event:

> It is a proven fact that the members of states and other social units which have lost their claim to a position of highest rank in the elimination struggles of their day often require a long time, even centuries, to come to terms with this changed situation and the

> consequent lowering of their self-esteem. And perhaps they never manage it. Britain in the recent past is a moving example of the difficulties a great power of the first rank has had in adjusting to its sinking to being a second- or third-class power.[2]

The loss of power was particularly traumatic for the Serbs. Not only did Serbia lose the status of a regional power, it completely disappeared as a political entity. The Serbs became second-class subjects of the sultan. This condition lasted from the fifteenth to the nineteenth century, during which time the Serbs assiduously cultivated myths of their great past and a great future.

Like other countries that reemerged as sovereign nation-states in the nineteenth century after a long period of foreign domination or political fragmentation, Serbia displayed a strong expansionist trend. In the words of George Kennan, "it was hard for people who had recently achieved so much, and this so suddenly, to know where to stop. Dreams of new glories to flow from new territorial expansion bemused many minds. The air was clouded by visions of a greater this or that: a 'greater Serbia,' a 'greater Bulgaria,' and so on."[3] Serbia's expansionist drive was evident in the outbreak of the two Balkan Wars in 1912–13, and although Serbia did not *cause* the First World War, the 1914 murder in Sarajevo it sponsored in order to destabilize the Austro-Hungarian monarchy (which stood in the way of its northward and westward expansion) provoked the conflict.

It would be an error to assume that the memory of the Serbian medieval empire necessarily led to the latest war for a Greater Serbia, but equally erroneous to deny a connection between the two. The myths and legends created soon after the Battle of Kosovo were reinvigorated by the Serbian intelligentsia to fan their compatriots' nationalist passions in the 1980s. The myths dealing with the loss of the medieval empire served to create a nationalist frenzy at the moment when the anticipated breakdown of the postwar order imposed by the communists and the Serbian domination of communist Yugoslavia's armed forces (the fourth largest in Europe) seemed to provide a unique opportunity for the realization of the central promise of Serbian national mythology—the creation of the Second Serbian Empire.

Myths have played an essential role in other twentieth-century genocidal campaigns as well. After the combination of fear, hatred, and imperialist ambitions fueled by myths and lies led to the Nazi and Fascist aggressions, a serious effort was made to understand the spread of these movements in terms of the type of persons who supported them. The best-known attempt of this kind yielded the F-scale (*F* stands for *Fascist*), which was supposed to identify the type of person who would likely follow a Hitler and engage in atrocities for him (little effort was made to check whether the scale would fit Stalin's followers).[4] The most researched sociopsychological topic of the 1950s, it succeeded at best in identifying only some traits of the followers of the Nazi movement, and eventually this model was abandoned.

One cannot explain a nation's violent expansionist adventure merely in terms of the psychological makeup of its members. Psychology cannot explain why a nation that has not displayed an excessive inclination to violence in its history can suddenly engage in large-scale massacres of entire segments of its population. Moreover, individuals and groups engaged in or advocating violence as protection against alleged conspiracies are present in some of the most democratic and prosperous nations. Biographies of most leaders and followers of genocidal movements do not reveal any particular psychological abnormalities.[5] They are characterized by banality rather than by demonism.

There is a psychological mechanism that makes it possible for large numbers of basically normal citizens to engage in collective crimes or to accept them without protest. It is based on strong links between members of a group. The passion aroused by the performance of a group's sports team is a manifestation of the intensity of the bonds of collective identity. Group cohesiveness may serve the same function in the human as in the animal world—self-preservation—but its unfortunate consequence is the ease with which one group can develop hatred of another, to the point of seeking its annihilation.

Various circumstances may facilitate the eruption of a collective murderous frenzy. Particularly important is the fear of being annihilated by an enemy and the confidence in one's own strength to annihilate the enemy instead. The modern age has added another motive for genocide: the utopian promise of a perfect society through the elimination of the groups accused of preventing its realization.

Thus, the primary driving force leading to genocide is not the pathology of the individuals organizing and committing the genocide, but the pathology of the ideas guiding them. These ideas are often produced and propagated by relatively normal people who may be unaware of the consequences of their escape from reality into myths.

In a perverse way, the ideology that generates a genocide demonstrates at the same time that most people committing it believe they are following their conscience. The self-defensive "kill so that you may not be killed" is usually not sufficient to mobilize the masses; the victim must be seen as a demon, and his killing as a universally beneficial act. Even at his worst, man likes to think that he is doing good.

This multidisciplinary essay explores the process through which the old myth of an innocent, suffering Serbia, and the concomitant myth of foreign evildoers who conspire against its very existence, influenced the behavior of Serbs at the close of the twentieth century. The study concentrates on the following features of Serbian historical experience that nourished these myths and contributed to the recent violent attempt to create a Second Serbian Empire: the entwining of church, state, and nation, with a resulting secularization of the first and deification of the last two entities; the drastic and lengthy interruption of national development by the Turkish conquest; the endemic violence of the Balkan highlands; the Romanticist glorification of blood and soil; and the policy of some Western powers that created conditions that stimulated Serbian expansionism.

Heavenly Serbia is the dominant Serbian national myth. As chapter 1 relates, it was created after the Turkish penetration into Serbia in the late fourteenth century. The myth attributed the Serbs' defeat at the Battle of Kosovo to their commitment to the heavenly kingdom, that is, to the choice of moral purity over military victory. Originally, the myth performed a useful function by helping the Serbs bear the humiliation of defeat and the centuries-long domination by a foreign culture. However, even when statehood was regained in the nineteenth century, the myth retained its vigor because it carried the promise that Serbia would resurrect as a mighty empire, instead of remaining a small, landlocked country. A prominent Serbian historian recently reaffirmed the myth's promise of a new empire: "By committing themselves to the heavenly empire, the Serbs took their earthly empire with them for a future that will come after the purification."[6] Myth and history, the eschatological and the temporal, are intertwined in the legend of Kosovo, as another modern Serbian intellectual asserts:

> The sacred story of the Serbian people, especially in the traditional form of oral decasyllabic songs, can be compared not only with the best works on battles in world history but even with mankind's best holy stories. This is a story about history, and even more about man's fate on earth and in the universe, about sin, sacrifice, salvation, and resurrection. Its model is the story of stories, the Gospel. It is Christian and evangelic, and therefore universally human. But it is also deeply national. Kosovo is the New Jerusalem, but a Jerusalem in the Balkans, in Serbia.[7]

The followers of the myth have detected the choice of the heavenly kingdom in all critical moments of their history. For example, after the dictator-king Aleksandar Karadordević was assassinated in 1934, the editor of a Belgrade newspaper wrote that "Aleksandar chose the heavenly kingdom in order to secure the future of Yugoslavia."[8] More recently, a Serbian Orthodox bishop reaffirmed the myth, which casts the crushing of "unheavenly" neighbors as a struggle against evil, even after the Serbs engaged in aggressions against Slovenia and Croatia in 1991: "I think that the *Kosovo covenant* of the Serbian people, that is, their general orientation toward, and in critical situations definite commitment to, the Heavenly Kingdom, and not to an earthly one, must be pointed out as a special characteristic of the spiritual life of Orthodox Serbs."[9]

Each of the three groups engaged in the wars that marked the disintegration of Yugoslavia (disregarding the very brief one in Slovenia) is characterized by a different religion. This fact has led some observers to believe that we are dealing here with religious wars. However, while religion is undoubtedly a very important identity mark for Serbs, Croats, and Bosnian Muslims, the persons most responsible for the outbreak of the wars have been characterized by an utter absence of religious convictions rather than by religious zeal. This is particularly obvious in the case of the principal culprits—the Serbs. As the last section of the first chapter indicates, their church, extremely closely connected with their state and nation, long ago neglected the gospel and devoted itself to political issues seemingly to a higher degree than any other Christian church.

The brief second chapter deals with the impact of the Turkish conquest on Serbian national consciousness. It was manifested not only in the myth of Heavenly Serbia but also in the myth of a heroic Serbian resistance, and in the expectation of the resurrection of the lost empire. Another consequence of the Ottoman domination was the further erosion of the Serbian Orthodox Church's religious function.

The unifying topic of chapter 3 is endemic violence in the Balkan highlands. In combination with a truly caesaropapist system in that area—the only such system in modern Europe—it created the environment in which the head of a nominally Christian church wrote the most influential and pernicious work of Serbian and Montenegrin literatures: a poem glorifying genocide.

Among writers who belong to a culture with a much greater separation between ecclesiastic and political powers one finds a strikingly different attitude toward the enemy. I frequently use comparisons between Serbia (or Montenegro) and Croatia in this study to highlight the differences between Eastern and Western Christian cultures. Such comparisons are particularly suitable, because we are dealing here with ethnically and linguistically very similar peoples who have developed distinct national identities through exposure to different civilizations. Most of these comparisons are drawn from a time when most Croats were anchored in Western cultural and political spheres, and the Serbs were an underdeveloped Eastern Orthodox nation submerged in the Ottoman Empire. The differences between the two nations have considerably diminished over time, and both have reached their moral nadir during the twentieth century. However, the differences—especially between their churches—have by no means disappeared. There is one more reason for references to Croatia in this study: the relatively new myth of a demonic Croatia is a complement to the myth of a Heavenly Serbia, both of which were embraced by a significant segment of the Western intelligentsia and reflected in the Western media.

In chapter 4, close contact with Western culture, established by diaspora Serbs during the eighteenth century, is shown to have provided the elements that transformed traditional tribalism and the church-centered national idea into modern Serbian nationalist ideology. Of particular importance were the Romanticist interest in folk art as the expression of a nation's uncorrupted soul, and the emphasis on language as the main identifier of a nation, which formed the basis for the modern concept of Serbia's national territory. The same chapter also shows some unpleasant consequences of the pre-1990s efforts to transform that territory into a homogeneous Serbian nation-state.

Chapter 5 examines the creation of the psychological climate for the recent wars for a Greater Serbia. This chapter explores some of the most prominent works by Serbian historians, theologians, novelists, and other intellectuals and artists who cultivated the myth of an innocent, suffering Serbia. These works (many of which were published in the 1980s—the decade preceding those wars) propagated the theses that Serbs, because of their goodness, have always been victims of others; that their enemies conspire to annihilate them; and that the time had come to act aggressively to avenge past wrongs and become the dominant power in the area.

All genocidal campaigns, whether guided by nationalist or universalist myths, are based on lies that portray a particular community as superior to others but threatened by those others. Since the progress of technology has produced extremely powerful means of mass destruction and centralized mass communication, it is of vital importance to combat myths that breed hatreds and conflicts. The urgency of contesting falsifications of history has been pointed out by Eric Hobsbawm on the occasion of the opening of the Central European University:

> We must resist the *formation* of national, ethnic, and other myths, as they are being formed. It will not make us popular. Thomas Masaryk, founder of the Czechoslovak republic, was not popular when he entered politics as the man who proved, with regret but without hesitation, that the medieval manuscripts on which much of the Czech national myth was based were fakes. But it has to be done.[10]

The fact that the Serbs have recently traversed the morally worst period of their entire history has already prompted an examination of their traditional myths and cultural icons. A Serbian scholar, has emphasized the importance of such an endeavor:

> The defeat of political projects based on historical reminiscences, and above all their tragic consequences that have endangered the life of every individual and of the nation as a whole, have created a fertile ground for the awakening of doubts about many deeply rooted historical ideas, and have thereby also made the public receptive to their reexamination. This defeat has, namely, made it obvious that the disencumbering of our historical consciousness of myths, fictions, and prejudices is, in fact, in our vital interest.[11]

Another Serbian scholar, Miodrag Popović expressed the same idea very succinctly in the concluding lines of his superb study of mythical layers in Serbian culture: "We must recognize that we are what we are, so that, emancipated from blind slavery to whatever we have inherited since time immemorial, we could be what we would like to be."[12]

A pragmatic national policy can be based only on a realistic assessment of a country's place in the world. But is it possible suddenly to reverse one's attitude toward crucial historical events, personalities, and myths cherished for a very long time, and realize that false gods have been worshiped? Efforts to dethrone false idols and expose bitter truth as a better foundation for the future always encounter strong resistance. However, total victory over fateful myths, violent habits, and national traumas is not necessary. It is sufficient to weaken them by showing that unrealistic visions of the past and expectations of the future lead to mistakes, and that national identity can be strengthened with a celebration of real achievements in the nation's past. If the reexamination of deeply entrenched ideas and attitudes gathers sufficient vigor, the direction in which a nation has been moving can be changed.

The Serbs are not the only ones deluded by their vision of themselves and their history. In the course of the nineteenth and twentieth centuries, the world, for various reasons, uncritically accepted many Serbian myths. This acceptance made them more credible, and thereby more destructive, in the country of origin. As the last chapter demonstrates, widespread ignorance about Serbia and the former Yugoslavia as a whole, coupled with indifference toward small, distant countries, made it difficult to make rational decisions when tensions started to rise in the Balkans. It would have been easy to prevent the war in 1991 had the dominant powers had a realistic view of the situation in that country, and the will to prevent the tragedy. Instead, they have also used myths and lies to justify their actions, or inactions. Therefore the liberation of politics from myths, lies, delusions, and sheer inexcusable ignorance is not a task for the Serbs only. It is a universal obligation.

1

Heavenly Serbia

The Birth of the Myth

Folk singers played a very important role in the illiterate and eliteless Serbian society following the Turkish conquest. Accompanying their chanting with a one-stringed fiddle called the *gusle,* they were not merely entertainers but bards who transmitted to their audiences a vision of the nation's past and future. However, they were not necessarily the creators of the myths propagated by their songs. The story of how Prince Lazar opted for the heavenly kingdom in the 1389 battle on the Field of Kosovo seems to have originated with the *Narration about Prince Lazar* by Serbian Patriarch Danilo III (who transferred the relics of the slain prince from the church of St. Spas in Priština to Ravanica Monastery in 1391), the noblewoman Jefimija's embroidered *Encomium to Prince Lazar,* and several texts by anonymous authors, written within thirty years after the battle.[1] These texts all interpret Prince Lazar's fate at Kosovo as a martyr's victory and a triumph of the commitment to the "heavenly kingdom" over the "earthly kingdom." Very few people have read the actual texts, but the folk songs based on their theme have had huge audiences over the centuries.

The best-known song about Prince Lazar's choice of the heavenly kingdom is "The Downfall of the Kingdom of Serbia." It tells of the prince's decision after a messenger sent by Saint Elias presented him with a choice:

> Oh, Tsar Lazar, of honorable descent,
> which kingdom will you choose?
> Do you prefer the heavenly kingdom,

> Or do you prefer the earthly kingdom?
> If you prefer the earthly kingdom,
> saddle the horses, tighten the girths!
> You knights, belt on your sabers,
> and charge against the Turks:
> the entire Turkish army will perish!
> But if you prefer the heavenly kingdom,
> build a church at Kosovo,
> do not make its foundation of marble,
> but of pure silk and scarlet,
> and make the army take Communion and prepare;
> your entire army will perish,
> and you, prince, will perish with it.[2]

The prince chose the heavenly kingdom, built a tent-church, "and called the Serbian patriarch / and twelve grand bishops, / and made the army take Communion and prepare."[3] The song then describes the ensuing fierce battle, in which the Serbian army perished together with its leader.

Another important folk song about the Kosovo legend is "The Prince's Supper" ("Kneževa večera"), which tells about Prince Lazar's supper with his knights on the eve of the battle. The analogy with Christ's Last Supper is obvious, as a commentator observes: "What is the Kosovo Supper but a repetition of the Last Supper? The Sacrificial Victim presides over both. At the Last Supper it is Christ, God, who sacrifices himself; at the Kosovo Supper, a ruler and a people sacrifice themselves."[4] In more than one figurative representation of the Kosovo Supper in Serbian churches and monasteries, Lazar appears as though seated at the Last Supper, surrounded by twelve apostle warriors. The analogy with the Last Supper is further enhanced by the presence of an alleged traitor among the twelve.[5]

The original—and perfectly normal—function of the legend of Prince Lazar's choice of the heavenly kingdom was to transform an alleged military defeat into a moral victory. The legend was gradually expanded to portray people who at every decisive turn in their history opt for the heavenly kingdom by taking the moral high ground. Archimandrate Justin Popović (1894–1979), a prominent theologian and university professor, is one of the modern proponents of this idea:

> The greatness of our people consists in the fact that they have, through Saint Sava, adopted evangelic justice and transformed it into their own. In the course of centuries they have developed such an affinity with this justice that it became their everyday, customary gospel. Only this can explain why our people have in all fateful moments of their history always preferred the heavenly to the earthly, the immortal to the mortal, the eternal to the transitory.[6]

Unheavenly Heroes

The Kosovo legend contains a contradiction. On the one hand, it praises Prince Lazar, the leader of the Serbian army at Kosovo, for choosing the heavenly kingdom, even at the cost of defeat and slavery. On the other hand, the most admired hero of the Kosovo cycle—Miloš Obilić—is guided by a pagan-heroic rather than Christian ethic.

Obilić is celebrated for a single action, which combined trickery with heroic self-sacrifice.[7] According to one version of his legend, Obilić came to see Sultan Murad I during the Battle of Kosovo pretending that he wanted to become his vassal, but when he was granted an audience he pulled out a knife hidden in his clothes and slaughtered the Ottoman chief. Some versions of the legend feature different locations, but the hero always uses a ruse to approach the sultan and kill him.

The extent of the Obilić cult is attested by the fact that he is sometimes represented as a saint. For example, in Grabovac Monastery, south of Niš, "[o]n the wall at the altar there is a picture of Prince Lazar, and Miloš Obilić next to him. Around Miloš's head there is the traditional saintly halo and the inscription: Saint Miloš Obilić!"[8] Hilandar, a prestigious Serbian monastery on Mount Athos in Greece, also holds a picture of Miloš Obilić as a saint.

While Obilić is the most admired legendary Serbian hero, Prince

Marko is the most popular one. Hundreds of folk songs describe his many feats, often involving cunning and extraordinary strength. But unlike Obilić's deceitfulness and violence, which can be justified as acts of war, Marko's violent acts often serve no purpose other than the venting of his rage. In comparison with other legendary heroes, Prince Marko displays an astonishing number of negative traits, such as duplicity, brutality, and collaboration with the conqueror of his country. Ruse has been used by many famous heroes ever since Ulysses devised the famous horse, and some of them are occasionally very cruel, but none match Marko in the scope of his deceitfulness and brutality against the weak. Women, even those who love and help him, are not spared.

In the folk song "Marko Kraljević and the Daughter of the Moorish King," Prince Marko tells his mother about the Moorish princess who saved him from prison. She fell in love with Marko while he was imprisoned by her father, and helped him escape after he had sworn that he would marry her. But the prince did not meet the princess's expectations. Instead, he killed her when he regained his freedom:

> And the Moorish maiden took me,
> Encircling me with her black arms,
> And when I looked on her, mother,
> On her black face and white teeth,
> A loathing gat hold of me;
> I drew the rich-wrought sabre,
> And smote her on the silken girdle,
> That the sabre cut clean through her.[9]

Such treatment of women is not unusual for Prince Marko. D. H. Low's collection of twenty-nine popular songs about the legendary prince contains several in which the hero's violent temper is directed against women. In one of them, "A Damsel Outwits Marko," the woman is spared from the sabre only by her wit, but in another the victim is brutally maimed. The protagonist of "The Sister of Leka Kapetan," the beautiful and outspoken Rosanda, enrages Marko by rejecting his offer of marriage:

> Liever had I remain unwed,
> In this our realm of Prizren
> Than go to Prilep castle,
> And be called Marko's wife.
> For Marko holds of the Sultan,
> He fights and smites for the Turks,
> ....
> Wherefore with all my beauty should I be wife to a
> Turkish minion?

Marko decides to punish Rosanda. In order to do so he entices her to come closer to him:

> O damsel, O proud Rosanda,
> I beseech thee of thy youthfulness,
> Send from thee thy maidens
> And turn thy face to me!
> For I was sore abashed, Rosa,
> Before thy brother in the čardak [closed balcony]
> So that I saw thee not well.
> And when I go to Prilep castle,
> My sister will weary me
> Asking: "Was Rosa fair to look upon?"
> Turn thee, that I may see thy face.

When Rosanda complies with the request, she is brutally attacked:

> Marko raged and was wroth out of wit,
> One step he made and a mighty spring,
> And by the hand he seized the damsel,
> He drew the sharp dagger from his girdle,
> And cut off her right arm;
> He cut off her arm at the shoulder,
> And gave the right arm into her left hand,
> And with the dagger he put out her eyes,
> And wrapped them in a silken kerchief,
> And thrust them into her bosom.[10]

Rosanda's rejection of Prince Marko points to still another negative feature of the hero: he was a collaborator. Several songs in the same collection refer to Marko serving the sultan and being rewarded for it. This trait of the legendary Prince Marko reflects the behavior of his historical prototype, King Marko Mrnjavčević (1335?–94). The real Marko, who became king in 1371, was a Turkish vassal who put himself and his army at the service of the Turks and died in the Battle of Rovine on May 17, 1394, fighting for the sultan against the Wallachian Prince Mircea.

The literary historian Svetozar Koljević states that Marko appears as an "ideal figure," noble and generous, in only three or four poems, in which he does not deal with human beings but with hawks or eagles.[11] Yet even in these instances, Marko's choice of a predatory animal that consumes human flesh and blood involves violence. An eagle saved by Marko relates how it became incapacitated on the Kosovo battlefield:

> Up to the stirrups of the steed that day the red blood ran,
> Unto the silken girdle of many a fighting man;
> Horses and heroes swam, steed by steed, and hero hero by,
> And we flew up hungry and thirsty, the vultures of the sky;
> We fed on human flesh, we drank our fill of human blood.[12]

As the sun dried the blood in its feathers the eagle could no longer fly, but Prince Marko put it on his horse and saved it from death. In another version of the song, the grateful bird reminds Marko that he himself gave it human flesh and blood: "you fed me the flesh of heroes, / you gave me red blood to drink."[13]

The legends of Prince Marko and Miloš Obilić followed different paths. The songs about Prince Marko were most popular during the first centuries of the Ottoman occupation, when the Serbian Orthodox Church enjoyed a privileged position in the Ottoman Empire and many Serbs served as martologues—Christian soldiers in the Ottoman army. During the same period the Obilić legend was cultivated mainly in the south Slavic areas not conquered by the Turks and farther west. The Obilić cult was revived in Serbia when the tension between the Serbian *raya* (the poor non-Muslim population in the Ottoman Empire) and the Turkish authorities began to grow. At that time, and particularly during the nineteenth-century Serbian struggle for independence, folk singers made Marko less brutal and more patriotic, so that both Marko and Obilić were seen as heroes of Serbian resistance against the Turks.

Serbian Patriarch Gavrilo (1881–1950) embraced the two heroes (together with a few other characters equally associated with violence in the service of the nation, as will later be demonstrated) as pillars of what he calls the "Kosovo ethics." In a text celebrating a 1941 Belgrade coup d'état, he glorified them as models to be followed:

> [T]he Kosovo ethics ... has elevated our past and exalted the spirit of Obilić, who became an ideal and a model of heroism, as well as the scope of Prince Marko, a protector of justice and a hero who defeated the enemy. All of this is best formulated in the characters of Bishop Danilo and his heroes as presented in *The Mountain Wreath,* where Njegoš's genius vividly and accurately describes the drama of the Serbian people in their fall and eventual rise in full victory over the enemy. The same Kosovo spirit inspired Karađorđe and Miloš [Obrenović] to build a new foundation for the Serbian state, which rose ever higher, and this clearly proves that the entire ascent of the Serbian people in history was won only and exclusively by the sword, in a sea of spilled blood and countless victims, which means that without all of this there is no victory, as there is no resurrection without death.[14]

The Byzantine Heritage

The Byzantine Empire provided the model for medieval Serbia's institutions and culture. It is therefore tempting to explain the violence and the cult of blood among the Serbs as a part of their Byzantine heritage. There is no difficulty in finding examples of extreme violence in the long history of that empire, such as the blinding in 1014 of an entire fifteen thousand-man Bulgarian army by the order of the Byzantine emperor Basil II, nicknamed the Bulgar-slayer (every hundredth soldier was left with one eye so he could lead the others home), or the fate of many Byzantine rulers:

Of the 109 sovereigns twenty-three ended by being assassinated. Twelve died in a convent or prison. Three died of starvation. Eighteen were mutilated by castration, or had their eyes gouged, or nose or hands cut off; and, apart from the thirty-four who died in their beds, and eight that were killed in a war or accident, the others were poisoned, suffocated, strangled, stabbed, hurled from the top of a pillar, or driven away ignominiously. Altogether, within 1058 years there were sixty-five palace-, street-, or barracks revolutions, and sixty-five dethronements.[15]

Harsh punishment stipulated by the law, which often involved cutting off noses, putting out eyes, and tearing off ears, were additional manifestations of cruelty in the Byzantine civilization.

However, it is no less difficult to compile a list of atrocities committed by Western Europeans in the struggle for power or in the service of state and church. The orgy of killing, rape, and looting unleashed by the Crusaders in Jerusalem and Constantinople upon the conquest of these cities, or the burning of heretics, sorcerers, and witches at the stake over several centuries are just a few pages of Western history that could justify a view of Western civilization as an extremely violent one. The traditional Western view of Byzantium as a corrupt and violent empire has been facilitated by the general inclination of every group to see its own crimes as aberrations, and those of the rival as paradigmatic. As for violence at the top of the power pyramid, the Ottoman Empire—where a newly elected sultan customarily killed all the relatives who might challenge his position—provides additional evidence that a high level of violence at the top does not necessarily mean that the other strata of the society are equally violent.

The Byzantine Empire, as the surviving half of the Roman Empire, was the center of civilized life in the then-known world, and it performed an important civilizing function. At a time when Western Europe was plunged into chaos and poverty, the empire based in Constantinople, the "New Rome," preserved the rich heritage of Hellenic and Roman cultures, and combining them with Christianity, achieved great results in the arts and crafts, philosophy, theology, jurisprudence, and other realms of culture. The architectural marvel of Hagia Sophia in Istanbul still stands as a testimony to the glory of Byzantine culture. The empire had an excellent civil service, the status of women was higher than in other contemporary civilizations, and the care of the poor and weak was well organized.

In addition to preserving and building on many achievements of Greco-Roman civilization, Constantinople extended its civilizing function to barbarian tribes that settled in central and eastern Europe during the era of migrations. It sent missionaries to the primitive Slavs in central and eastern Europe, who had invaded the Roman Empire, to convert them to Christianity and give them access to a more developed culture. One of these missionaries, Saint Cyril of Salonika (826/827–69), is regarded as the author of the Glagolitic alphabet, which was used by most western Slavs. The followers of Saint Cyril and the other "Slavic Apostle," Saint Methodius, are credited with the development of the Cyrillic alphabet, which is still used by Orthodox Slavs.

Christianity played a significant role in the civilizing efforts of Byzantium. Like any higher religion, it has strived to tame violence, in part by diverting man's attention from the immediate to the transcendent. It condemned the abuse of power, wealth, and sensual pleasures, and emphasized humility and equality of men before God.

This basic message of Christianity, and of other higher religions, is constantly threatened by the very organizations set up to propagate it. It is an unavoidable paradox: as a church acquires power and wealth, it becomes exposed to the very temptations it should combat. This is why churches often reach the highest spiritual levels when they are persecuted, and are at their worst when corrupted by the exercise of power. It is no accident that some of the worst collective crimes in the history of Western Christendom were committed by the Crusaders, a product of a very close link between ecclesiastic and political powers.

The strong bond between church and state represented a weakness of Byzantine civilization. The subordination of the church to the state was institutionalized, especially under Emperor Justinian, and the state became the master of the church. In Joseph Brodsky's words, instead of being "the bride of Christ," the church became "the spouse of the state."[16] This way the church, instead of limiting temporal power, legitimized the power exercised by the state and its absolute ruler. The difference between Western and Eastern Christianity in this regard is relative, but it has been an important relative difference. The Frankish kingdom and the Holy Roman Empire, as well as other Western states (especially after the Reformation), established state churches in Western Europe, but none of them were able to assert a continuous control over the church. The often fierce rivalry between the ecclesiastic and political spheres—with neither side being able to permanently dominate the other—was a source of many bloody conflicts, but it prevented either side from establishing absolute power. The independence of the church fostered the emergence of other independent social entities, and thus contributed to political, economic, and intellectual liberties.[17] A political scientist points out the uniqueness of the situation:

> In no other historical tradition was it conceivable that a powerful secular ruler like Emperor Henry IV would undertake a penitent's pilgrimage, in a hair shirt and with a rope around his neck, to expiate his politico-religious sins or, in power terms, to recognize the religious authority of Pope Gregory VII, whom he had unsuccessfully challenged. The idea of the tsar of Muscovy or the Byzantine emperor or the Ottoman sultan performing an analogous penance is an inherent absurdity.[18]

Specific circumstances, however, limited the corrupting effects of the subordination of the church to the state in the Byzantine Empire. One of them was the strength of the religious spirit of the Byzantines. Even though the emperor appointed the patriarch and bishops, they were not wholly subservient to him because the church was a powerful institution enjoying great moral authority. The function of maintaining the moral consciousness of the empire was performed particularly by the numerous monks and hermits, whose prestige made them very influential.

Second, as long as Byzantium was a multinational empire, its church as well was supranational. But when a strong Bulgarian state and then a Serbian state emerged on the northern fringe of the empire, the two states followed the Byzantine model of the relationship between church and state, and formed autocephalous churches that did not recognize any higher outside authority. With the formation of the Bulgarian autocephalous church (first created around 927, revived in 1235) and the Serbian autocephalous church (in 1219), the church of the Byzantine Empire was essentially reduced to a Greek church. The "ecumenical" patriarch of Constantinople still enjoyed special honor as the head of the oldest Orthodox church, but had no authority over the patriarchs of other Orthodox churches. He became the leader of a national church.

The formation of autocephalous Bulgarian and Serbian churches did not merely imitate the Byzantine state-church relationship. It also had the important political function of strengthening these nations against Byzantine imperial designs, supported by the church hierarchy in Constantinople. The presence of national churches in turn stimulated Bulgarian and Serbian imperialisms. At the points of their greatest strength, both Bulgaria and Serbia attempted to form a new Byzantine empire where Bulgarians, or Serbs, would hold both the political and ecclesiastic power. Thus the loss of the ecclesiastic unity of the Orthodox Balkan countries exacerbated the existing political rivalries and prevented the three countries from forming an alliance to withstand the Turkish assault. They even formed alliances with the Turks against their Christian Orthodox rivals.

There was a significant contrast between the disunity in the Orthodox Balkans and the situation in the Catholic world farther west, where the union of Croatia with Hungary and then the multinational Habsburg Empire formed a barrier against Ottoman penetration. Church unity was an important factor in this political solidarity. But the solidarity of Western Christians was at best limited to their own particular brand of Christianity. Their conquest of Constantinople in 1204 gave Byzantium a blow from which it never fully recovered, and they stood by while the Turks conquered the city in 1453.

In addition to the close church-state relationship, there was also a close "state-heaven" relationship in Byzantium, a direct relationship between the political and the divine spheres that bypassed the church. This relationship was largely responsible for the carnage in the Byzantine court. The idea that every emperor attains his position by God's will was taken so literally that every usurper, regardless of his background and the means by which he came to power, was hailed as the one chosen by God as soon as he triumphed. The automatic celestial backing of whoever climbed to the top of the political pyramid encouraged coups and struggles for power, and was therefore a destabilizing factor in the empire:

> Without any doubt, it is the theocratic ideology itself that, in Byzantium, carries in itself a seed of instability. Just as God gives power, God can withdraw it, and it is a Christian's duty to obediently follow the ebb and flow of the divine will: in the face of this essential duty there is no friendship, gratitude, or even political trends and social ties that count. The very word "fidelity" did not have the sense we ascribe to it: to be faithful in Byzantium means to be on God's side, that is, on the side of the stronger.[19]

The concept of a Heavenly Serbia was facilitated by the close relationship between the imperial and celestial spheres in Byzantine culture. Another Byzantinologist comments on this relationship:

> The Byzantines imagined God and the Heavenly Kingdom as a vastly enlarged replica of the imperial court at Constantinople. If questioned on this point, they would probably have expressed the relation in the reverse order by saying that the emperor's court was a diminished reflection of the heavenly court. Whichever of the two was the "archetype" and whichever the copy, their mutual resemblance was taken for granted and it explains many manifestations of Byzantine religiosity.[20]

The difference between Byzantium and Serbia in this regard is that the Byzantines regarded the emperor and his court as heavenly, whereas the Serbs conferred heavenly status on the nation as a whole. The earthly Serbia is holy Serbia. "Therefore," says Bishop Atanasije Jevtić, dean of the Orthodox Theological School in Belgrade, "we Orthodox Serbs, as well as other Orthodox peoples, are at the same time fighters for the earthly kingdom and for the Heavenly Kingdom."[21] He sees the two realms fused in the Serbian national character:

> It is the well-known Christian, humane (more precisely: divine-humane, *Christlike*) character of our national soul, readiness for self-sacrifice and suffering, forbearance and forgiveness, tolerance and magnanimity, and captivity for the sake of justice and freedom. In a word, a permanent and definitive commitment to the Heavenly Kingdom, which has been manifested particularly in the Kosovo and post-Kosovo events.[22]

In authentic Christian thought the Church, that is, the community of believers, constitutes the mystical body of Christ. The identification of the church with the nation favors instead the concept of the nation as the mystical body.

Saint-Savaism: Radical Nationalization of a Church

The close connection between the Serbian Orthodox Church and the Serbian state and nation dates back to 1219, when the church was established. Saint Sava, the founder of the church, was the youngest son of the founder of the Nemanja dynasty, and brother of the first Serbian king. He was himself actively involved in affairs of the state, and the definitive inclusion of Serbia in the Byzantine world was his achievement. His brother Stefan received both the royal insignia and the crown from Pope Honorius III in 1217, but the fear that Western Christianity might establish itself in Serbia (the fear may have been unwarranted because of the intense dissatisfaction among the Serbian clergy with the king's ties with Rome) contributed to the decision of the Byzantine emperor and the ecumenical patriarch to grant autonomy to the Orthodox Church in Serbia in 1219. Another reason for Sava's success in obtaining autocephalous status for his church—which also meant the recognition of Serbia's sovereignty—was the weakness of Byzantium. The Latins had conquered Constantinople in 1204, and both the emperor and the patriarch sought refuge in Nicaea.

The link between state and church remained strong throughout the rule of the Nemanja dynasty, as the lineup of Serbian saints shows. Besides the saints it shares with other Orthodox churches, the Serbian church celebrates fifty-nine national saints.[23] Twenty-six of them were rulers or members of the ruling families, predominantly from the Nemanja dynasty, and twenty-three were members of the church hierarchy (including seven patriarchs and eleven archbishops). Four saints, including Makarije, a sixteenth-century Serbian patriarch closely related to a powerful Ottoman grand vizier, form part of both groups.

Several ruling families have contributed more than one saint. The first such family is that of Saint Sava himself: his father, mother, and brother are also Serbian saints. Another four-saint family is composed of Despot Mother Angelina, her husband, Despot Stefan the Blind, and their sons Archbishop Maksim and Despot Jovan.[24]

A few of the canonized rulers were genuinely pious. Saint Sava's father, Stefan Nemanja, became a monk after turning power over to another son. Most kings built beautiful monasteries, but the moral standards of most of them would not qualify them as saints. King Milutin (reigned 1282–1321), for example, a child of two saints— King Stefan Uroš I and his wife, Jelena—and a saint himself, had his son—the future King Stefan Uroš III Dečanski, a saint in his own right—blinded, because he had plotted to overthrow his father. Despot Stefan Lazarević, who, as a Turkish vassal, made significant contributions to the expansion of the Ottoman Empire, has been canonized too.

Even some of the saints unrelated to ruling families have become tools of national ideology. A Montenegrin scholar points out the ideological metamorphosis of two such saints:

> Concrete historical personalities are elevated to mythic symbols, and an ideological substance ... is mostly concentrated around figures with the aura of liberation and sainthood. Saint Peter of Cetinje and Saint Basil of Ostrog, whose cults strongly deviate from usual Christian mysticism, have lost almost all religious content and become national liberation symbols, under which Montenegrin tribes obtain moral cleansing and motivation for new ventures.[25]

Turkish rule in Serbia did not end the politicization of the Serbian Orthodox Church but only changed its nature. When the autocephalous Serbian Orthodox Church was reestablished as a patriarchate with the seat in the Kosovo town of Peć in 1557, it no longer served the Serbian state because that state had ceased to exist; but it served the Ottoman state, and as the only surviving national institution, it became the main carrier of Serbian national identity. Its nonreligious functions were even expanded under the Turkish system of millets—ethnoreligious communities of non-Islamic peoples, which enjoyed a considerable degree of religious and cultural autonomy and were in charge of administrative duties such as the collection of taxes. The historian Michael B. Petrovich points out that "This role of the Serbian church had little to do with religion either as theology or as a set of personal beliefs and convictions. Rather, the Serbian church was a cultural and quasi-political institution, which embodied and expressed the ethos of the Serbian people to such a degree that nationality and religion fused into a distinctive 'Serbian faith.' "[26] Another scholar described the Serbian Orthodox Church, at the time of the Peć patriarchate, as "a sort of a vassal clerocratic state within the framework of the powerful military-feudal empire."[27]

The Christianization of Serbia, which was rather advanced among the upper classes and urban population under the Nemanja dynasty, suffered a setback under Turkish rule, although the decline was somewhat checked with the establishment of the patriarchate of Peć (1557–1766). The number of priests was greatly reduced and their education neglected. Under these circumstances, pagan beliefs, which had never disappeared, especially among the rural population, resurfaced. They shaped the popular image of the founder of the church, as the pioneer Serbian historian of religion, Veselin Čajkanović, observes:

> Formally, and in name, the traditional Saint Sava is a Christian saint, and a very zealous propagator of the Christian faith; essentially, however, by his character and temperament, and by the myths and beliefs linked with him, he still belongs in the old, pre-Christian time. . . . One of the main character traits attributed to our saint in

folk literature is a strong propensity to anger, and readiness to punish. Anger and punishment are frequently mentioned. In Ćorović's
anthology the saint's anger, or act of punishment, represents a motif,
often the *main* motif, in no less than forty-two stories! The anger is
frequently insufficiently motivated and unjustified, and the punishment excessive.[28]

The reaffirmation of pre-Christian tribal attitudes in Serbia was a
gradual process, facilitated by the chaos accompanying the demise
of the Serbian medieval state and the abolition of the patriarchate
of Peć in 1766. A further step in the same direction took place in
the late eighteenth and nineteenth centuries, when the ideas of the
purity of primitive societies and the nation as the guardian of the
people's authentic spirit reinforced the beliefs opposed to Christian
ethics.

The drastic neglect of the religious function of the Serbian Orthodox Church may account for the unusually low popular interest in
religion among present-day Serbs. "Opinion polls reported by *Ilus-
trovana politika* (February 23, 1982) revealed that in traditionally
Catholic regions one-third of the youth are religious, one-third
atheists, and one-third either passive believers or uncertain. In traditionally Serbian Orthodox regions, by contrast, only 3 percent of
the youth felt religious, while 90 percent claimed to feel positive
aversion toward religion."[29]

A survey of 4,800 employed persons in all Yugoslav republics and
autonomous provinces, made in November 1985, gave the following
data about the percentages of the population professing religious
faith:[30]

Kosovo	44
Croatia	33
Slovenia	26
Macedonia	19
Bosnia-Herzegovina	17
Serbia	11
Vojvodina	10
Montenegro	10

Surveys of religiosity in communist Yugoslavia are not always reliable, but all of them show Serbs and Montenegrins at the bottom of
the scale. Moreover, the lack of religious spirit among the Serbs
does not seem to be a recent phenomenon. A Polish visitor was
struck by it at the beginning of the century, and reported it in an
article in a Moscow weekly:

> The Serbs are the most irreligious of all the peoples with whom I
> have had the opportunity to deal. In this they are very different from
> both Poles and Russians. All of the best works of the Polish mind in
> poetry and philosophy have their origin in the depth of religious
> idealism. Analogously, the creative work of the greatest Russian art-
> ists and thinkers is concentrated on the religious issue. But the
> religious issue does not exist for the Serbs; they are completely
> absorbed by the temporal; they are immersed in the trifles of every-
> day political struggle and find neither the will nor the time to lift
> their thoughts to the area of the absolute. They have churches and
> monasteries—but the churches are always empty. . . .
>
> When I communicated my observations on Serbian religiosity to
> my Serbian acquaintances in Sarajevo, they not only did not perceive
> them as a reproach but accepted them with pride as a proof of what
> they regarded as their advantage. "The word Serb," they explained
> to me, "is a synonym of radicalism in the Slavic south. Religious,
> social, political radicalism constitutes their distinctive mark and, at
> the same time, a source of their strength."[31]

The Russian philosopher Vladimir Soloviev points out a correlation
between religious indifference and the political use of the church:
"The religious indifference of the Serbs is as well known as their
mania for using Orthodoxy as a political weapon in their fratricidal
struggle against the Catholic Croats."[32] The author of a study of
tombstone inscriptions in western Serbia points out the Serbian
peasants' indifference and even hostility to the church:

> Although it is an indisputable psychological fact that village folk
> believed in god, feared him and prayed to him, the peasant most
> frequently revealed himself as an inveterate pagan, warrior, haiduk,
> offender, and blasphemer! Many peasants did not take communion
> for as long as fifty years, and crossed themselves only when drinking

a glass of brandy because "one has to." And nobody could curse god and the saints more foully than the Serbian peasant! He aimed curses at all the saints in heaven, debased and disdained them when things went wrong. He made fun of priests and monks, god's representatives, in his mockeries. Only on tombstones, facing horrible death, would he come back to god and "nice Christian behavior."[33]

One measure of the political function of the church in the Eastern Orthodox world is that no nation that forms part of it possesses full legitimacy without its own national church. This explains the apparent paradox that the Yugoslav communist regime, in the process of formally establishing Macedonia as a nation after the Second World War, insisted on the formation of the Macedonian Orthodox Church against strong objections by the existing Orthodox churches. Similarly, the abolition of the autonomous Montenegrin Orthodox Church (which was de facto autocephalous after the abolition of the patriarchate of Peć in 1766) in 1918 was an important step in Serbian efforts to make Montenegro an integral part of Serbia.

Since an autocephalous national church can be controlled more easily than a universal church whose leadership resides outside the borders of the empire, Ottoman rulers gave greater privileges to the Orthodox than to the Catholic Church. For the same reason, communist regimes put a great deal of pressure on Catholic hierarchies in their countries to sever their ties with the Vatican and establish national churches.

A church may not be unhappy with its subordination to a state as long as it can use the power of the state to expand its own power. The Serbian Orthodox Church greatly expanded under Ottoman rule, and under Stalin the Russian Orthodox Church expanded in Ukraine—specifically at the expense of the Uniate Church, which maintained the Eastern Rite in its liturgy but acknowledged papal authority in doctrine. At the same time, the traditional right of the state to appoint bishops of the Orthodox Church, preserved even under a ruler who persecuted the church, such as Joseph Stalin, made it possible for the regime to plant collaborators in the hierarchy of the Russian Orthodox Church.

Nevertheless, the Russian church hierarchy seems to have had a genuine respect for the communist leader. Gleb Yakunin, a prominent Russian human rights activist and former Orthodox priest, lists the titles the patriarch of the Russian Orthodox Church Alexis bestowed on Stalin: "Supreme leader, Supreme leader of the Russian people, Wise Leader, Leader of Genius, Great Leader, the Great and Wise Leader, the Great Head of our State, the Wise Builder of the People's Well-Being, and the Great Builder of the People's Happiness." Yakunin does not think that this was just a result of pressure by the regime: "astonishing as it may seem, Patriarch Alexis and some other leaders of the Patriarchate were, beyond any doubt, largely sincere in their attitude towards Stalin."[34]

The fusion of the ecclesiastic and political spheres corrupts both. The institution that should impose moral restraints on political power removes them and instead confers a sacral or quasi-sacral status to the carriers of power. The traditional subservience of the Orthodox Church to the state may be an important reason why communist totalitarianism first came to power in an Orthodox country, and why Orthodox countries have had greater difficulties than Catholic and Protestant countries fighting and dismantling communist regimes. It also explains why one of Stalin's closest associates showed such enthusiasm upon the discovery that a Yugoslav ambassador to the Soviet Union shared the Orthodox heritage, as the latter reports in his memoirs:

> Voroshilov asked me where I came from. When he heard me say that I was a Montenegrin, he was simply overjoyed. He asked me with some hesitation whether the Montenegrins belonged to the Orthodox faith. When I confirmed that they are Orthodox, explained that Montenegro is on the dividing line between the Moslem and Catholic worlds, and that the Montenegrins are therefore "genuine Orthodox," Voroshilov's face lit up as though he had received a piece of unexpected good news. He seized me by the hand and assured me that everything between us would now be different and better and that all obstacles in the way of our friendship had been removed. He did not ask me whether I was a member of the Central Committee of the Communist Party in Yugoslavia, but whether, as a

Montenegrin, I belonged to the Orthodox Church. The latter was
more important to him, it appears, than the former.[35]

The affinity between the Eastern Orthodox and the modern totalitarian deification of the state and nation was noted by one of the
two most influential twentieth-century Serbian Orthodox theologians, Bishop Nikolaj Velimirović (1880–1956). He praised Adolf Hitler for doing what the founder of the Serbian Orthodox Church did
in the thirteenth century: "One must render homage to the present
German leader, who, as a simple craftsman and man of the people,
realized that nationalism without religion is an anomaly, a cold and
insecure mechanism. Thus in the twentieth century he arrived at
Saint Sava's idea, and as a layman undertook the most important
task in his nation that befits a saint, genius, and hero."[36]

Saint-Savaism (*Svetosavlje*) is a common Serbian term for the
peculiar blend of church, state, and nation that was established by
Saint Sava in the early thirteenth century. A Serbian theologian
defined it as "Orthodoxy ennobled by a healthy Serbian nationalism."[37] It was formulated as a messianic ideology in the 1930s, when
the Serbian church's support of the Yugoslav government's pan-
Serb policies met strong resistance from the Roman Catholic
Church in the newly formed Yugoslav union. The review *Svetosavlje*,
published in Belgrade from 1932 to 1940, was instrumental in
spreading the ideology, which was strongly influenced by Russian
Slavophile messianism and based on the conviction that only Orthodoxy has preserved the purity of the original Christianity. Danilo
Medan, one of its promoters, wrote that Saint-Savaism was symbolic
of the pan-Slavist idea of the union of all Slavs, whose mission is
universal: "It must give the world true Christianity in an Orthodox
interpretation, whose authentic sources have been obscured by the
Roman Catholicism and Protestantism of the West."[38]

Saint-Savaism regards the nation as holy because of its identification with the only true faith. This conviction is reflected in Bishop
Velimirović's reference to the nation in terms usually reserved for a
divinity: "Although the Serbs are numerically not a great nation,
their life and history are a filigree work of ineffable harmony and

beauty."[39] Archimandrate Justin Popović, a disciple of Velimirović, expressed the fusion of religion and politics even more explicitly: "Our national history is a very eloquent proof of Christ's resurrection and power."[40] The blurring of the border between the temporal and the transcendent is also evident in the theocratic ideal expressed by Velimirović on the occasion of a Vid's Day celebration: "If somebody asked what the ideal of the mass of our working people is, he could be given a dependable answer right away: Holiness. With all their heart the people want a holy church, holy school, holy culture, holy dynasty, holy authorities, holy state, and—holy army."[41]

The annihilation of whatever stands in the way of such a holy nation is a duty. War as a tool for achieving holy unity acquires great importance. "War is the basis of every art and every higher human virtue and ability," while "Peace and civic vices flourish together,"[42] wrote the same advocate of Saint-Savaism. A friend of the late bishop reported that "up to 1912 [when Serbia took part in the First Balkan War] Nikolaj was afraid that his generation would not see a war."[43] The association of war with Serbia's salvation, the core of the Kosovo myth, was first developed as a response to the trauma caused by the Turkish conquest.

2

The Encounter with the Turks

Ottoman Religious Tolerance

The union of Serbian church and nation, a Byzantine heritage, became even tighter after the Ottoman Turkish conquest, when Serbia ceased to exist as a territorial and political entity. Since the nation was no longer associated with a state, its link with the national religion became still more pronounced. The myth of the Heavenly Serbia was a manifestation of the radical union of nation and church. The Ottoman domination contributed to the development of the Serbs' self-image of a holy people whose moral superiority makes them victims of the immorality of others.

The centuries-old submergence of Serbia in the Ottoman Empire was undoubtedly a national tragedy. The Serbs lost their political and cultural elites and their national institutions—with the exception of the Serbian Orthodox Church. They were reduced to a society of peasants and small merchants in an empire dominated by a foreign civilization. However, in spite of the undeniable negative consequences of the Ottoman domination, there is a limit to the Turks' responsibility for the difficulties Serbia and other Orthodox Balkan nations have experienced since becoming independent in the nineteenth century.

The high degree of ethnic and religious intolerance in Orthodox Balkan countries certainly was not an imitation of the Turkish model. The Ottoman Empire, like the Omayyad Arab empire that ruled Spain, showed a high degree of religious tolerance in comparison with Byzantium and Catholic or Protestant countries. For example, while Catholic Spain expelled the Jews, the Ottoman Empire received them and let them live in peace as long as the empire existed. The nearly total destruction of the hundreds of mosques built in Serbia during the centuries of the Turkish rule (in Belgrade only one was spared) was not patterned after Turkish behavior either, but corresponds to the obliteration of the legacy of Turkish rule in liberated Western Christian areas. Most Serbian medieval monasteries survived the long Ottoman rule, and some of the churches and monasteries built during the Ottoman period rival those built by Serbian medieval kings. A Serbian cultural historian points out the extent of the Ottoman Turks' religious tolerance:

> Despite its subordination to the Ottoman state, the Orthodox church enjoyed full religious freedom and cultural autonomy de jure and mostly de facto, too, at the time of the patriarchate of Peć, which means from 1557 on. In its churches, prayers were sung and services held to Serbian king-saints, and from the walls, in the middle of the Ottoman empire, Orthodox saints and warriors greeted the congregation. Old Serbian books were treated as holy objects by the Turks, too, and monasteries were protected by the sultan's special charter. An example of extreme religious tolerance was the Turkish tacit disregard of the *Service to Holy Prince Lazar,* which was sung in church on June 15 every year. The "Service" referred to the Turks as godless people used by Prince Lazar as "fuel for the eternal flame."[1]

The same author notes that about two hundred monks lived and worked in a Serbian religious center at Rača (by the Drina River) in the late seventeenth century. However, religious tolerance in the Ottoman Empire was combined with social and political discrimination. Only non-Muslims had to pay a poll tax and contribute free labor. They were also subjected to many restrictions, including some very visible ones, such as prohibitions against wearing weapons or bright colors.

While Turkish rule was often brutal, the high degree of violence endemic to some parts of the Balkans is not entirely the fault of the Turks either. Historical records do not indicate that the Ottoman army was more cruel than other armies at the time. The worst aspect of the Ottoman expansion was the devastation and depopulation that frequently preceded the conquest of new territories.

(Large-scale atrocities against the population at large at that stage were generally not committed by regular Turkish army but by unpaid Tatar horsemen and other Ottoman subjects who engaged in the terrifying raids for the reward of plunder and slaves.) But once the conquered territories were secured, their populations enjoyed a *pax ottomana*. Formerly sovereign states that had become parts of the empire no longer could wage wars with one another; it can be argued that there was generally more order until the empire started to decline in the late seventeenth century. Had the Ottoman rule been based on terror alone, it probably would not have lasted so long. Violence increased during the last two centuries of the Ottoman Empire, when the Turkish capacity to keep order declined and economic difficulties led to heavier taxation, especially when wars for national liberation started in the nineteenth century. Notably, one of the most violent areas in the Balkans, Montenegro, was never completely dominated by the Turks.

Turkish rule was praised by a fifteenth-century Serb. Konstantin Mihailović was a member of a Serbian unit that aided the Turks in the final attack on Constantinople in 1453. He later joined the Turkish elite units, the Janissaries, and participated in the Turkish attack on Bosnia. Captured by the Hungarians there, he eventually settled in Poland, where he wrote a book titled *A Janissary's Memoirs, or A Turkish Chronicle.*[2] One purpose of the book was to advise the king of Poland how to fight the Turks more effectively. Although Mihailović resented Turkish domination of his homeland, he expressed admiration for the Turkish system of promotion on the basis of personal merits, and he praised other features of the Ottoman state that were, in his opinion, superior to what he saw in European countries at the time: "there is a lot of justice among the pagans. They are just in their mutual dealings. They are also just toward all of their subjects, Christians as well as Jews and all the others ruled by them, because the emperor himself takes care of that."[3]

However, while Western Europe progressed economically after the time when Mihailović made those observations and developed religious tolerance in the eighteenth century, the decline of the

Ottoman Empire led to internal disorder and increasing violence. A great deal of the Christian population's dissatisfaction was caused by the Janissaries, who gradually changed from a disciplined elite force into an unruly privileged class that created grave problems for both the population and the authorities in Istanbul and was abolished in 1826. Another source of dissatisfaction was the local landed potentates, who displayed a greater affinity with the worst aspects of European feudalism than with the traditional Ottoman *timar* system, which awarded estates conditionally, in exchange for military service.

The Short-Lived Serbian Empire

The Turkish conquest was made more traumatic for the Serbs by the fact that it began only sixteen years after the death of Emperor Dušan the Mighty, under whom Serbia had experienced the greatest expansion in its history. Tsar Dušan, who acceded to the throne in 1331 (after imprisoning and, according to some sources, murdering his father), conquered the Byzantine territories of Macedonia, Albania, Epirus, and Thessaly, seizing from Byzantium more than half its remaining territory. The distance from Serbia's new border to Athens was only one hundred kilometers.

Serbia had become a significant Balkan power under King Uroš (reigned 1243–76), when its emerging mining industry (developed primarily by the Saxons from Hungary) and increased trade provided funds for a mercenary army. Serbia's growing power led to its expansion, mainly toward the south, at the expense of Byzantium, whose economic power was rapidly crumbling. Serbian victories, especially under King Milutin (1282–1321), made Byzantium even weaker. When Dušan embarked on his conquests, the Byzantine Empire was additionally weakened by its second civil war. The internal struggles that crippled and ruined the Byzantine Empire made it easy for Dušan to build his empire. He won cities entirely by sieges without a single open-field battle.

On Easter Sunday in 1346, Dušan had himself crowned emperor

and autocrat of the Serbs and Greeks, an indication of his intention to replace the Byzantine Empire with a new Serbo-Greek empire. He intended to launch an expedition against Constantinople but died in 1355 before he could realize his plan. However, Dušan's Serbian empire was as weak as the moribund Byzantine Empire. His Greek subjects felt no allegiance to a conqueror who was excommunicated along with the Serbian patriarch by the ecumenical patriarch in Constantinople.[4] Moreover, Serbian attacks prompted Byzantine Emperor John VI Cantacuzen (1347–54) to turn to the Turks for assistance. The Ottomans helped the emperor but, in the process, established a foothold on European soil at Gallipoli. Thus, Dušan's construction of a Serbian empire at the expense of Byzantium indirectly facilitated the eventual subjugation of Serbia by the Turks.

Dušan's empire is seen by latter-day Serbs as the moment of medieval Serbia's greatest glory and an inspiration for the future, but some of Dušan's contemporaries and near contemporaries perceived it as a betrayal of the ecclesiastico-political traditions of the Nemanja dynasty. As a Serbian historian notes,

> It is significant that the dynastic hagio-biography ignores the imperial period, from 1345 to 1371, corresponding to the reigns of Tsars Dušan and Uroš, to the point of interrupting the biography of Stefan Dušan before the proclamation of the empire. The imperial idea did not agree with the traditional ideology. The last part of *The Lives of Serbian Holy Kings and Archbishops* does not speak of the two tsars except to express a severe judgment regarding their political work, and particularly that of Dušan.[5]

Dušan's empire lacked the allegiance of a large part of its subjects and the appropriate administrative and institutional framework for governing the drastically expanded state, while nobles of uncertain loyalty retained great authority in their domains. For these reasons the empire began crumbling immediately after Dušan's death, having existed for barely twenty-five years. But despite the empire's short life, in the popular memory it is seen as the culmination of the medieval Serbian state, and its embellished memory has ever since nourished the Serbs' conviction that Serbia is destined to become an empire again. The belief was just as strong during the centuries of Turkish domination as it was during the nineteenth-century struggle for independence, or in the late twentieth century, when the Serbs engaged in genocidal wars to realize the old dream.

Dušan's son and successor, Tsar Uroš V (1356–71), ruled only over central Serbian lands. Several peripheral areas seceded, and others became virtually independent. Among the nobles who ruled quite independently while recognizing the suzerainty of Uroš were the brothers Vukašin and Uglješa Mrnjavčević. Unable to dominate them, in 1365 Uroš crowned Vukašin king and Uglješa despot. Vukašin, in turn, named his son Marko "kraljević" (little king or prince), expecting that he would succeed the childless Tsar Uroš.

In the meantime, the Turks continued their advance in the Balkans and became a threat to Despot Uglješa, whose eastern Macedonian domain was most exposed to their attack. Uglješa's attempt to create a coalition with other Serb lords against the Turks failed; only his brother King Vukašin responded. In the Battle of Chernomen in 1371 their forces were destroyed, and both brothers lost their lives.

Resistance and Collaboration

After the catastrophe at Chernomen, the Serbs were even more divided, because several warlords in the south had become Turkish vassals. These vassals failed to join the Christian forces at the Kosovo battlefield in 1389, not only out of fear of Turkish might but

> partly also because of the lack of true national solidarity and because, in pursuit of particular interests, the feeling for the nation as a whole was lost. Selfish individuals did not sufficiently understand that the loss of the main national center and its significance would make their own position toward the victor graver and weaker. Konstantin Dejanović even catered to the Turkish army, which passed through his land on the way to Kosovo, and gave it his auxiliary troops.[6]

Nevertheless, the Battle of Kosovo on June 28, 1389, did not end in a Turkish victory. The leaders in both camps—Serbian Prince Lazar Hrebeljanović and Ottoman Sultan Murad I—were killed, and the Turkish army suffered losses so heavy that it could not continue the campaign and had to return home. Among the preserved sources from 1389, not a single one speaks of a Turkish success, and the majority testify to a Turkish defeat.[7] However, it was easier for the Turks, a considerably greater power, to recover from the losses sustained in the battle. Only in this sense was the outcome of the battle favorable for the Turks. This event marked one stage in the gradual loss of Serbia's independence, which began with the Battle of Chernomen and was completed with the fall of Smederevo in 1459, eighty-eight years later. The process was slowed by the Turks' confrontation with the forces of Tamerlane in Asia, the resistance of some Serbs, and significant Bosnian, Albanian, Wallachian, and especially Hungarian engagement to stop the Turkish advance.

The Serbs contributed to their own subjugation by participating in Ottoman military campaigns. They fought for the Turks much more vigorously than one would expect of unwilling vassals, and they decisively influenced the outcome of several important battles. The cavalry of Despot Stefan Lazarević (the son of Prince Lazar, who was killed by the Turks at Kosovo in 1389), ruler of Serbia from 1389 to 1427, was a crucial factor in the Turkish victory in the battle at Nicopolis on September 25, 1396. This victory of the forces of Sultan Bayezid I over an alliance of European forces led by the Hungarian King Sigismund consolidated Turkish control over the Balkan peninsula. According to *The Cambridge Medieval History,* "[t]he rashness of the proud French chivalry, the retreat of the Wallachian prince, and the strategy of the Sultan, were responsible for the overwhelming defeat of the Christians, while it was reserved for Stephen Lazarević and his 15,000 Serbs, at a critical moment, to strike the decisive blow for the Turks."[8]

Barbara Tuchman points out that the Serbs could have avoided assisting the Ottoman army: "As a vassal of the Sultan, the Serbian Despot, Stephen Lazarevich, might have chosen passive neutrality like the Bulgarians on whose soil the struggle was being fought, but he hated the Hungarians more than the Turks, and chose active fidelity to his Moslem overlord. His intervention was decisive. Sigismund's forces were overwhelmed."[9]

Despot Lazarević put his army at the service of the sultan every year during the first thirteen years of his reign. In 1398 his soldiers participated in the first great Turkish invasion of Bosnia; in 1402 he assisted Bayezid at the fatal battle of Angora with five thousand (according to some sources, ten thousand) armored lancers:

> When the fortune of the day had already decided against the Sultan, the Serbian horsemen twice cut their way through the Tartar bowmen, whose arrows rebounded from their iron cuirasses. Seeing that all was lost, Stephen in vain urged Bayazid to flee; and, when the latter refused to leave the field, the Serbian prince saved the life of the Sultan's eldest son Sulaiman, and escaped with him to Brusa.[10]

According to the legend, as recorded by a chronicler at the court of Despot Lazarević, King Marko fought unwillingly for the Turks and prayed before the 1394 Battle of Rovine (in which he lost his life) that the Turkish side would lose.[11] Historical records, however, show that Serbian military assistance was often considerable. Serbs provided significant support to the Turks at the Battle of Chamorlú near Samokov, on July 10, 1413, when the fate of the Turkish Empire and with it that of the Balkan Slavs were decided. Two Serbian rulers, Stefan Lazarević and his nephew, contributed on that day, one with the troops he sent and the other with personal bravery, to the consolidation of Ottoman power, and thus unwittingly prepared the way for the complete conquest of their country later on.

The last attempt of medieval Christendom to push the Turks back and free Bulgaria was made in 1444, nine years before the fall of Constantinople, and fifteen years before the full subjugation of Serbia. The decisive battle between the Turks and a crusade composed of Poles, Hungarians, Austrians, and Frenchmen, led by the Polish and Hungarian King Vladislav and the brilliant military strategist Janos Hunyadi, was fought at Varna on November 10. Serbian Despot Đurađ Branković, who had succeeded Despot Lazarević in 1427, contributed to the disastrous defeat of the Christians by informing Sultan Murad of the Christian advance and barring the road by which the Albanian leader Skanderbeg had intended to traverse Serbia to join the Christian forces at Varna. He acted similarly four years later, when Hunyadi again attacked the Turks. "On this occasion, too, Branković betrayed the Christian cause by warning Murād of the coming Hungarian invasion."[12]

On October 17, 1448, Turkish and Christian armies clashed once more on the fateful field of Kosovo, but this time the Serbs did not participate in the fight. Instead they "lurked in the mountain passes which led out of the plain, ready to fall upon and plunder the fugitives."[13] The Serbian despot's armed neutrality, while others fought at Varna and Kosovo, was not his only crime against the common cause of the Balkan Christians: with the sultan's permission, he extended his frontiers at the expense of Bosnia, ignoring the threat the growing Turkish power would pose to himself.

Such historical facts explain why Serbian folk singers turned a Turkish vassal into a national hero: at the time when the oldest extant Serbian heroic folk songs were created, that is, the time of the Ottoman penetration into the Balkans, most Serbian rulers were Turkish vassals, and the prowess of a Serbian knight was admired even when he served a foreign master. The renowned nineteenth-century German historian Leopold Ranke made the following comment on Serbian vassalage and Prince Marko:

> It appears as though the nation had intended to represent in this hero its own vassalage, at the period when, after the battle of Kossovo, the Servian army assisted almost every year in the wars of Bajazet; yet maintaining its independent character, and still appearing formidable in its force even to the Sultan himself. At this time the nation was possessed of vast strength, and unbroken courage, and yet—it served the Turks. This the Servian poets have represented in their hero, whom they portray with all the characteristics of the national sentiments—even with the barbarism of a blood-thirsty cruelty mingled with the love of gain—concentrating in him the glories of their more ancient heroes.[14]

The Serbs contributed to the loss of their independence not only by cooperating with the Turks but also by fighting among themselves.

For example, in one of the lesser-known battles on the Field of Kosovo in 1402, fourteen years after the famous Kosovo battle, the army of Despot Lazarević, who ruled over a large part of Serbia, clashed with the army of Đurađ Branković, who wanted to expand his small domain around Priština. The parties in such inter-Serbian clashes often asked the Turks for assistance. And, as the Serbian historian Stanoje Stanojević pointed out, "throughout the period of struggles with the Turks, there has not been a single instance of a joint action against them by the entire Serbian people."[15]

The fear of losing their identity is the reason the Serbs preferred to become Turkish, rather than Hungarian, vassals. They saw, not without justification, the domination of a Catholic king as a greater threat to their national church than Muslim rule. For the same reason, the Russians fought the Swedes and Livonian and Teutonic knights with greater determination than they resisted the Mongols. But by serving as Turkish vassals, the Serbian nobility contributed to its own disappearance.

The collaboration of the Serbs with the conqueror of their country brought some rewards. Appreciating their help in the conquest of southern Hungary, and especially of the Banat, in 1557 the Turks reestablished the patriarchate of Peć, which had been abolished in 1459.[16] Following the established pattern of the close link between state and church in Serbia, Grand Vizier Mehmed Pasha Sokollu appointed a close relative as the patriarch.[17] Because of the close link between the Orthodox Church and nation, the reemergence of the autonomous Serbian Orthodox Church and the huge expansion of its jurisdiction had very important consequences for the future of Serbia and its neighbors. The privileged position of the Serbian Orthodox Church in the Ottoman Empire and the population migrations caused by Turkish conquests resulted in the presence of large numbers of Serbs in western Bosnia and the parts of Croatia bordering with that empire.

Turkish conquests of new territories were often accompanied by severe depopulation, because of the killing and exodus of large numbers of natives. The Turks took care to resettle the newly acquired areas in order to facilitate their defense. Most of the new settlers they brought in were Vlachs, the most nomadic people in the Balkans and the most loyal non-Muslim subjects of the sultan.

The words *Vlach* and *Wallach* have the same root as the word *Welsh,* but the Vlachs were not of Celtic origin.[18] In the Balkans the word *Vlach* was applied mostly to the people who spoke a form of Latin. They were descendants of a mixture of ancient Roman colonists and Romanized natives, like those who form the bulk of the population of modern Romania. Most had probably been originally members of Thracian and Illyrian tribes. After the barbarian invasion of the Roman Empire, many of them took refuge in the mountains, where sheepherding became their dominant occupation. The majority of Vlachs were Orthodox Christians, converted to Christianity by Byzantium, but many in the western Balkans, under the jurisdiction of Rome, became Catholics.

Native Vlach inhabitants of Croatia, Bosnia, and Herzegovina, as well as most of those who settled there after the Turkish conquest, adopted the language of the Slavic majority even before the arrival of the Turks. Nevertheless, they still identified themselves as Vlachs. This is why the 1630 codes defining the rights and obligations of the population in some areas of the Habsburg Military Frontier where Vlachs formed a majority of the population were called *Statuta Valachorum* (1630). The Vlachs' eventual ethnic identification as Croats or Serbs was essentially determined by their religious affiliation. The majority became members of the Serbian Orthodox Church and developed Serbian national consciousness. Analogously, most Catholic Vlachs came to regard themselves as members of the Croatian nation. This process was largely completed with the emergence of modern nationalism in the Balkans in the nineteenth century.

The Serbianized Vlachs, still often called Vlachs (Vlasi), formed the bulk of the Serbian population in western Bosnia and southern Croatia until their exodus in the summer of 1995. The transformation of Vlachs into Serbs explains why until 1995 there was a higher concentration of Serbs in parts of Bosnia and Croatia distant from Serbia than in some areas adjacent to it. These remote Serb enclaves have influenced Serbian conceptions of Serbia's western border.

Turkish rule was certainly not an apocalyptic evil, and Serbs were not innocent victims of history, as popular tradition based on the Kosovo legend maintains; nevertheless, consequences of the disruption of national life by the prolonged Ottoman domination are still adversely affecting the destiny of Serbia.

3

Dinaric Highlanders and Their Songs

The Violent Balkan Highlands

The idolatry of state and nation, nourished by their fusion with a national church, is an important source of violence in the Balkans, but not the only one. A high level of endemic violence can be found among the inhabitants of the Dinaric Mountains (covering the hinterland of Dalmatian Croatia, Herzegovina, Montenegro, and parts of Bosnia and Serbia) and throughout the mountain chain that extends, under different names, through Albania and Greece. A patriarchal-heroic culture as violent as that in Montenegro developed on the Mani Peninsula at the southern end of the Peloponnesus, a part of ancient Sparta.[1] The tendency toward violence is not limited to any particular church or religion: Catholics and Muslims in this area share it with the Orthodox.[2] What has distinguished the Orthodox Dinaric culture was the combination of traditional endemic violence with the highest degree of union between church and state. A result of this combination was a literary work that glorifies mass violence. By becoming the most popular book in Serbia and Montenegro, it spread the cult of violence far beyond the Dinaric area.

Sociologists regard the way of life of mountain herdsmen—in contrast to that of the more pacific land tillers in the plain—as an important source of violence among Balkan highlanders. The poverty of the people fighting for survival on the barren soil of these mountains, the absence of cities, the isolation, and the preservation of a tribal social structure are important additional factors that contributed to the high level of endemic violence in the area.[3]

No higher civilization—Byzantine, Islamic, or Western—fully replaced the pagan-tribal culture of the inhabitants of the Dinaric Mountains. Illiteracy, still widespread among the highlanders in the first half of the twentieth century, reinforced their isolation and contributed to their preservation of heroic oral folk songs—an artistic expression of tribal-heroic culture—long after those exposed to urban culture had lost interest in it. Among highlanders, folk songs were an essential instrument of education. Illiteracy, the soil in which folk songs flourished, was not uncommon even among clergymen, especially the Orthodox. As a result of their isolation and lack of education, clergymen identified with their congregations to such a degree that they accepted the community's existing moral standards instead of imposing higher ones based on religious precepts.

Violence in the Dinaric areas has been directed not only at different ethnic and religious groups but also at members of the same community. Montenegrin clans, for example, frequently engaged in mutual conflicts, and even called on the Turks to help them fight against fellow Montenegrins. The blood feud, widely practiced by the Montenegrins and Albanians until recently, is another example of violence aimed at members of the same ethnic or religious community.[4] There were numerous cases of Christian Montenegrins fleeing to Turkish territory from vendetta-seeking coreligionists and killing fellow Christians with the same ardor with which they had been killing Muslims.[5]

Collaboration with an external enemy against domestic enemies also occurred under the Austrian occupation during the First World War, as Milovan Djilas relates:

> We Montenegrins did not hold a grudge against the enemy alone, but against one another as well. Indeed, our enemy—the Austrians and their minions—were called to intervene and to help in these quarrels. Two notable clans entered into a blood feud. No one really knew what it was all about. While one side did their shooting as guerrillas, the other side joined the Austrians. The Austrian shadow

hovered over all these crimes. But the root was in ourselves, in Montenegro.[6]

The blood feud made life miserable and weakened the defense against external enemies, but as an integral part of daily life, it also contributed to social order, as an American anthropologist noted:

As in Albania, the blood feud had important functions as a social sanction, in spite of the obvious immediate disruption it brought. Threat of vendetta helped to hold individuals within the marriage pattern. It heightened the degree of group integration within the *brastvo*, and ensured that the *brastvo* would attempt to control behavior of its members. It checked the raiding pattern, especially within the tribe but also in the immediate area; and it extended the protection of the *brastvo* and tribe to isolated houses. While dysfunctional aspects were dramatic, especially during political crises calling for intertribal military solidarity, individual tribes usually remained viable as political units under the vendetta system because truces usually could be made when needed.[7]

The custom of killing the older members of a household when they became a burden, practiced in the Balkan Mountains of eastern Serbia until recently, is a reminder that endemic violence is not limited to the Dinaric Mountains but is present in other Balkan highland areas also. This form of intrafamilial violence (which has not been recorded in Montenegro) was called the *lapot*. In the area of Homolje, Zaječar, and Negotin Krajina, the ritual existed and was practiced on a large scale until the end of the nineteenth century, and even in the early twentieth century:[8]

According to tradition, as G. Trojanović has recorded, when someone got old and weak in the village of Prisjan near Pirot, the family decided to kill that person. The killing was public, in the presence of people. The bailiff went from house to house shouting, "There's a *lapot* in such and such a village, such and such a house, come to the *podušje!*" Family members used to kill the old man or woman in front of the gathering, mostly with a stick, less frequently with rocks or an ax. . . . The killing was done primarily by the victim's children. In Krepoljin and some other places in eastern Serbia, members of the household used to prepare cornmush, put it on the old man's or woman's head, and strike it with an ax until the person died. They did it this way to make it appear that the mush was the killer, not themselves.[9]

The sociologist Dinko Tomasic noted that in Dinaric society, from earliest times to the present, sharp father-son clashes were a regular occurrence, and patricides and infanticides were common. In more recent times, politics and ideology have been an important source of intrafamilial violence. During World War II, for instance, in Dinaric families, fathers and sons often found themselves in opposite camps. Particularly "in Montenegro there were a number of instances in which sons who fought with the Partisans executed their own fathers who were made prisoners while fighting with the Chetniks."[10]

The reckless assertion of personal power at every level of Dinaric society is a basic source of violence. In such an environment, violent self-assertion brings respect, as an incident between Milovan Djilas and his elder brother illustrates: "He could not endure being crossed by a youngster, and I could not endure being struck, I grabbed a knife from the table. The stab in his thigh was deep and wide; the blood spurted across the room. . . . After that he never turned on me. Apparently he understood, all of a sudden, that I was sufficiently mature so that beatings could solve no disputes."[11]

Dinaric willingness to resort to violence is glorified by nationalist ideologues as a part of a heroic lifestyle dedicated to freedom and independence, but it is essentially a manifestation of lawlessness. Dinaric violence is a way of administering justice where the aggrieved party both accuses and punishes in the absence of the rule of law. However, the same man who uses unrestrained violence against his adversaries may be quite submissive to an authority backed by force. A nineteenth-century observer of life in Montenegro noticed this paradox of the Dinaric man: "He is as courageous in combat as he is fearful of harsh authorities. Harsh authorities can turn him into a true slave."[12] This explains why the Balkan highlanders' willingness to fight has never resulted in true political freedom, although it has helped the struggle for independence. Guerrilla-type warfare that goes on for generations has a very negative impact on respect for the rule of law and human life, and thus on the ability to achieve freedom from domestic oppressors once the foreign ones are ousted.

Dinaric lawlessness also has had a strong economic incentive. Robbery, looting, and rustling represented an important source of income among highlanders. Haiduks were notorious Dinaric highwaymen in the Ottoman Empire.[13] Folk songs celebrate them as apostles of justice and freedom in the fight against the Turks, but robbery was usually the primary motive of their activity. Ranke relates that the haiduk Veljko, who participated in the Serbian uprising against the Turks, "was fond of war, not for the attainment of any specific object, but for its own sake," and that, being advised by the Russians not to call himself *haiduk* because it signified a *robber,* he replied, "I should be sorry if there were any greater robber than I am."[14]

In Balkan highland culture, violence is often taken for granted, without any sense of guilt or sorrow for the victims. In haiduk folk songs "there is no trace of awareness that the hanging of prisoners and the cutting off of ears as keepsakes might give rise to any other human feeling but mirth."[15] A high level of violence and the condoning of the most vicious cruelty as just punishment can be observed in the Serbian folk song "Grujo's Wife's Treachery."

The plot of the song begins with Maximia, the beautiful wife of the haiduk Grujo, hitting her little son, Stevan, to prevent him from waking up his father and warning him that three Turks are approaching. She hits him so hard that "the child rolled over three times, lost three sound teeth, and disjointed four."[16] She then helps the Turks capture Grujo, but a barmaid's ruse and the son's help set him free. There is violence again, when Stevan cuts the rope with which his father's hands were tied; too small to handle the knife properly, he cuts his father's hand, too. The child is horrified at the sight of blood, but his father comforts him by saying that the rope, not the hand, is bleeding. After several episodes, including the killing of the three Turks, Grujo sets out to punish his wife. After taking her clothes off,

> He smeared his wife with wax and tar,
> And sulphur and fast powder,
> Wrapped her in soft cotton,
> Poured strong brandy over her,
> Buried her up to her waist,
> Lit the hair on her head,
> And sat down to drink cool wine,
> While she cast light like a bright candle.[17]

Grujo was not moved by Maximia's entreaties as she was burning, but when the flames consumed her breasts the son burst out in tears and said, "My mother's breasts have burned, / The breasts that nursed me, father, / And put me on my feet." His son's words moved Grujo to tears too. "He extinguished what was left, / And buried it nicely."[18] This ending, and the "bleeding rope" episode, clearly show an intent to portray the outlaw Grujo as a good and sensitive man who gives deserved punishment to a wicked woman; "the terrifying lines which describe the torture are meant to ring as a kind of hymn to justice."[19]

Grujo engages in similar savagery in another folk song, in which he, as a child, maims his mother. His father, Old Novak,[20] lets the son cut off his mother's right breast and both arms, and after setting her afire they both warm themselves by the flame.[21] The selection of severed organs is not random. They are the ones most directly engaged in the act of nursing: the mother holds the child in her arms while it feeds on her breast. The misogyny of patriarchal-heroic culture reaches its absolute peak here: violence is directed against motherhood and thus against life itself.

By calling the haiduk a devil, the folk singer seems to acknowledge the evil of the haiduks' way of life, yet he finds the devil fascinating:

> If one could have seen this!
> A devil riding on a devil's back,
> A mountain haiduk on a furious white horse.[22]

The Prince-Bishop's "Song of Horror"

Byzantium and other Orthodox societies are often called caesaro-papist because of the subordination of the church to the state, although the two institutions have been ruled by different persons. In one Orthodox country, however, caesaropapism reached its most radical form: archbishops of Cetinje, who also had the title of *vladikas*, were heads of the Montenegrin Orthodox Church and simultaneously the rulers of Montenegro. The office was hereditary, passing from uncle to nephew. This exercise of supreme political and ecclesiastic rule by one person lasted until 1852.[23]

One of these caesaropapist rulers, Vladika Petar Petrović Njegoš (1813–51), was also a poet, generally regarded as the founder of modern Montenegrin and Serbian literatures.[24] His most celebrated work is the dramatic poem *Gorski vijenac (The Mountain Wreath)*, first published in 1847. It is worth examining this work in some detail, because its combination of high artistic value (which cannot be fully appreciated in any of the existing English translations), religious symbolism, and glorification of genocide may well be unparalleled in world literature.

The poem was inspired by a massacre of Muslims, popularly known as "Christmas Eve" or "The Extermination of the Turks" (the "Turks" in question were actually native Slavs who converted to Islam during the Turkish rule). It originally carried the subtitle "a historical event from the end of the seventeenth century."[25] The main theme of the poem is the conflict between Christian and Muslim Montenegrins, resolved through the massacre of the latter.

The poem starts with an explosion of hatred. In the opening monologue by the principal character, Vladika Danilo, the "Turks" are variously called devils, the devil's tribe, the devil's large maw, accursed litter, and loathsome degenerates, and they are compared to locusts and to an owl gulping a bird. But the vladika has a solution to the blight:

> The blasphemers of Christ's name
> we will baptize with water or with blood!

> We'll drive the plague out of the pen!
> Let the song of horror ring forth,
> a true altar on a blood-stained rock.[26]

The plot is simple. Two assemblies of Christian Montenegrin chieftains, one held on the highest peak in their country on the eve of Pentecost, the other on the day of the Nativity of the Virgin Mary, result in the decision "to cleanse the country of infidels."[27] After they fail to persuade the Muslims to change their faith, they decide to kill all those who refuse to convert. The massacres take place on Christmas Eve.

The connection of the plot with important dates in the Christian calendar is enhanced by a natural phenomenon: during the first assembly, in stormy weather atop the mountain, two lightnings "made a cross of live fire / What a marvelous sight it was! / Nobody in the world has ever / heard of or seen such a cross."[28]

The climactic penultimate scene takes place on Christmas Day. A student cheerfully informs the blind Abbot Stefan about the clouds of smoke rising from burned villages and the slaughter: "there's a slaughter, and a big one, too; / delighted, I listened to it for one hour!"[29] The abbot associates the smoke with the holiday: "How can a national sacrifice / be made without clouds of smoke?"[30] A large group of blood-spattered people appears next and addresses the vladika:

> The tidings are good, our Lord.
> . . . .
> As large as Cetinje Valley is,
> not a single witness escaped
> to tell what happened there.
> We put under our sabers all those
> who did not want to be baptized;
> But those who bowed to the Holy Child,
> and crossed themselves with the Christian cross,
> we accepted as our brothers.
> We burned all Turkish houses,
> that there might be no abode nor trace
> of our infidel domestic enemy.[31]

The prince-bishop is delighted by the news:

> What a joy, my falcons,
> what a joy, heroic liberty!
> This morning you've marvelously resurrected
> from the tombs of our forefathers![32]

Unlike the vladika, who combines ecclesiastic and political roles, old Abbot Stefan is conceived of as a purely spiritual figure. This adds weight to his invitation to the slayers to receive the sacrament: "Come here, brothers, and take the Holy Communion / without fast and without confession, / I will take it all upon my soul."[33]

The final scene takes place on New Year's Day. The vladika and the abbot receive the news of the slaughter of Muslims in yet another district:

> The slaughter lasted one day and one night:
> The Crmnica River was filled with Turks,
>
> . . . .
> There is no longer in our district
> any trace of the Turkish presence
> except for headless corpses or ruins.[34]

The vladika weeps for the Christians that perished in the expedition, but the abbot laughs and says,

> If I could weep for joy,
> I would weep more sweetly than ever,
> But with me, when my soul is singing,
> my tears dry up from joy.[35]

Still another warrior, Vuk Mandušić, arrives, blood-spattered and holding a broken rifle. At a meeting of Montenegrin leaders at the beginning of the poem, he had proposed to cleanse the country of infidels, and vowed that "our struggle will not end / until the extermination, Turkish or ours."[36] Now he describes one more bloody event and weeps over his rifle, ruined by the enemy's bullet:

> I mourn my old rifle more
> than I would my own arm had it been hit.

> I mourn it as if it were my only son,
> I mourn it as if it were my own brother,
> because it was a gun above all guns.
> It brought good luck, and it was deadly.[37]

The poem ends with the prince-bishop giving Vuk a new rifle, "for in the hands of Vuk Mandušić / every rifle will be deadly." This conclusion conveys the message that the task, which has not been completed, must be carried on, and the abrupt end of the poem reinforces the impression that it is not the true end, and that the extermination of infidels must be pursued to the end.

The rejoicing over the massacres and their depiction as a baptism in blood that leads to the nation's rebirth make the poem a hymn to genocide.[38] The author is aware that he is making a pact with the devil, but he believes that future generations will enjoy the flowers of the evil:

> Let Hell devour, and Satan mow down!
> Flowers will grow at the graveyard
> for some remote future generation.[39]

In addition to hatred of Islam and a lament for fallen Byzantium, the poem displays a strong contempt for the West, conveyed through the various characters' comments on Venice. In Njegoš's time, Venice had long passed the zenith of its power but still offered many attractions to a visitor. Nevertheless, Njegoš, the autocratic ruler of a country where impaled human heads were always on display on a tower visible from his residence, disparaged Venetian cuisine and entertainment, including music, and found the people of Venice sickly, effeminate, and sly.[40] While his Montenegrin characters are heroic, healthy, and freedom-loving, cowardly Venetians live in constant fear of the oppressive police state: "However large Venice is from end to end, / there was not a single person there / who did not believe any fellow citizen / to be a secret agent and a spy."[41] This exaggeration is even more curious in view of the kind of regime the author of these verses established in his own country. Even a sympathetic biographer noted that Njegoš himself introduced spying and secret murders, mostly by ambush, in his native country.[42] Similarly, the criticism of dismal conditions in Venice's notorious Piombi prison by a character in *The Mountain Wreath* becomes hollow when he suggests the execution of inmates as a better alternative: "Why don't you kill them off bravely?"[43]

The Mountain Wreath is a most vivid illustration of how religion may be distorted when it is dominated by the spirit of tribalism. Bishop Nikolaj Velimirović, a passionate eulogist of Njegoš's work, pointed out that the name most frequently mentioned in it, after God, is Miloš Obilić, the slayer of Sultan Murad at Kosovo, and that "this knight is to our poet some kind of divinity; this is why we speak of Obilić's altar."[44] In another poem, Njegoš expresses an equally exalted view of the slaying of a national enemy: "God's dearest sacrifice is / a boiling stream of tyrant's blood."[45]

The author of a 1930s anthropological study of the Yugoslavs noted the discrepancy between Njegoš's ideas and Christ's teaching: "Unlike the gentle Nazarene, teacher of love and forgiveness, God Sabbaoth, Christ Pantocrator, Archangel Michael, and Saint George are symbols of a heroized Christianity. . . . Njegoš, the philosopher of this religion, has no deeper bond with the personality of Christ."[46] Bishop Velimirović made the same judgment: "Njegoš's Christology is almost rudimentary. No Christian priest has ever said less about Christ than this metropolitan from Cetinje."[47]

The glorification of murder is not the only deviation from Christianity to be found in Njegoš's work: the idea of the world as an evil place is another anti-Christian view. In the words of Abbot Stefan, "This world is a tyrant to the tyrant, / let alone to a noble soul! / It is work of infernal discord: / in it the soul is at war with the flesh."[48] These verses are followed by a powerful passage listing the elements constantly at war with each other, and ending with man seeing a monkey in the mirror. The ideas of an eternal struggle between good and evil and the imprisonment of the soul in the body, clearly expressed in these verses, are central ideas of cosmological dualism, usually called Manicheism.[49]

Believers in cosmological dualism—such as the Albigenses, Cathars, and Bogomils—taught that good and evil are two equally powerful eternal forces. The world itself is evil, and man should escape from it through ascetic behavior, including vegetarianism and the refusal to procreate. The theme of *The Mountain Wreath*, however, is not the cosmic struggle between good and evil but the struggle for a homogeneous Orthodox theocracy. Such a community is celebrated as the supreme good, and any means toward its realization are permitted. This is the spirit of a primitive tribal religion in which the neighbor of a different faith is the devil and must be annihilated: "Strike the devil, leave no trace of him."[50] And revenge is "a holy potion, consecrated by God."[51]

Although Njegoš thought of Orthodox Christianity and Islam as epitomizing good versus evil, the methods advocated in *The Mountain Wreath* to achieve the victory of Orthodoxy make the conflict between the two religions as devoid of morality as a fight between gladiators: "Our faiths will swim in blood, / the better one will not sink."[52] His nihilism and necrophilia are even more explicit in the following verses: "The Crescent and the Cross, two dreadful symbols—/ their kingdoms rule over tombs."[53]

It is noteworthy that the theme of the struggle against the Turks was not a part of the Serbian folk singers' repertory in the sixteenth and seventeenth centuries. During this period of Turkish rule, the Serbs enjoyed peace and the benefits of a well-administered empire; their church had substantial autonomy; and service in the Ottoman army provided income for many Serbs. Under these conditions, interest in the conflict between Serbs and Turks waned, and Prince Marko, who served the Turks, rather than Prince Lazar or Miloš Obilić, who died fighting them, became by far the most popular Serbian hero. During the same period, folk singers and poets in those parts of Croatia not conquered by the Turks and in the countries farther to the west sang the glory of Lazar, Miloš, and other Serbian heroes who confronted the Turks. However, the mythical component of the struggle was largely absent from the songs and poems cultivated in those countries engaged in military confrontation with the Ottoman Empire. Another trait absent from the poems produced in Western Christian areas is the intense and overt hatred displayed in *The Mountain Wreath*.

Ivan Gundulić (1589–1638), the author of a major work of Croatian Baroque literature, the epic poem *Osman*, was a native of Dubrovnik, geographically very close to Montenegro, yet his attitude toward the Turks is vastly different. Although Gundulić longs for the liberation of Christians and glorifies the Polish king for his victory over the Turks, he deals rather sympathetically with the tragic story of Sultan Osman. Osman is portrayed as more noble and humane than historic records indicate, and his downfall is seen as a manifestation of the fickleness of fate.

One of the major Hungarian literary works of the seventeenth century is the epic poem *Szigeti veszedelem* (The Siege of Sziget) by Miklos Zrinyi (1620–1664), a nobleman from the powerful Croatian feudal family Zrinski. The poem deals with the 1566 siege of the castle at Sziget by the army of Suleiman the Magnificent, who decided to capture the fortress on his way to Vienna. The defenders, commanded by the poet's great-grandfather, a viceroy, bravely resisted. When faced with an inevitable defeat by vastly superior forces, they chose to die in a sortie. In spite of the fact that other members of the Zrinski family, including the author himself, also participated and some died in fierce battles with the Turks, the poem never demonizes them. The Turks are portrayed as human beings, and a love story between Deliman the Tatar and the sultan's daughter Cumilla is interwoven into the main plot. The following verses about the sultan illustrate the poet's respect for the enemy:

> The truth I must write, let all hear it now,
> Although Sultan Suleiman was our enemy,
> Excepting that he was a pagan, there
> had never been such a lord among the Turks.

> But even without the exception, I can boldly state
> There has never been on this earth, even among pagans,
> Such a wise man and hero who in so many battles,
> And in so many countries had been triumphant.[54]

Pavao Ritter Vitezović (1652–1713) is another Croatian nobleman-warrior-poet who wrote about the Sziget tragedy. His poem *Odiljenje sigetsko* (The Sziget Farewell), first published in 1684, reminisces about the event without rancor or cry for revenge. The last of the four cantos, titled "Tombstones," consists of epitaphs for the Croatian and Turkish warriors who died during the siege, paying equal respect to both. The following is the epitaph for a Croatian warrior:

> I bloodied, stained, and dulled my saber,
> blood gave glory and distinction to me,
> Ivan Novaković of the Debeljak clan,
> whom songs praise as a brave man.
> I sent Murtuzan Pasha to Mohammed
> together with other Muslims at Sziget.
> But I myself fell where the viceroy and the city fell,
> God has given me life in heavens for this death.[55]

The epitaph for Murtuzan Pasha is essentially identical to that of his slayer:

> Here below Sziget
> a father and son, Murtuzan and Ahmed,
> lie, to the sultan's honor:
> We fought so hard that we gave our lives.
> Among soldiers our bodies
> rest here, our names forever,
> our souls in heavenly glory.[56]

A collection of poems written by the Croatian Franciscan priest Andrija Kačić-Miošić (1704–60) under the title *Razgovor ugodni naroda slovinskoga* (A Pleasant Discourse of Slavic People) is of lesser artistic value than Njegoš's poem but rivaled *The Mountain Wreath* in popularity for a long time. Most of these poems deal with bloody battles between Christians and Muslims, yet the author evidences respect for the enemy. For example, the final poem of the collection, "The Last Poem about Glorious Bosnia," treats the warriors in both camps equally; after praising the Christian heroes, the poet celebrates the Slavic Muslims who distinguished themselves in battles, and concludes with the following verses:

> All of them are Bosnians of old,
> Bosnians or Herzegovinians,

who converted to Islam
when the Turks conquered Bosnia,

together with countless other heroes,
old Bosnian knights,
who cut more Christian heads
than there are grass leaves in the Coastland.

Farewell, Milovan!
Pray to God, forget the battles:
everything is nothing, everything will turn to dust;
repent for your sins, one must meet God.[57]

The author of *The Mountain Wreath,* an avid multilingual reader, must have known most of these poems as well as other works in which the Western Christian tradition imposed restraints on the expression of anger and hatred. But his work is no less exceptional in comparison with the literature of Orthodox Russia. A particularly apt comparison here is with Alexander Pushkin's *Eugene Onegin.* Even in Eastern Europe, where poets have traditionally played a significantly more important social role than in the West, the popularity of Pushkin's *Eugene Onegin* with the Russians and Njegoš's *Mountain Wreath* with the Serbs and Montenegrins is unparalleled. Many people from all social strata in the respective countries know large segments of these long poems by heart. The Russian critic Vissarion Belinski called *Eugene Onegin* an encyclopedia of Russian life. *The Mountain Wreath,* whose meager plot is enriched with colorful episodes depicting many aspects of life in Montenegro, can as appropriately be called an encyclopedia of Montenegrin life. Both works were created at approximately the same time (only fourteen years separate their publication) in Slavic countries sharing the same religion, yet they could hardly be more different.

One of the differences consists in the role and stature of male and female characters. Reflecting the patriarchal world of Montenegro, Njegoš's poem has only male characters—violent highlanders engaged in slaughtering their neighbors of a different religion. One woman does speak in the poem, but she has no name. Identified only as a sister of one of the heroes, she delivers a lament for the slain brother and then kills herself.[58] The men have no significant individual traits either; they are all immersed in the collective.[59]

Pushkin's Onegin, on the other hand, is a decadent antihero. The aimless existence of this spoiled, bored, blasé aristocrat is contrasted with the real hero of the work—Tatiana, a woman of integrity, simplicity, and strength, capable of experiencing intense love. She has been the model for several heroines of Tolstoy and other Russian writers.[60]

In *The Mountain Wreath* the poet hails the massacre as the road to national rebirth, whereas Pushkin makes the reader feel the absurdity of violence through the killing of a principal character.[61] Great Russian novelists such as Tolstoy and Dostoevsky follow Pushkin by showing the futility of violence.

The contrast between the two most popular literary works of these Slavic nations reflects the contrast between the sophistication of Russia's upper classes and the roughness of the Balkan highlands. It also reflects certain differences between the respective churches. Like any other Orthodox Church, the Russian church has been corrupted by its close relationship with political power and national aspirations. But in contrast to Serbia and Montenegro, the subordination to politics has not permeated all levels of the Russian Orthodox church. The lower clergy in Russia often rebelled against the hierarchy and preserved an intense religious spirit. Besides, there have been powerful religious sects in Russia outside the state church. In the two Balkan nations, however, there have been no rebellions against the politicization of the church and no rival sects.[62]

Moreover, the glorification of genocide in *The Mountain Wreath* cannot be attributed to external influences. Many foreign influences can be detected, but not in the sphere of ethics. The un-Christian ethos of *The Mountain Wreath* has two main roots. One is the old pagan cult of revenge, particularly strong in Dinaric tribal societies, and expressed in the kind of folk poetry that experienced an enthusiastic revival in the late eighteenth and early nineteenth centuries— the time of Njegoš, himself a collector of folk poetry. Another major impetus to hatred came from the demonization of the enemy in the teachings of the Serbian Orthodox Church. Miodrag Popović notes this influence:

> Folk poetry took over the idea of Sultan Murad as a mythical evil from the church tradition. Already in the Kosovo *Narrations,* and especially in the *Service to Holy Prince Lazar,* in the sections that talk about Turks, we find expressions such as true snake, wild beast, infernal dragon, Satan, children of beast and dragon, which shows that the Church saw them as a mythical evil long before folk tradition did.[63]

The Chorus

The importance and influence of Njegoš's powerful poetic work in Serbian and Montenegrin cultures cannot be overemphasized. The Bosnian Serb historian Milorad Ekmečić, who became the chief ideologist of Serbian aggression against Bosnia in the 1990s, mentions that it "was published in twenty editions between 1847 and 1913, to become the most widely read literary work among the Serbs. It was *The Mountain Wreath* together with the myth of Kosovo that provided the Serbian nationalist movement with its ethic in the following century."[64] Its influence is comparable to that of the Bible in Protestant countries or the Qur'an in the Islamic world, but its message is very different.[65] Through the authority of its author and the appeal of its verse, the immensely popular poem sanctioned and reinforced the endemic violence from which it sprang.

It can only be speculated to what degree a massacre of Muslims in the newly formed Yugoslavia (long after the Turks had left) was inspired by Njegoš's poetry, because that bloody raid committed by Montenegrins had numerous precedents in the violent history of the area. However, there is no doubt that the participants in the raid knew Njegoš's most popular poem very well. The raid is described by Montenegrin-born Milovan Djilas (1911–95), a prominent Yugoslav communist leader and subsequently a dissident, in an autobiographical work aptly titled *Land without Justice*. Djilas's father was one of the leaders of the raid.

In the autumn of 1924, a Montenegrin chieftain was killed in an ambush. It was not known who killed him (later it was found that he had been killed by rival Montenegrin chieftains), yet a raid was staged and about 350 Muslims were killed. There had been no war at the time, not even a local conflict. Djilas recognizes that the Muslim population under attack "was unarmed, and most were not warlike."[66] Raids were frequent in the area, and according to Djilas, "raiding parties, which engaged also in sheep rustling, were a branch of the local economy, and one of the most profitable at that."[67] However, the scope and level of violence in this raid made it very different from those raids motivated by personal gain:

> After those prisoners in Šahovići were mowed down, one of our villagers, Sekula, went from corpse to corpse and severed the ligaments at their heels. This is what is done in the village with oxen after they are struck down by a blow of the ax, to keep them from getting up again if they should revive. Some who went through the pockets of the dead found bloody cubes of sugar there and ate them. Babes were taken from the arms of mothers and sisters and slaughtered before their eyes. These same murderers later tried to justify themselves by saying that they would not have cut their throats but only shot them had their mothers and sisters not been there. The beards of the Moslem religious leaders were torn out and crosses were carved into their foreheads. In one village a group was tied around a haystack with wire and fire set to it. . . .
>
> One group attacked an isolated Moslem homestead. They found the peasant skinning a lamb. They intended to shoot him and burn down the house, but the skinning of the lamb inspired them to hang the peasant by his heels on the same plum tree. A skilled butcher split open the peasant's head with an ax, but very carefully, so as not to harm the torso. Then he cut open the chest. The heart was still pulsating. The butcher plucked it out with his hand and threw it to a dog.[68]

Yugoslav authorities did not even attempt to identify or punish the perpetrators of the crime. There was no investigation of any kind.

Because of this and other massacres, the Muslims of that region began to migrate to Turkey, selling their homesteads for a trifle, and Orthodox Montenegrin settlers replaced them. It was a successful act of "ethnic cleansing," to use the euphemism the Serbs made popular about seventy years later.

Djilas's honesty and courage in relating the hideous event in which his own father played a leading role must be admired, as one must also admire his courage in denouncing communism after he became disappointed with it. Nevertheless, his break with communism did not mean a break with the cult of violence (although as a dissident he no longer had the opportunity to practice it). Djilas's first book in his postcommunist phase was a tribute to Njegoš, "the poet of massacres in which the cutting off of heads was a sacred and heroic act."[69]

Djilas justified Njegoš's advocacy of violence. He recognized that violence was evil, yet found its use in the service of Serbia's national goals permissible because "Serbianism is a concrete form of the human desire for good, for freedom."[70] The title Djilas gave to the central chapter of his study of Njegoš—"Poet of Serbian Cosmic Misfortune"—indicates that he supported the popular idea that Serbia faced the indifference or hostility of practically the entire world, in spite, or perhaps because, of its goodness.

Djilas's biographer Vladimir Dedijer stated that Djilas knew *The Mountain Wreath* by heart and recited it frequently as a leader of the communist resistance movement during World War II.[71] It may well have contributed to his cruelty and fanaticism. Djilas himself cut the throat of at least one war prisoner; he describes the act in his book *Wartime*.[72] Dedijer offers numerous additional instances of Djilas's fondness for killing during World War II.[73] And Richard West offers an example from the postwar period: "Once, when he was minister of information, he printed in the newspaper *Borba* a long complaint that two black marketeers had been given prison terms instead of the death sentence; as a result of this they were hanged."[74]

Djilas's apology for Njegoš's violence was therefore simultaneously an apology for his own deeds: "Foreigners reproached [Nje-

goš] for cruelty because of the taking of heads. They did not com-
prehend our sufferings and passions."[75] Years after his disillusionment with communist ideology, Djilas justified the cruelties
committed in its name: "we had to have an ideology that would
inspire general confidence and impress on our fighting men that we
were struggling for a just, the only just, cause. That belief demanded
the use of means which, under different circumstances, I would
have repudiated and rejected."[76] Such sophistry allowed Djilas to
find beauty and virtue even in massacres:

> Njegoš's massacre was the first, or at least among the very rare, to be
> a poetic and even a humanistic motif, one in which the very deed is
> magnified. What is new is the light he casts on this deed, the dem-
> onstration of its inevitability and justice, and, above all, its poetic
> expression. Njegoš was the first to experience passionately and to
> give expression to a massacre as an aspect of human destiny, as a
> higher ordinance. Herein lies its originality and its greatness.[77]

Thus, in his early postcommunist stage, Djilas did not come any
closer to the Western concept of humanism: "Njegoš's humanism,
and ours—the mastery over evil through evil—is dark and
bloody."[78] Later in his life, Djilas fought state-sponsored violence as
a human rights activist and a harsh critic of the abuse of power, but
he never repudiated his enthusiasm for the "poet of massacres."

Djilas was joined by others in singing uncritical praise of Njegoš's
alleged love of fellow men and freedom. The Nobel laureate Ivo
Andrić, for example, concluded an essay titled "Njegoš's Humaneness" by stating that "every celebration of Njegoš's poetic work is
simultaneously a celebration of humaneness and man's struggle for
humaneness"![79] Leaders of the Serbian Orthodox Church have
rivaled secular Serbian nationalists and communist ideologues in
their praise of Njegoš. For example, Bishop Velimirović maintained
that Njegoš was a humane and noble man and that his approval of
violence, including headhunting and impalement, was based on a
keen sense of justice: "The Turks are [tyrants and] enemies of
justice, thus they are evil, and the evil has to be crushed until it is
eradicated. In a row of dried up heads, Njegoš did not see human

heads but only heads of the enemies of justice. These rows of heads served as trophies of avenged justice."[80]

In the almost one and a half centuries between the appearance of *The Mountain Wreath* and the outbreak of the 1990s war in the Balkans that attempted to carry out the message contained in the poem, no scholar anywhere unequivocally condemned the antihumanist and antireligious character of the work, which has been translated into a number of languages.[81] In a study published in 1985, the Bosnian Muslim literary historian Muhsin Rizvić went further than most in recognizing the presence of an ethical problem in the poem, but he also went to great lengths to minimize Njegoš's attachment to violence and to attribute it to Western influences. Rizvić pointed out Casimir Delavigne's *Vêpres siciliennes*, Gianbattista Niccolini's *Giovanni da Procida*, and especially Friedrich Schiller's *Wilhelm Tell* as models for the massacre in Njegoš's dramatic poem.[82] According to him, "the romantic motif of a general massacre connected with the idea of national liberation was alive in German literary life at the time" (that is, the time when Njegoš's tutor, the writer Sima Milutinović, lived in Germany).

In his attempt to trace Njegoš's praise of genocide to a Western source, Rizvić incorrectly stated that "in Schiller's play the conspirators make the decision to exterminate all foreigners."[83] In fact, in *Wilhelm Tell*, most of the Swiss confederates are opposed to the use of violence. They feel they have justice on their side and that God will provide a way to freedom without bloodshed. In Schiller's play, anger is controlled by moral forces; in Njegoš's poem, hatred eliminates morality.[84] A comparison of the endings of the two works highlights the extent of the ethical difference between them. Schiller's play concludes with social peace achieved by the nobles' renunciation of their privileges and the granting of freedom to their subjects; Njegoš's poem ends with massacres followed by the blessing of a gun. The Romanticist spirit comes much closer to *The Mountain Wreath* in the verses of "La Marseillaise," "Let impure blood / drench our fields," than in *Wilhelm Tell*.

When an area is saturated with myths, and especially when the myths are vigorously promoted by the state and other institutions, specialists in the area often accept those myths and end up being more ignorant in important aspects of their field than sober-minded nonspecialists. Reactions to the English translation of Djilas's *Njegoš: Poet, Prince, Bishop* illustrate this paradox. Most reviewers of the book—educated persons guided by common sense and common morality—noted serious deficiencies of the work, both in style and content. The *Time* reviewer found it "turgid in style and parochial in scope."[85] John Simon stated in *Book Week* that, "for the most part, Djilas rambles and repeats himself, moralizes and philosophizes away windily, and untidily struggles to resolve moral ambivalences about his subject and life in general"; displays "a kind of peasant hamminess that thinks itself elegant"; and shows "propensity for bad, usually chauvinistic prose poetry."[86] The reviewer for an American Library Association publication remarked that Djilas was "in grave difficulties with Western humanism, which, judging by this book, he does not wish to understand," and added, "A world of Njegošes would be a blood bath. Djilas, in our time, champions Njegoš, although, clearly, had he been Njegoš' prisoner (and not Tito's), he would have been impaled years ago."[87] Anthony West noted in the *New Yorker* that "[i]deas remarkably close to [Djilas's ideas about massacres] were used by Hitler's accomplices and accessories to justify their participation in his crimes against humanity," and ended with this eloquent statement: "Njegoš was, in sober truth, the embodiment of everything that a free nation must outgrow, and in holding him up for our admiration Djilas helps to perpetuate the tyranny of local and regional loyalties that has made man the cruelest and most destructive of the animals."[88]

A Harvard University professor of Slavic literature, on the other hand, was enthusiastic about Djilas's book. Albert B. Lord, whom the Serbian Orthodox Church—quite appropriately—decorated with the Order of Saint Sava, found the work "extraordinary" (the adjective is used three times), "important," "superb," "penetrating," "inspired," "pertinent," "remarkable," "powerful," consisting of "small masterpieces," and possessing "deep emotion and sincerity."[89]

The general failure (until very recently) of the Njegoš and Balkan area experts to comment on the glaring ethical problem in *The Mountain Wreath* is particularly striking. One of the reasons for the phenomenon is "eternal Romanticism"—man's seemingly immutable fascination with dark passions and violence, as long as they do not threaten him personally. A more prosaic reason is that the monarchist and communist Yugoslavias, both of which glorified Njegoš as a noble mind, fighter for freedom, and champion of Yugoslavism, rewarded those who accepted their myths and closed the door to those who did not.

Serbia's 1990s wars have finally prompted a wide recognition of the obvious: Njegoš's *Mountain Wreath* is a call to genocide. Some Serbs and Montenegrins are beginning to admit it as well. Indeed, the author of the first monograph addressing the criminal aspect of the work is the Montenegrin writer Stanko Cerović.

4

The Dilemmas of Modern Serbian National Identity

The Legacy of the Enlightenment and Romanticism

The cultural history of Serbia, like that of Russia and other Eastern European Orthodox countries, followed a development different from that of Catholic and Protestant Europe. In Orthodox countries, the equivalent of the Middle Ages—the period during which the church was the dominant bearer of cultural heritage—lasted until the late seventeenth and early eighteenth centuries. Strong ties were then established with the West, at the time when the Enlightenment had laid the foundation for modern secular culture. This contact, uninterrupted since, has led to a large-scale assimilation of Western culture by the Serbs.

However, the anti-Western attitude, nourished primarily by the Serbian Orthodox Church and by the old pagan-tribal ethos, did not disappear but has reasserted itself as a lasting and powerful current in Serbian culture. The elevation of an old pagan war god to the patron saint of the nation is the most conspicuous manifestation of the reaffirmation of tribal attitudes in the era of Westernization. The Western ideology of Romanticism, with its cult of supposedly pure primitive cultures, aided the revival of Serbian pagan-heroic culture, which is indifferent or even hostile to a social order based on the rights of the individual citizen.

Another Romanticist idea—that vernacular language and folk art represent the purest expressions of the soul of a nation and the most important criterion for its identity—has served as the foundation for the modern concept of a Greater Serbia (as well as for the Yugoslav idea). The desire to achieve that Greater Serbia, as opposed to a smaller Serbia based on the rule of law, represents another dilemma of modern Serbian history.

While the Westernization of Russia was suddenly launched by Tsar Peter the Great, the Serbs' Westernization started more gradually, from below, with the Serbian community in the Habsburg territory north of the Sava and Danube Rivers. Serbs started settling in those Hungarian and Croatian lands in the fifteenth century, during the last stage of Serbian resistance to the Turkish advance. Next came the Serbs who served in the Ottoman army, and were given land that had become vacant owing to Turkish raids. The expulsion of the Turks in the late seventeenth century again provided a lot of vacant land that attracted more settlers from the south as well as from all Habsburg lands.

Serbian nineteenth-century historiography, however, depicted the Serbs' settlement in the Pannonian plain principally as a result of an allegedly cataclysmic exodus in 1690, called the Great Migration. Among the consequences of that migration, according to the legend, was the transformation of Kosovo from a purely Serbian into a predominantly Albanian-inhabited area. The actual exodus, which was of relatively modest proportions, was caused by a reversal of military fortunes. In a series of victories over Ottoman forces in 1689, the Austrian army advanced as far south as Skopje. Some local inhabitants joined it as auxiliary troops. The next year the Ottoman forces and their Tatar auxiliaries pushed the Austrians back and committed large-scale atrocities as a punishment for the revolt. Some Serbs fled to the mountains. The number of those who fled to Habsburg territory, led by the patriarch of Peć, Arsenije III Čarnojević, appears to have been less than forty thousand, about one-fourth of them from Kosovo.[1]

The most significant result of the 1690 wave of settlers was that it brought the head of the Serbian Orthodox Church to Habsburg territory. The arrival of Patriarch Arsenije led to the establishment of the Serbian Orthodox metropolinate in the city of Karlovci in the Slavonian Military Frontier in 1713. The Austrians, who wanted to weaken the power of the Hungarian nobility, offered the Serbian church a status not very different from the one it enjoyed in the Ottoman Empire. There was no millet system in the Habsburg lands, but the Viennese court granted a series of special privileges to the Serbian church, so that, in a predominantly Catholic empire, Serbian Orthodox metropolitans exercised a higher degree of political authority than did the Catholic prelates.

As the situation of the Ottoman Serbs worsened with the abolition of the patriarchate of Peć and the subordination of the Serbian Orthodox Church to the patriarchate in Istanbul in 1766, the Serb diaspora in the Habsburg Empire became the main vehicle of Serbian religious and cultural life. The city of Novi Sad remained the center of Serbian culture until the mid-nineteenth century.

The dominant cultural trend at the time when Pannonian Serbs developed a prosperous and educated middle class was the Enlightenment (which arrived in this part of Europe with a delay of about two decades), a movement drastically different from the tribal-heroic culture of their Dinaric ancestors. The most prominent Serb thinker to emerge in this new cultural climate was Dositej Obradović (1739–1811), a modernizer who strove to eliminate old pagan customs and beliefs from Serbian culture. He advocated tolerance and regarded folk poetry as a negative influence. Obradović wanted to orient Serbia toward the West rather than Russia. Thus, there is a striking contrast between Njegoš's disdain for Venice and Obradović's enthusiasm for the capital of the Habsburg Empire: "The entire city of Vienna seemed to be mine, because I could stroll in it as much as I wanted. . . . The world-famous Vienna masked ball, comedies, Italian operas, concerts, imperial libraries, all these merry and useful entertainments and delights I could enjoy, and did enjoy as much as upper-class people do."[2]

Together with Stefan Stratimirović, Lukijan Mušicki, and other followers of the Enlightenment, Obradović wanted to uproot paganism among the Serbs. Not surprisingly, Njegoš, who, together with Vuk Karadžić and other Romanticists, introduced pagan elements of folk heritage and tribal-heroic culture to modern Serbian literature, was very hostile to the rationalists' efforts. On August 3, 1837, Njegoš wrote a letter to the ruler of Serbia, Prince Miloš Obrenović, asking him to ban Obradović's writings.[3] However, at a later stage Obradović also embraced a Romanticism through which he was "enraptured by the old Serbian glory from the time before the Turks."[4] This led to a shift in Obradović's position toward folk art, as Milorad Pavić noted: "Although Dositej initially had reservations against oral literature, . . . he later changed this attitude regarding oral creation and started to record folk art (stories, songs, sayings) and write poems in the verse of folk epics."[5]

The Serbian scholar Vojislav Đurić saw in Saint Sava and Dositej Obradović two pivotal figures in Serbian culture:

> There are two epochs in the history of Serbian culture: the old, from Saint Sava to Dositej, and the new, from Dositej to our days. Sava is the first Serbian writer, Dositej the first modern Serbian writer. But, far more than that, both are great founders, portentous organizers, creators of programs that trace the line of development of an entire nation for centuries. Sava determined the framework and the themes—the ecclesio-feudal ones, based on the Byzantine (that is, the best at the time) models, but aiming at autonomous development—for architecture, visual arts, literature, and for our entire first culture. Marked by works of timeless value, they pulled us out of pagan darkness, and after the collapse of the old state, under the Turks, played the crucial role in the struggle for our national survival. And at the moment when, by a strange paradox of history, the continuation of the old culture had long been an anachronism and yet an irreplaceable weapon against both Turkification and Uniatization, that is, Germanization and Magyarization, the moment before the uprising and during the uprising in Serbia, after the Serbian middle class in Vojvodina became rather strong—at this opportune moment Dositej launched a merciless criticism of our medieval backwardness and created a broad long-term program and the first examples of the new culture, secular and popular.[6]

What Đurić says here is true but it is not the whole truth. For, together with their positive achievements, Saint Sava and Obradović have each bequeathed one fateful flaw to Serbian culture: Saint Sava was the architect of the close association between church, state, and nation, in which state interests and national ambitions have proved stronger than the Christian spirit;[7] Obradović, a rationalist, pro-Western critic of church bigotry and an advocate of tolerance, was the first to formulate the modern, linguistically based Pan-Serbism.

In 1783 Obradović dedicated his writings to the "Slavoserbian people," that is, to "the inhabitants of Serbia, Bosnia, Herzegovina, Montenegro, Dalmatia, Croatia, Syrmium, Banat and Bačka."[8] They are all his "Serbian brethren, regardless of their church and religion."[9] Obradović remained faithful to the pan-Serb idea; in his last work, *Mezimac*, he stated,

> The Serbs are called differently in different kingdoms and provinces: in Serbia Serbians, ... in Bosnia Bosnians, in Dalmatia Dalmatians, in Herzegovina Herzegovinians, and in Montenegro Montenegrins. ... The most ordinary Serb from Banat or Bačka finds in Serbia, in Bosnia and Herzegovina, in Dalmatia, especially in Croatia, in Slavonia and Srem, his own native language and his people, whether they be of Eastern or Roman faith.[10]

The other two early proponents of modern Pan-Serbism were also members of the Habsburg Serb community. The historian Jovan Rajić (1726–1801) in the second volume of his *History of Various Slavic Peoples, Especially Bulgars, Croats and Serbs*,[11] written in 1786, counts Bosnia and Herzegovina, Dalmatia, and Slavonia as Serbian lands. And in 1806 Sava Tekelija (1761–1842), a lawyer and politician, published a map of "Serbian lands," which included Montenegro, Bosnia, Herzegovina, Dubrovnik, and Dalmatia. However, their Pan-Serbism was not imperialist; nor was Obradović's. They seem to have sincerely believed that the anticipated triumph of rationalism over religion would eliminate the barriers between the Orthodox, Catholic, and Muslim south Slavs, and that they would all see themselves as parts of one—Serbian—nation.

The idea of using brute force to eliminate religious and cultural barriers to a homogeneous nation was expressed with brutal directness by Njegoš, a towering figure in the period Đurić calls Obradović's. In fact, Njegoš has marked the modern period of Serbian culture no less than Obradović, and many Serbs think that Njegoš dominates it. Milovan Djilas, an admirer of Njegoš, expressed such an opinion: "We have had only one humanistic thinker in the West European sense of that term—Dositej Obradović—and even he, a Westerner, remained misunderstood and without successors, as someone great and useful, but not really one of us."[12] However, the search for a single dominant figure in modern Serbian culture seems to be misdirected; Obradović and Njegoš represent its equally powerful poles. Indeed, ever since Serbs came into close contact with the West, they have been torn between the model of Western civil society and ethnic tribalism.

Consequently, there are three pivotal figures in Serbian culture: Saint Sava, who united church and state; Obradović, who tried to separate them; and Njegoš, who revealed the terrifying consequences of a radical union of the two. Only Obradović favored an orientation toward the West.

The historian Miodrag Popović, aware of the importance of Njegoš as the leading modern representative of the mythical trend in Serbian culture, concluded a chapter on the two trends in Serbian religious and national thought in the early nineteenth century with the question "whether this conflict between Dositej and Njegoš, as a conflict between the mythical and the rational, has ended or if it has tacitly continued until the present."[13] Just about the time he posed this question, in the late 1970s, the mythical, irrational current started to erupt with great force.

Language and Territory

Modern Pan-Serbism emerged as a result of the Romanticist idea that vernacular language is the main criterion for the identity of a nation, combined with the thesis that all štokavian dialects are Serbian. Since all Bosnians, Herzegovinians, and Montenegrins and most Croats speak štokavian, this thesis transforms them into Serbs. One of the two non-štokavian Croatian dialects, the kajkavian, superficially similar to the Slovene language, was often seen as a branch of the latter; the other one, the čakavian, spoken in a narrow area along the Adriatic coast and on the islands, was consequently the only one usually regarded as a genuinely Croatian idiom.[14]

Linguistically based Pan-Serbism, which is only outlined in Obradović's thought, is a dominant idea of the most celebrated Serbian linguist, Vuk Stefanović Karadžić (1787–1864). Born in Serbia to a poor family of Montenegrin descent, Karadžić did not receive a good education, but he was an intelligent man who was given valuable help by prominent Central European scholars passionately interested in folk culture and the development of a literary language based on the speech of ordinary, illiterate people. The Italian linguist Sergio Bonazza notes that a strong demand for a Serbian scholar who would carry out the tasks of great interest to contemporary Central European culture significantly contributed to Karadžić's professional success, and that the Slovenian linguist Jernej (Bartholomäus) Kopitar (1780–1844), based in Vienna, played a particularly important role in Karadžić's career by helping him meet that demand:

> Kopitar wrote the program for the creation of a modern Serbian literary language and for the revival of Serbian culture three years before he met Vuk Karadžić. For three years he had been looking for a Serb possessing literary talent who would be able to execute the program, until he finally discovered Vuk Karadžić, who carried out Kopitar's linguistic-literary program for Serbs in a short time and with great success.[15]

Karadžić is best known for his collection of "Serbian" folk songs and stories (the collection is misnamed because it includes oral literature of Croats and Bosnian Muslims, who were all Serbs in his view), and for the development of the modern Serbian language, based on the speech of the common folk rather than on traditional Serbian literary languages. In order to make the new language a better tool for making all štokavian speakers members of the Serbian nation, he did not base it on a dialect spoken in Serbia but on one spoken in Herzegovina, an area of mixed Catholic, Muslim, and Orthodox population, geographically distant from Serbia.

Karadžić did not need to fight for acceptance of the idea that all štokavian speakers were Serbs. The Czech Jozef Dobrovský (1753–1829) proposed the identification of štokavian (or "Illyrian") with Serbian before Karadžić, and promoted that thesis successfully. In fact, Dobrovský went much further than proclaiming that all štokavian south Slavic speakers were Serbs: on the basis of an incorrect analysis of the word "Serb," he concluded that formerly all Slavic peoples called themselves Serbs, and that the term "Serb" is older than "Slav." His follower, the Slovak linguist Pavel Šafařík (1795–1861), also insisted that "the Slavs" own oldest name, used by all or a large part of the peoples composing this family, was, as we have proved . . . Srbs, Serbs."[16] Karadžić and other Serbs eagerly accepted this thesis,[17] although doubts about it were expressed as early as 1837,[18] and another Czech scholar eventually proved it untenable.[19] But while Dobrovský's and Šafařík's attempts to introduce the word *Serb* as a synonym for *Slav* failed, the identification of most southern Slavs as Serbs became widely accepted. It fit the Romanticist tendency to base the identity of a nation on a common language and folk culture, while neglecting the role of religion and urban culture.

Great figures of German Romanticism—Herder, Therese von Jakob (Talvj), the brothers Grimm, Goethe, and Ranke—were enthusiastic about south Slavic folk culture. The famous philologist Jacob Grimm (1785–1863) advised Vuk Karadžić about collecting folklore and translated his *Little Serbian Grammar* as well as a large number of south Slavic folk songs.[20] Goethe's translation of the song "Hasan Aga's Wife" made this poetry a part of world literature.[21] All of them—following Kopitar, Dobrovský, and Karadžić—regarded every štokavian-speaking south Slav as a Serb. Thus Goethe stated, "Most Serbs (Serb-speaking people) are, as is well known, Christian, partly of Greek and partly of Latin faith; a part professes Muslim faith."[22]

Karadžić's language-nation equation brought him into conflict with the Serbian Orthodox Church and its church-nation equation. His rejection of traditional Serbian literary idioms, which were strongly influenced by the Old Church Slavonic and Russian languages, was another reason for the initial hostility of the Serbian church to his linguistic reforms. But resistance was soon overcome, and the conflict between the language-nation and church-nation equations subsided, partly because it had no bearing on the concept of Greater Serbia. The area where štokavian dialects are spoken to a large degree coincided with the jurisdiction of the patriarchate of Peć after the Turkish conquests.

The fact that even Obradović, a rationalist and tolerant thinker, did not recognize a separate ethnic and political identity of a nation such as the Croats, whose statehood had not been interrupted since it was established in the seventh century (although their sovereignty was), cannot be sufficiently explained by his idealistic vision of a Slavo-Serb brotherhood. The Croatian Illyrian Movement (1835–48) also had a program of a unification of south Slavs (originally also including the Bulgarians) into a community based on the language and ethnos, but did not envision it as a Greater Croatia.[23] This is why they chose the name Illyria for the proposed union.[24] A pan-Croatian ideology, claiming that Serbs were actually Croats, ethnically or politically, was first formulated after 1849 by Ante Starčević.[25] He and his followers subsequently abandoned the claim to Serbia, but persisted in regarding Bosnia as a Croatian land. However, unlike Serb nationalists who regarded the Muslims as renegades, "Starčević was one of the first Christian thinkers anywhere to express admiration for Islam, describing the Bosnian Muslim elite as . . . the 'oldest and purest nobility in Europe.' "[26]

South Slavic unification could be seen as either a union of equal peoples or assimilation into Greater Serbia. The conflict between these two approaches, that is, between the assimilationist nature of Serbian national ideologies and the integrative character of Croatian national thought, remained a constant in the period preceding the formation of Yugoslavia and throughout its existence.[27]

A comparative study of Serbian and Croatian elementary school textbooks from the late nineteenth and early twentieth centuries vividly illustrates the difference between the two approaches:

In the Serbian readers, the language was always referred to as Serbian, and written in Cyrillic. In the Croatian, it was called Croatian or

Serbian, and written in both alphabets. Both also stressed literature. In the Serbian readers, the literature was identified as Serbian, or Catholic and Western, two euphemisms for Croatian literature. Although the emphasis in the Croatian readers was on Croatian literature, Serbian authors and their writings were also readily discussed.

The same pattern was evident in their presentation of historical subjects. The Serbian books concentrated on Serbian history, ignoring Croatian. Without slighting their own past, the Croatian readers presented Serbian history as positively as they did their own. In other words, in the readers, the most important books for the elementary school students, information that could contribute to South Slavic understanding was found in the Croatian books, but not the Serbian.[28]

In the Serbian books, Croats lived in lands that were considered Serbian; no Croatian history of the period before the Balkan Wars was discussed. In contrast, Serbian affairs were well covered in the Croatian readers and textbooks. Moreover, the Serbs were presented in a favorable light in the history books, but as a separate Slavic nation.[29]

The same contrast appears in the teaching of geography:

The Serbian books laid claim to all the Croatian lands—Croatia, Slavonia, and Dalmatia. They based their case primarily on a linguistic argument. In addition, they used facts, figures, and historical arguments to support their claims to these lands. The Croatian books concentrated on describing the lands of the Triune Kingdom [Croatia, Slavonia, and Dalmatia], and they made it clear that other peoples, including Serbs, lived there. . . . None of the Croatian books, however, advanced any claims to Serbia, Montenegro, Old Serbia [Kosovo], or Macedonia, which were regarded as Serb domains.[30]

The inculcation of pan-Serbian ideology at an early age explains by itself why the Yugoslav union was doomed to failure.

The asymmetry in the acceptance of fellow Slavic peoples as separate entities is due to the different historical experiences of the Serbs and Croats. When the Turks consolidated their control of the Balkans, Serbia was obliterated as a political and cultural entity in the Ottoman Empire. There was no Serbian state at all, and the principal mark of Serbian national identity was membership in the Serbian Orthodox Church. The Serbian millet, that is, the Ottoman ethnoreligious community under the jurisdiction of the Serbian Orthodox Church, covered an area much wider than the medieval Serbian state, but a millet had no territorial exclusivity; various millets could coexist on the same territory. Nevertheless, in the absence of Serbia as a political entity, the Serbs interpreted their millet as an indicator of their national territory. This identification was fully accepted by Serbian ecclesiastic circles in the course of the seventeenth century. Thus Serbian monks who traveled to Russia to collect alms at the time invariably identified themselves as coming "from such and such city, or such and such monastery in the Serbian land," regardless of whether the city or monastery in question was in Serbia, Montenegro, Bosnia, or Croatia.[31]

The drastic separation of ethnicity from polity in the Serbian experience explains why even well-intended Serbs paid little or no attention to the long existence and relatively high territorial stability of entities like Bosnia, Croatia, and Montenegro,[32] and assumed that the territory of Serbia was determined by the presence of the Serbian Orthodox Church, "Serbian graves," or the štokavian speech, with total disregard for political history. This contrasts with the Croatians' insistence on their historical state rights.

Vuk Karadžić was very much aware of the primacy of ethnicity over polity in the quest for a Greater Serbia. This is why, contrary to historical evidence, he claimed the supremacy of the ethnos over the demos even in medieval Serbia: "I think that the name *Serbia* appeared in recent times, after the Serbian Empire ceased to exist; and I wonder whether it can be found anywhere that any of our kings or emperors were called the king or emperor of *Serbia*, rather than of the *Serbs*."[33]

Modern Pan-Serbism was originally not militant. Obradović seems to have sincerely believed that Catholic and Muslim speakers of štokavian dialects would willingly accept their identification as Serbs. But in the course of Serbia's struggle for independence, and subsequently for aggrandizement, when the intensity of the štokavian-speaking Catholics' and Muslims' resistance to assimilation became obvious, Pan-Serbism became ever more associated with the ethos of Njegoš's *Mountain Wreath*, that is, the advocacy of violence as a tool for the realization of a homogeneous Greater Serbia, united both by faith and by language. The presence of a pagan-heroic tradition in modern Pan-Serbism was also manifested in the rising cult of the pre-Christian god Vid.

The Resurrection and International Recognition of a Pagan War God

Except for Njegoš, the inhabitants of the Dinaric Mountains, where old pagan-heroic tribalism was still very strong, were not the principal revivers of that tradition under Romanticist influence. The Serbian intelligentsia, located mostly in the Pannonian urban environment rather than in the harsh southern mountains, played the dominant role in the resurgence of tribalism. The literary historian Radomir Konstantinović called attention to the rejection of outsiders in Serbian literature of the Romanticist period:

> The entire Serbian Romanticism, especially in its final period, is imbued with the fear of man outside the kin, the man who is "only" a man, as a monster: at each low tide of the tribal (national) rapture this diabolic man, an incarnation of hatred and "cosmopolitan malice," stood up, the same way he disappeared, if only for a moment, with the renewal of tribal ecstasy. This is why it can be assumed, not without ground, that the search for the "holy war," which fills the entire Romanticist period, is also inspired by the fear of the non-kindred man as a monster: to the Romanticist in this culture man can be either a Serb or a monster. . . . This has been determined by a mental technique of the tribal-patriarchal civilization, developed over the centuries.[34]

According to the Serbian historian Miodrag Popović, it was the intelligentsia who turned the Kosovo myth—the promise of avenging the defeat and resurrecting the Serbian empire—into the core of modern Serbian national ideology:

The Kosovo myth acquired the central position in the spiritual life of the Serbian intelligentsia in the nineteenth century. It lived outside poetry, too: among politicians, the military, scientists, professors, artists, clergy, physicians, merchants, tradesmen, and especially among college and high school students. It gradually became an integral part of their national ideology. Gradually, the Kosovo myth became the spiritual bridge between the bourgeois intelligentsia and the still present followers of the god Vid in our patriarchal-heroic world.[35]

Vid is a pre-Christian Slavic sun and war god whose memory was never obliterated by the Christianization of Serbia. His growing prominence in the course of the nineteenth and early twentieth centuries has been one of the most conspicuous manifestations of the assertion of pagan-heroic values in modern Serbia.

Information about pre-Christian Slavic religions is very scarce, and most of the written sources refer to the Slavs of what is now Russia and to those who settled the Baltic coast. There are no references to the god Vid anywhere outside the south Slavic area, but the Baltic Slavs had several divinities whose names ended with the suffix -*vit*: Sventovit, Iarovit, Porevit, and Rugevit.[36] They were sun gods as well as warrior gods, as indicated by the weapons on their statues. According to some sources, the northern Slavs' supreme god was Sventovit. His sanctuary in Arkona on the Baltic island of Rügen contained a statue of the four-headed deity as late as 1168, when the Christian Danes stormed the place and removed the statue and the treasure guarded there. A detailed description of the temple, statue, and cult of Sventovit in Arkona is provided by Saxo Grammaticus, a Danish monk who wrote his history of the Danes in the late twelfth century, soon after the destruction of the temple:

> In the temple stood a huge image, far overtopping all human stature, marvelous for its four heads and four necks. . . . Not far off a bridle and saddle and many emblems of godhead were visible. Men's marvel at these things was increased by a sword of notable size, whose scabbard and hilt were not only excellently graven, but also graced outside with silver. . . . This god also had 300 horses appointed to it,

and as many men-at-arms riding them, all of whose gains, either by arms or theft, were put in the care of the priest. . . . This statue was worshiped with the tributes of all Sclavonia, and neighboring kings did not fail to honour its sacrifice with gifts. . . . Also it possessed a special white horse. . . . On this horse, in the belief of Rügen, Suanto-Vitus—so the image was called—rode to war against the foes of his religion.[37]

Saxo also described the temple of Rugevit, whose name he spelled "Rugie-Vitus"—the Vit of Rügen. The statue in this temple had seven heads, "and the workman had also bound by its side in a single belt seven real swords with their scabbards. The eighth is held in its hand drawn; this was fitted in the wrist and fixed very fast with an iron nail."[38]

There is no concrete evidence of a connection between the cult of the south Slavic god Vid and that of the northern gods, but the fact that Vid was celebrated on the day of the summer solstice indicates his role as a sun god. In one of the scant extant references to Vid, a south Slavic folk song refers to his warrior nature. It describes the return of "White Vid" after a prolonged war campaign:

> You waged war, oh, White Vid, koledo! [*koledo* is a ritual
> refrain]
> Three years with accursed Turks,
> And four with black Hungarians.[39]

The song also mentions Vid's horses.

The fact that the 1389 Battle of Kosovo was fought on the day of the summer solstice (the time of the celebration of the god Vid) was probably coincidental, but the elevation of this battle (in which no side obtained clear victory) to the pivotal moment of the disappearance of the Serbian state and to the centerpiece of Serbian national mythology is hardly an accident. The connection of the mythic defeat at Kosovo with the celebration of the important sun and war god, whose cult was weakened but never completely suppressed with the acceptance of Christianity, has made the glorification of the event not just a masochistic obsession with a lost war, but an affirmation of the belief that, with the god's help, the defeat would be avenged and Serbia resurrected as a mighty empire. The association of the Battle of Kosovo with the god Vid may be one of the reasons why in national memory it completely overshadowed the strategically more significant battles at Chernomen (1371) and Nicopolis (1396), in which Christian armies experienced catastrophic defeats.

The association of the legendary battle with a pagan war god and a Christian prince opting for the heavenly kingdom may seem contradictory, but in popular perception the saintly prince is himself warlike. A Serbian scholar points out the warlike character of both Saint Lazar and Saint Sava, the two greatest Serbian Orthodox saints, and the pagan influences in the cult that surrounds them:

> Deeply rooted in the old Serbian religion before the conversion to Christianity and before the settlement in the Balkans, the holiday, Vid's Day, dedicated to the war god Vid, who has been substituted in Christianity by Sava Nemanjić, Sava's father Simeon, and Prince Lazar, has constituted the age-old link between the fallen and the living. Sava and Simeon Nemanja march in front of Serbian warriors in defense against foreign tribesmen. Lazar appears in the role of a kind of war god not only in the *Service* but also in Jefimija's *Encomium*, where he and other "holy martyrs" constitute some kind of war council.[40]

The martial disposition of these prominent Serbian saints has also been influenced by the Byzantine military saints, such as George, Demetrios, Nestor, Theodore Teron, Theodore Stratelates, Merkourios, and Prokopios, whose celebrated actions include assistance to armies and defense of cities.[41] Some of them are depicted, fully armed, on the walls of Serbian churches and monasteries.

Since Vid's Day commemorates a pagan god,[42] the holiday was not celebrated in the Serbian Orthodox Church, nor was it marked in old Serbian calendars (all of which were church calendars).[43] Those calendars assigned June 15 (the date of Vid's Day in the Julian calendar) to the Old Testament prophet Amos and to Saint Lazar, the prince who perished in the Battle of Kosovo. Vid's Day appeared in calendars for the first time in the 1860s, the time of the triumph of Vuk Karadžić's ideas and nationalist exuberance caused by progressive liberation from Turkish rule.

At first, Vid's Day was listed together with Prophet Amos and Prince Lazar, and was printed in regular black letters, meaning that it was not a national or church holiday. Around 1889, the five hundredth anniversary of the Battle of Kosovo, the Serbian public started demanding that Vid's Day be named an official holiday of the Serbian Orthodox Church. It was marked in red letters for the first time in the official calendar of the church for 1892 in the following way: "Prophet Amos and Prince Lazar (Vid's Day)." Vacillation about proclaiming Vid's Day an official national and church holiday continued during the early twentieth century. Only after the 1913 victory over the Turks in the First Balkan War was Vid's Day officially introduced as a national, church, and folk holiday.[44]

In the course of the twentieth century, Vid's Day has gained further significance. On that day (June 28 in the Gregorian calendar) in 1914, a Serbian nationalist celebrated the war god by assassinating the heir to the Austro-Hungarian throne, Archduke Franz Ferdinand, thereby igniting the First World War. By choosing to sign the Versailles Peace Treaty on the same day in 1919, the victorious Western Allies provided the war with a symmetry: the same war god that sponsored its beginning became the patron of the flawed peace treaty that would provide fertile ground for new wars. On June 28, 1921, Serbian political parties passed the "Vid's Day Constitution" for the new State of Serbs, Croats, and Slovenes, which provided the legal basis for Serbian hegemony and made the new country unstable because of the refusal of non-Serbs to accept it. The importance attached to the holiday in monarchist Yugoslavia was also reflected in the choice of Vid's Day as the end of the school year throughout the country. Stalin chose Vid's Day 1948 to issue the condemnation of the Yugoslav leadership by the Comintern, convinced that this act would bring down Tito's regime. Forty-one years later, Slobodan Milošević for the first time threatened to use military force to reshape Yugoslavia in his speech at Kosovo on Vid's Day 1989, the six hundredth anniversary of the Battle of Kosovo. And French president François Mitterrand chose June 28, 1992, for his visit to

Sarajevo. The visit, at the height of the massacres of Muslims in northern and eastern Bosnia, prevented a NATO strike against the Serbs and continued the Franco-Serbian alliance, which, ironically, was initiated with a murder in the same city and on the same day seventy-eight years earlier.

The acceptance of Vid's Day as the main Serbian national holiday symbolized the triumph of the Dinaric pagan-heroic ethos and a marriage of this ethos to imperial ambitions.[45] The old pagan sun god became the patron of the nation, and his spirit infused all Serbian professions and institutions, including the Serbian Orthodox Church. Miodrag Popović pointed out some disquieting implications of this cult:

> The Vid's Day cult, which blends historical actuality with mythical reality, a real struggle for freedom with the preserved pagan propensities (revenge, slaughter, and offering of sacrifice, the revival of the heroic ancestor), potentially contains all the traits of environments characterized by untamed mythical impulses. The cult was historically necessary as a specific phase in the development of national thought. But as a permanent state of mind, the Vid's Day cult can be fatal to the people unable to extricate themselves from its pseudo mythical and pseudo historical webs. Through them, contemporary intellect and spirit can experience a new Kosovo: an intellectual and ethical defeat.[46]

The Bloody Rebirth of the Serbian State

While the Habsburg Serb community, enjoying prosperity and an absence of violence, assimilated Western culture and became a vanguard in the modernization of Serbia, the Serbs in the decaying Ottoman Empire concentrated their energies on the struggle for independence. However, the liberation from Turkish rule, which started with the First Serbian Uprising in 1804 and ended with the achievement of full sovereignty in 1878, did not mean a liberation from violence. On the contrary, prolonged warfare nourished violence and resulted in the first "ethnic cleansings."

The leader of the First Serbian Uprising was an illiterate pig farmer and haiduk, Kara Đorđe (Black George) Petrović, the founder of the Karađorđević dynasty. He displayed the traditional Dinaric violence that would mark modern Serbia. He shot his stepfather when the latter refused to flee Serbia with him before a successful Turkish counteroffensive "and ordered one of his companions to give the death-blow to the old man, who was writhing in agony."[47] Once he assaulted his own mother by forcing a hive of bees on her head. He ordered that his only brother, whom he loved, be hanged at the door of the house, and forbade his mother to mourn outwardly for her son. If irritated by another person, "he would not even pause to tell his *Momkes* [personal guard] to beat the offender to the ground, but he would himself slay his adversary: and he spared none."[48]

From 1817—when Kara Đorđe was killed (and his severed head sent to the sultan) by his rival, Miloš Obrenović, leader of the Second Serbian Uprising and the founder of the Obrenović dynasty —until 1903, three of the seven rulers of Serbia (members of the two rival dynasties) were assassinated, all of them by fellow Serbs. Of the remaining four, one died less than a month after being installed gravely ill, one was overthrown, and one abdicated.

The church in Serbia could not do much to improve the general violence and lawlessness because, unlike the Serbian Orthodox Church in the Habsburg monarchy, it had little prestige and influence. "Like the other peasants, [the priests] were mostly poor because their entire income consisted mainly of irregular and meager income from baptisms, weddings, funeral services, and other ceremonials. They served in church very seldom, sometimes no more than once a year."[49] Metropolitan Petar Jovanović, the primate of Serbia from 1833 to 1859, was modern Serbia's first bishop to have a formal higher education. But the intellectual deficiency of the church was not its only shortcoming, as an American historian explains:

> The Serbian clergy were not only on a low level of culture, but also riddled with men of no particular religious vocation or moral qualities. Their ranks were filled with scoundrels of every sort—thieves,

drunkards, rapists, charlatan healers, and the like. One vagabond priest had the dubious distinction of having been suspended by three different bishops. Another stole the purse of a colleague who was on his deathbed. The monks of whole monasteries refused to live by their rule. Parish priests denied the sacraments to those who would not pay their illegally exorbitant fees.[50]

Prince Miloš Obrenović (who ruled 1815–39 and 1858–60) was an illiterate tyrant, a murderer, and an extortioner, but at the same time a pious man, who started to impose discipline on the church. As a result of the efforts of Miloš, Metropolitan Petar, and others, conditions in the church gradually improved.

The last change of the ruling dynasty in Serbia took place in 1903, when pro-Austrian King Aleksandar Obrenović was killed by a faction that wanted to bring a pro-Russian Karađorđević back to the throne. The *New York Times* reported on the brutal regicide:

The King fell upon his knees and begged for life, offering to yield to every demand, to sign any document, to agree to leave the country, or to send Queen Draga away—anything, everything, if they only would not kill him.

The officers answered roughly: "It is too late," and fired at him. The Queen also fell on her knees and asked pardon for her conduct, but one of the officers, calling her a degrading epithet, told her she had been Queen long enough. One of the conspirators, after submitting the Queen to gross indignities, slashed her with his sword, and the other officers fired at her. The King was also slashed with sabres. The conspirators then dragged the King and Queen into the front apartment and threw them over the balcony upon the lawn in front of the palace. . . . The King and Queen lived between one and two hours afterward.

Meanwhile two of the officers summoned the Queen's two brothers from their home to the house of the commander of the Belgrade division, where they were offered a glass of water and told to bid each other farewell. In the very instant they embraced the officers shot and killed them.[51]

One year before these murders took place, an ominous text appeared in the most prestigious literary magazine in Belgrade, expressing an attitude that would lead to many more murders. In the article titled "Serbs and Croats," an ethnic Serb from Croatia, Nikola Stojanović, proclaimed that "the struggle [between the two peoples] must be carried on 'until the extermination, yours or ours.' One side must succumb."[52] The blood-curdling slogan was set in quotation marks because it was an adaptation of Njegoš's verse "Until the extermination, Turkish or ours."[53]

Petar I (1903–14), installed by the military officers who had plotted, apparently without his knowledge, the murder of King Aleksandar Obrenović, made a sincere effort to stop the vicious circle of violence and transform Serbia into a civilized country based on the rule of law. He initiated reforms to free Serbia from the legacy of oppression and violence. The publication of John Stuart Mill's *On Liberty*, which the king himself had translated, was one manifestation of his intention to free Serbia from the burden of its heritage.

An important reason that the king's good intentions did not bear more fruit was his country's militant anti-Austrian and anti-Turkish policy, reinforced by his own pro-Russian orientation and, especially, by the influence of the military. It was Serbia's misfortune that its war actions were so successful. Victories in the two Balkan Wars of 1912 and 1913 resulted in the acquisition of substantial territories—the Sandžak, Kosovo, and Macedonia—containing large non-Serbian majorities. Suddenly, Serbia changed from an ethnically homogeneous state into one where Serbs constituted less than two-thirds of the population. Serbia's expansion proved an obstacle to its development, because the energies that could have been used to modernize Serbia and make it a stable country ruled by law were diverted to the tasks of dominating and assimilating the large number of non-Serbs within its borders. Terror was the method employed to rule over the subjects whose rights and national identities were denied.

Nevertheless, the relative enlightenment of King Petar I's rule gave rise to what one Serbian analyst calls the myth of the golden age of modern Serbia:

This myth immediately became a significant political instrument, used to legitimize the brutal assassinations of the royal couple, the political persecutions by the new regime, and the boycott of the international community, which, with varying intensity, lasted until the end of this period, and to hide the strong political influence of the army. After the 1918 unification, the myth of the "golden age" was used . . . as an argument supporting the thesis that in Yugoslavia, Serbia was the only inheritor of modern, liberal public-law and political traditions, which provided legitimization to a clearly Serb-marked centralism. Historiography, especially post–World War II, also made a significant contribution to the preservation of this myth, even when, as a historiography of communist provenance, it was far from glorifying this regime.[54]

This does not mean that strong yearnings for the rule of law were not present in early twentieth-century Serbia, but only that they were neutralized by the expectation of a rebirth of the Serbian empire, promised by the national mythology.

The High Cost of Imperial Ambitions

Serbia's expansion in the early twentieth century was hardly spontaneous. Plans for the creation of a Greater Serbia were drawn in the mid-nineteenth century, and from that time the creation of a Second Serbian Empire became the basis of Serbia's foreign policy. The most important political document outlining Serbia's future expansion was the *Načertanije* (Program), written by Ilija Garašanin, minister of internal affairs of the principality of Serbia, in 1844 as a secret political document.[55] It was written just three years before the publication of the other work of fundamental importance in the shaping of modern Pan-Serbism: Njegoš's *Mountain Wreath*. Garašanin was one of the most important political figures in Serbia between 1843 and 1867, and his program explicitly set the resurrection of Dušan's fourteenth-century empire as the goal of Serbia's foreign policy:

The Serbian rulers, it may be remembered, began to assume the position held by the Greek Empire and almost succeeded in making an end of it, replacing the collapsed Eastern Roman Empire with a Serbian-Slavic one. Emperor Dushan the Mighty had even adopted the crest of the Greek Empire. The arrival of the Turks in the Balkans interrupted this change, and prevented it from taking place for a long time. But now, since the Turkish power is broken and destroyed, so to speak, this interrupted process must commence once more in the same spirit and again be undertaken in the knowledge of that right.[56]

Garašanin's program was influenced by two documents. One was a memorandum titled "Conseils sur la conduite à suivre par la Serbie,"[57] written by the Polish aristocrat Adam Czartoryski in 1843. Prince Czartoryski was the leader of a group of Polish exiles in Paris, whose principal aim was to curb Russian influence. In an attempt to adapt the memorandum to make it more acceptable to the Serbs, Czartoryski's agent in Belgrade, the Czech František A. Zach, wrote a document known as "Zach's Plan."[58] The essential idea of both documents was that the Serbs should cooperate with other south Slavic peoples in the creation of a common state that would be independent of both Russia and Austria. Garašanin followed Zach's text very closely, even copying entire paragraphs almost verbatim, but wherever Zach used the term *south Slavs,* Garašanin replaced it with *Serbs* and turned a program of a south Slavic union, similar to that of the "Illyrians," into a blueprint for a Greater Serbia.

Garašanin's program outlined the steps necessary to make all south Slavic territories in the Ottoman Empire and northern Albania parts of Greater Serbia or dependent on it. "Serbia must destroy, stone by stone, the edifice of the Turkish state, taking from it whatever is salvageable, and upon the solid foundation of the old Serbian state erect a great new Serbian state."[59] Garašanin was aware that Serbia's plan "to absorb all the Serbian peoples around her"[60] meant a conflict with Austria: "Austria must always be the eternal enemy of a Serbian state."[61]

Garašanin followed Dušan in his ambition to control Constantinople, the birthplace of Eastern Orthodoxy (which, in the meantime, had become the Turkish Istanbul), and to dominate Bulgaria, which would have inevitably led to a conflict with Russia's foreign policy. This is the reason for the anti-Russian sentiment in the *Načertanije*, but the Serbs soon abandoned the highly unrealistic ambition regarding Istanbul, and occasional later designs for a union with Bulgaria were mostly of a federalist nature. However, the conquest of all of Macedonia, providing access to the Aegean Sea, remained high on the Serbian foreign policy agenda and was an important motivation behind Serbia's engagement in the 1912–13 Balkan Wars.

Only four years after Garašanin wrote his program, the revolutionary events of 1848 shook the Habsburg Empire to its foundations. This was an additional reason for Serbia to direct its main expansionist thrust to the west and north, that is, to Bosnia-Herzegovina, Croatia, Montenegro, and Vojvodina, most of which had never been a part of the Serbian state. Instead of common religion and culture, which were to be the unifying features of Dušan's Serbo-Byzantine empire, language and ethnicity became the main criteria for the formation of the modern Serbian empire.

The Serbs' military successes in the Balkan Wars of 1912–13 satisfied most of their territorial ambitions in the east and south, but the Austro-Hungarian Empire, which included Bosnia-Herzegovina, Croatia, and Vojvodina, stood in the way of westward and northward expansion. Therefore the destabilization of that multinational empire became the most urgent goal of Serbia's foreign policy. Such was the situation when a Serbian terrorist fired the shots that killed Archduke Franz Ferdinand, heir to the Austro-Hungarian throne, and his wife in Sarajevo in 1914.

Some people regard terrorist acts as a necessary but unfortunate tool for the realization of their plans. The Sarajevo terrorists were more radical. They saw the bloodshed as a sacrament essential to the well-being of the nation. "The life of the nation consists in blood, blood is the god of the nation, death is superseded by resurrection, and the assassination is the Resurrection of the nation," wrote a coconspirator in his diary after hearing that the attempt on the life of Archduke Franz Ferdinand had succeeded.[62] Nationalism was the religion of the conspirators, and, following Njegoš's precept, they erected its altar on blood. Gavrilo Princip, the assassin, knew *The Mountain Wreath* by heart. It is significant that the sultan-slayer Miloš Obilić is the most highly regarded hero in the poem.

The events unleashed by the Sarajevo assassination brought about an even larger territorial expansion of Serbia than expected, for the Serbs never viewed the Kingdom of Serbs, Croats, and Slovenes, which was created in 1918, as a union of equal peoples but as a Greater Serbia. This approach inevitably led to the institutionalization of terror.

In its first years, the new kingdom was formally a parliamentary democracy, but in practice it was an absolute monarchy. The power of the parliament, in which the Croats constituted the strongest opposition group, was severely limited, yet the king could not tolerate any opposition at all. His attitude was shared by many Serbs. *Politika*, the leading Serbian newspaper, *Samouprava*, the newspaper of the ruling Radical Party, and a Belgrade journal named *Jedinstvo* (Unity), subsidized by Premier Velja Vukičević, openly advocated the murder of the leaders of the opposition. An article in *Jedinstvo*, published on June 14, 1928, under the title "One Can Talk with Swine in Their Language Only" concluded with such a demand: "your first duty was and remains to kill Svetozar Pribićević in Belgrade and Stjepan Radić in Zagreb on the same day."[63] Six days later, Puniša Račić, a Serbian deputy from Montenegro, acted on this exhortation by killing two Croat deputies on the floor of the parliament in Belgrade and wounding several others, including the leader of the Croatian opposition, Stjepan Radić, who died a few weeks later.[64]

Instead of expressing regret to the Croats and curbing the excesses of centralism, King Aleksandar responded with increased oppression. In the proclamation of his personal dictatorship on January 6, 1929, the king said that "Parliamentarism leads to spiritual decadence and disunity of the people, instead of strengthening the spirit of national and state unity." He banned all political activity and the display of Croatian, Slovenian, and even Serbian national symbols, and he redrew internal borders, so that Croatia as well as the other constituent parts of the kingdom, except for Slovenia but including Serbia, ceased to exist as geographic and political entities. This was the first time in over one thousand years that Croatia's statehood was suspended. The Kingdom of Serbs, Croats and Slovenes was renamed Yugoslavia. The Serbs' renunciation of their own national name (repeated with the formation of the rump Federal Republic of Yugoslavia in 1993) may seem like a concession to south Slavic unity, but it reflected the intention of transforming the multinational country into a one-nation state. The Czech writer Karel Havlíček's 1844 characterization of Russian Pan-Slavism applies equally well to Serbian Yugoslavism, if "Russian" is replaced with "Serb(ian)" and "Slav" with "Yugoslav": "The Serbs like to call Yugoslav whatever is Serbian in order to be able later to name Serbian whatever is Yugoslav."

The reign of terror, up to then practiced most savagely against the Albanians and Macedonians, was unleashed fully in Croatia as well, and a number of prominent Croats were assassinated or savagely beaten.[65] In this atmosphere, Vasa Čubrilović, a participant in the 1914 assassination plot against Archduke Franz Ferdinand in Sarajevo, outlined a program for the expulsion of the Albanians with all the measures to be taken to this purpose, emphasizing that "the only method and the only means is the brutal force of an organized governmental power, and we have always been above them in this."[66]

The French statesman Robert Schuman, the future architect of the European Community, wrote a report after his visit to Croatia and Slovenia in 1934. Here is an excerpt:

> The use of the words "Slovene" and "Croat" is generally forbidden; one must say "Yugoslav." Administrative units have been changed drastically in order to erase the memory of historical and ethnic borders.
>
> All functions of any importance have been reserved for the Serbs. Of 200 generals two are Croats, one of whom is on a mission in Albania. Only one prominent diplomat is Croatian. In Bosnia, 30 magistrates, 29 of whom are Croats, have been forced into retirement

under the pretext of economy. Among young candidates preference is always given to Serbs. Croatian teachers are sent in great numbers to Old Serbia and Macedonia, areas that are religiously and culturally completely different from their own.

The few Croats and somewhat more numerous Slovenes in the service of the regime have been won over with the lure of personal benefits.

The police are entirely Serbian; modeled on the Russian tsarist police, they inspire fear through the network of informants (in Zagreb, Split, etc., thousands of persons are on the police payroll); through the torture inflicted on the prisoners who refuse to denounce their friends; through the arbitrariness and severity of administrative sanctions the police can decree without the possibility of appeal to judicial forums. Mr. Trumbić, the first Yugoslav minister of foreign affairs, a signatory of the Treaty of Trianon, caused the sentencing of several friends of his whom he had invited to dinner in a restaurant during his trip to Split and Banja Luka last June; offence: participation in a political meeting; sanctions: several months in prison and fines amounting to 182,000 dinars (60,000 French francs). Such facts are reproduced each week.

Mr. Korošec, a Slovenian, the prime minister in late 1928 and member of the first dictatorial cabinet, has been interned for two years. He did not dare to meet his colleague Trumbić or myself (while I was at a distance of 100 meters from his residence). Other persons could meet me only after ten o'clock at night at a third person's, with infinite precautions. Others, finally, have asked me not to try to approach them.[67]

This was the setting in which a Croatian member of the dissolved Yugoslav Parliament, Ante Pavelić, formed an illegal movement called Ustaša (Insurgent), devoted to the dissolution of Yugoslavia by any means. One of its actions, in cooperation with Macedonian separatists, was the assassination of King Aleksandar during his visit to France in 1934.

The emergence of the Ustaša movement was a deplorable reaction to the Serbian terror. Never had there been organized political terrorism in Croatia before, and the movement attracted very few Croats. The *Yugoslav Encyclopedia* states that "an Ustaša organization was not formally set up in the country nor was the number of the Ustašas significant. There were small, regionally located groups, or isolated individuals who acted on the Ustaša platform."[68] The great majority of Croats rallied around the Croatian Peasant Party and its program of passive resistance and political compromise. Even a large number of ethnic Serbs joined the Croatian Peasant Party to express their opposition to the Serbian monarchist dicta- torship.[69] But in 1941, when Yugoslavia, sick with internal discord, was overrun by Axis forces, the Ustašas were put in power by Fascist Italy and Nazi Germany, after the Croatian Peasant Party leadership refused the Nazi offer of forming a collaborationist government. Along with the invading armies, Serbian Četniks, and multinational communist-led Partisans, Croatian Ustašas turned the disintegrated Yugoslavia into a slaughterhouse.

The Second World War concluded with a reconstituted Yugosla- via under communist rule. The promise of a federal solution in which every nation would have equal rights was an important factor in the success of the Partisan movement under Tito's leadership. But in practice, the federalism of Yugoslavia's early postwar period, like its Soviet model, was a facade for a rigidly centralized system. Centralism enabled the Serbs, the largest nationality, whose capital was also the federal capital, to assume the dominant position in the new state. Even when centralism was weakened and federalism taken more seriously, Serbs remained the dominant presence in the federal administration. According to data published in 1969, of 5,885 federal officials, 4,334 were Serbs. Montenegrins were also highly repre- sented, with 424 officials—a representation nearly three times larger than their proportion in the population of Yugoslavia. Ethnic Alba- nians, about two and a half times as numerous as the Montenegrins, were represented with only eleven federal officials.[70]

Aleksandar Ranković (1909–83), the founder of communist Yu- goslavia's secret police and the minister of internal affairs during the country's most oppressive period, was the official most notable for using the power of a centralized police state for Serbian nation- alist purposes. He took advantage of the security forces under his command to boost the power of Serbian minorities throughout

Yugoslavia, excelling particularly in the persecution of the Kosovo Albanians. He sabotaged economic reforms because any lessening of the regime's control over the economy would be favorable to those parts of Yugoslavia with a stronger work ethic and more developed industry than Serbia. This is why many Serbs regarded him as a national hero, while the other Yugoslavs saw him as the main instrument of totalitarian oppression. Serbian nostalgia for the Ranković era was manifested at his funeral in Belgrade in 1983, as the following news item demonstrates: "The 73-year old Serb, whose fifteen-year service was characterized by police state terror, died on Friday from a heart attack. According to newspaper reports, about 100,000 people gathered at the cemetery to give him their last farewell, applauding and cheering. A detachment of the People's Army fired several salvos for the 'Peoples Hero.' "[71]

Serbian preference for hard-line rule was also manifested in the 1969 elections, the only ones during Tito's reign that gave voters a choice between more than one candidate. Serbian and Montenegrin voters showed preference for hard-line candidates, while all the other Yugoslavs favored reformist candidates.[72] The last elections before the dissolution of Yugoslavia, in 1990 and 1991, repeated the same pattern: the communists lost power in all Yugoslav republics except Serbia and Montenegro.

The desire to preserve the dominant position in Yugoslavia was the main reason for the preference of many Serbs for a centralized, hard-line regime. Similarly, Croatia's and Slovenia's efforts to liberalize the Yugoslav communist regime and introduce a market economy were supported by the expectation that economic liberalization and decentralization would increase their power and protect them against Serbian hegemony. Thus, Serbian nationalism tended to align itself with strict state control, while Croatian and Slovenian nationalisms were more inclined toward free-market policies.

The ouster of Ranković in 1966 marked the beginning of a strong wave of liberalization. The process of liberalization went farthest in Croatia until, by late 1971, the Croatian reformists challenged the Yugoslav political system—which was still Leninist—and thereby Belgrade's monopoly on power. At that point Tito intervened, purging the entire Croatian communist leadership and replacing it with obedient hard-liners. As a result of the massive purge (including incarceration of many prominent intellectuals and closing of publications and institutions), the "Croatian spring" was replaced by the "Croatian silence," and Slovenia became the leader in the struggle for political and economic liberalization in the 1970s and 1980s.

In spite of the 1971–72 purge in Croatia, which was followed by similar purges on a smaller scale in the other republics, reformers again came to power in Croatia by the late 1980s. In Serbia the process went in the opposite direction: the hard-liners installed in 1972 were succeeded in the mid-1980s by even more radical communist and nationalist hard-liners led by Slobodan Milošević.

The use of hard-line communism as a tool for domination over other nationalities is not the only explanation for its prevalence in Serbia. The difference between the Croatian and Slovenian communists, on the one hand, and the Serbian and Montenegrin ones, on the other, also reflected the cultural divide that ran through the former Yugoslavia, as an analyst observed at the time of the conflict between the "Eurocommunists" and Moscow:

> An examination of the potential application of Eurocommunist ideas in Eastern Europe shows that it is precisely those areas of Eastern Europe that were not part of the Byzantine tradition (East Germany, Czechoslovakia, Poland, Hungary, and northern Yugoslavia) that are most susceptible.... The appeal of Eurocommunism, as distinguished from independent/national communism, apparently is minimal in Albania, Bulgaria, Romania, and southern Yugoslavia. In fact, whatever "Eurocommunization" has been taking place in Yugoslavia as an input into Titoism largely originates and is most widely practiced in Slovenia and Croatia.[73]

The line dividing the countries whose culture is rooted in Byzantium from those that have formed part of the Western community is not a rigid one. Ethnic or national tribalism was very strong in a number of Western European countries in the first half of the twentieth century, and Croatia presently displays greater affinity with Milošević's Serbia than with the countries with which it cohabited for centuries. On the other hand, in every Orthodox country there are people strongly committed to the establishment of modern civil society. A propitious international climate may help at least some of them achieve this goal.

The next chapter explores the opposite process—how unpropitious circumstances turned some long-standing negative aspects of the Serbian heritage into a paroxysm of tribal fears and hatreds that bred the 1990s wars.

5

A Vicious Circle of Lies and Fears

> The devil ... was a murderer from the first, and he has nothing to do with the truth, for there is no truth in him. When he tells a lie, he speaks in his true character, for he is a liar and the father of them.   —John 8:44

Fictional Data and Real Hatreds

Yugoslavia would have been less susceptible to violent disintegration if, at the end of World War II, there had been a reconciliation between the nations and factions that had fought one another. All of them, and especially the two most guilty ones, Croats and Serbs, should have admitted the mistakes and crimes committed since they entered the Yugoslav union and taken the steps necessary to prevent another conflict in the future. The enormity of the crimes committed by various parties made such action urgent. The reconciliation of France and Germany was a good model, but it could not be followed because one basic condition was missing: freedom, including the very important freedom of information.

One of communist Yugoslavia's most popular slogans was "brotherhood and unity," but the lies launched by the regime played a crucial role in undermining whatever feeling of brotherhood and unity that had emerged in the struggle against foreign occupiers during World War II. The most fatal of the lies spread by communist Yugoslavia's propaganda machine consisted in false accounts of World War II victims. Huge exaggerations of the number of war victims were launched to magnify Yugoslavia's losses in the Second World War and thus obtain larger war reparations payments, hide the extent of the crimes committed by the communists, and portray the latter as saviors both from external aggressors and from genocidal policies of domestic nationalists.

Yugoslav authorities gave the figure of 1,706,000 Yugoslav war victims to the International Reparations Commission in 1946, without any documentation. It is not known how they arrived at this number, but on the eve of the 1947 Paris Conference on Reparations, the Federal Bureau of Statistics in Belgrade ordered a new employee, the second-year mathematics student Vladeta Vučković, to compute "a significant number" of war victims, and gave him two weeks to do so.[1] Vučković estimated the number of wartime losses to be 1.7 million. The number did not denote real war victims, that is, people who were killed or died of war-related causes. Instead, it represented an estimate of demographic losses, that is, the difference between the population after the war and the projected population that would have been reached had there been no war. Never-conceived children were included in these losses. This important distinction was ignored, and 1.7 million remained the officially approved figure of Yugoslav war victims.

Many party and government officials were not aware of the magnitude of the distortion, or even that there was a distortion at all. However, a compilation of data on war victims made in 1964 provided a clear proof of the extent of the misrepresentation. The Federal Republic of Germany requested the compilation in order to finalize the agreement about the financial compensation for Yugoslav war victims.

The Yugoslav government ordered the preparation of the list of war victims in June 1964, and by November the data were collected. When they were processed in Belgrade in August 1966, they caused consternation because it turned out that the total number of Yugoslavs who died due to war actions and persecutions by the Axis forces and their collaborators (but excluding the victims of the communist-led forces) was lower than 600,000. When a review of the data produced only minor corrections, access to them was highly restricted, although they were given to the FRG. Yugoslavia's communist regime continued operating with the figure of 1.7 million even after it had been made obvious that it was an enormous exaggeration. Even in postcommunist Belgrade, access to the data on the 597,323 victims has remained restricted. The data were finally published in 1997, but in a very limited edition with a controlled distribution.[2]

Because of communist Yugoslavia's refusal to complete and publish data on World War II victims in the Yugoslav territory, a list of all victims is still not available, but the data produced in 1964 agree with the estimates by professional demographers. When the results of the first Yugoslav postwar census (1951) became available in the early fifties, Paul F. Myers and Arthur A. Campbell of the U.S. Bureau of the Census concluded in their 1954 study, on the basis of census data, demographic trends, and additional information, "that 1,067,000 persons in Yugoslavia lost their lives as a direct or indirect consequence of the war."[3] Two other researchers arrived at very similar conclusions in the 1980s. The Montenegrin Serb émigré Bogoljub Kočović published his study in London in 1985, while the Croatian Vladimir Žerjavić, working independently, published his in Zagreb in 1989 (when it became possible to publish such a study in the former Yugoslavia). These studies still provide the most reliable information on World War II losses in Yugoslavia.

According to Kočović, total demographic losses in Yugoslavia amounted to 1,985,000 (Žerjavić's figure is 2,022,000). By deducting from this number the losses caused by the drop in the birthrate and by expatriation, Kočović arrived at the number of 1,014,000 (Žerjavić: 1,027,000) actual war victims from the territory of the former Kingdom of Yugoslavia.[4] By further deducting the victims who were members of ethnic minorities, Kočović estimated the number of war victims among the constituent nationalities of the country— Croats, Macedonians, Montenegrins, Muslims, Serbs, and Slovenes— at 869,000. This figure is larger than the one arrived at in 1964, because it covers all categories of victims, including those regarded as collaborationists.

According to Kočović, there were 487,000 Serbs among the real war victims. (Žerjavić calculated the number of Serbian victims as high as 530,000.)[5] They were killed by Croats, Germans, Albanians, Muslims, Hungarians, Italians, Soviet forces, and, last but not least, other Serbs. They were also killed by bombing, including Allied air attacks, political liquidations, and various diseases, especially typhus. Among the other war victims in Kočović's study, there were 207,000 Croats, 86,000 Muslims, 60,000 Jews, and 50,000 Montenegrins. Relative losses within particular groups were as follows: Jews, 81.8 percent; Montenegrins, 10.4 percent;[6] Serbs, 6.9 percent; Muslims, 6.8 percent; Croats, 5.4 percent; Slovenes, 2.5 percent; and Macedonians, 0.9 percent.[7]

Kočović and Žerjavić differ in their estimates of wartime losses on the territory that forms the present-day Republic of Croatia, but the fact that the Croatian author came up with higher Serbian and lower Croatian losses than the Serbian author is an indication of the absence of nationalist bias in their studies. According to Kočović there were 124,000 Serb and 125,000 Croat war victims in Croatia, while according to Žerjavić the respective numbers are 131,000 and 106,000.[8]

There are also differences in the two authors' estimates of the number of Serb and Croat war victims in Bosnia-Herzegovina. Kočović gives the following figures: 209,000 Serbs, 79,000 Croats, 75,000 Muslims. Žerjavić's corresponding figures are 164,000, 64,000, and 75,000.[9]

The differences between Kočović and Žerjavić are insignificant in comparison with the difference of about 700,000 between their estimates of actual losses and the official figures from the Yugoslav communist regime. This discrepancy provided a fertile ground for various Yugoslav ethnic and political factions who took advantage of the phantom victims and the lack of documentation to produce inflated figures of their own losses. Thus Croats spoke of at least 300,000 Croatian casualties of the "Bleiburg massacre"[10] by the Yugoslav army, while the real number is probably under 50,000. The Muslims also spoke of a loss of 300,000 lives in their community. But the Serbs were most extreme in the numbers game: they accused Croats of having massacred 700,000 or more Serbs in one concentration camp alone.

Exaggerated claims of the number of war victims by various Yugoslav nationalities were published in ethnic émigré publications abroad. Within Yugoslavia, their dissemination was mostly oral. However, due to the Serbs' dominance in federal institutions in Belgrade—the capital of Serbia as well as Yugoslavia—and their disproportionate political influence in Bosnia-Herzegovina and Croatia, inflated accounts of Serbian wartime losses were propagated more openly, even through official channels.

The arbitrariness with which the numbers of victims were handled in the former Yugoslavia can be illustrated with the discrepancy within a single publication. In the entry on the Jasenovac concentration camp, a Yugoslav encyclopedia states that "about 500–600 thousand Serbs, Croats, and Jews were killed in this camp,"[11] while in the general entry on concentration camps, the same encyclopedia informs the reader that "according to incomplete and approximate data about 350,000 persons perished in the Jasenovac camp."[12]

Tito and his inner circle were aware of the destructive potential of falsehoods that fed nationalist rivalries in Yugoslavia. They imposed limited restraints on the propagation of nationalist distortions, but the only effective way of combating lies would have been full disclosure of the truth, not prohibition of selected texts and pronouncements, or incarceration of their authors by a regime that itself was the main source of the lies. With the fragmentation and weakening of the Yugoslav communist party after Tito's death in 1980, greater freedom of publication also meant a greater freedom for the dissemination of lies, even as it opened up new areas of historical research that had previously been off limits. As a consequence, the alleged number of Serbian World War II victims, already hugely inflated during Tito's lifetime, became even more extravagant. Thus General Velimir Terzić stated in an interview in 1983 that "in Jasenovac alone—according to the latest data—at least one million Serbs were killed from 1941 to 1945, not to count the victims of other nationalities."[13] In a book published in 1990, the number of persons allegedly killed at Jasenovac had grown to over

1,110,929.[14] And the prominent novelist and equally prominent politician Vuk Drašković wrote in a letter to a Zagreb newspaper in 1986 of "at least 1.5 million slaughtered Serbs in Pavelić's Croatia."[15]

The few researchers free of mythomania have arrived at far lower numbers of Jasenovac victims. The above-mentioned demographer Vladimir Žerjavić estimated that the approximate total number of people killed at Jasenovac could be around 100,000,[16] and that approximately half of them were Serbs,[17] the rest consisting mostly of Jews, Gypsies, Croats, and Muslims. In the second edition of his study of Word War II victims in Yugoslavia, Bogoljub Kočović, using a method different from Žerjavić's, arrived at the figure of about 83,000 victims who lost their lives at the Jasenovac camp.[18]

Antun Miletić, a researcher at the Military Archives in Belgrade, has collected data on the inmates killed at Jasenovac camp since 1979. One source of his information is lists of persons compiled in every village, town, and city in Yugoslavia, except for Macedonia and Slovenia. He has complemented these findings with the results obtained by various commissions on war crimes, and claims to have a list of 77,200 identified victims, of which 41,936 are Serbs,[19] but the list has not been published.

Miletić has expressed the opinion that the total number of victims could be substantially larger, stressing that his research did not cover Macedonia and Slovenia. However, very few people from these two areas—probably less than one hundred—lost their lives at Jasenovac. Moreover, the number of victims he has identified is very close to Žerjavić's and Kočović's estimates, and all of them are proportionate to reliable estimates of the total number of World War II victims in Yugoslavia.[20]

The outside world could have restrained the manipulations of the number of Yugoslav war victims—and mitigated their consequences—by not accepting them. An examination of widely available Yugoslav census data would have indicated gross misrepresentation. Moreover, as stated above, the results of such an analysis by two American demographers have been available in a U.S. government publication since 1954.

Another important source of postwar friction between various communities in the former Yugoslavia was the vilification of the Roman Catholic Church. Yugoslav communist authorities attacked the Catholic Church much more harshly than the Orthodox Church because they were not able to control a church whose supreme authority resided outside the country as they could the Serbian national Orthodox Church, traditionally obedient to political power. They put great pressure on the archbishop of Zagreb, Alojzije Stepinac, to loosen or sever ties with the Vatican and establish a national church. After he refused, he was accused of collaboration with the Ustaša regime in the wartime Croatian state and sentenced to a sixteen-year imprisonment and forced labor in October 1946. The American historian Sabrina Ramet notes that

> Some time after the trial, Milovan Djilas—at that time still a prominent member of the political establishment—admitted in private conversation that the real problem with Stepinac was not his politics vis-à-vis the Ustaše but his politics vis-à-vis the communists themselves, and in particular his fidelity to Rome. "If he had only proclaimed [the creation of] a Croatian Church, separate from Rome," said Djilas, "we would have raised him to the clouds."[21]

In fact, Stepinac had saved many people persecuted by the Ustaša regime and openly reproached the Ustaša authorities in his sermons. A British author who spent thirty years studying the churches in the former Yugoslavia and their relations with the state asserts that "Stepinac was strongly anti-Nazi as well as uncompromisingly and totally anti-communist; his credentials on this score cannot be faulted."[22]

The anti-Catholicism of a regime that did not tolerate any independent centers of power was reinforced by traditional Serbian Orthodox anti-Catholicism. A result of this symbiosis was a persistent hostility against the Catholic Church, which continued and sometimes reached the level of paranoia even after Tito's regime became less oppressive. An example of this paranoia is the following statement from a book on the 1941 disintegration of Yugoslavia by an army general and military historian, Velimir Terzić, published in 1963:

It is an irrefutable historical truth that the Vatican, with the pope at the helm, has been an open and brutal enemy of our country and our peoples, and that the entire Vatican policy for the last one thousand years has been directed to a single goal—to disunite and subjugate our peoples, and turn them into blind slaves of the Roman church.[23]

Some of General Terzić's "irrefutable" truths refer to concrete issues, which makes their falsity transparent:

It has been irrefutably proven that the Vatican participated in the preparation for the NDH [Independent State of Croatia] and that it gave full support and aid to Pavelić and Maček in their political and material-organizational preparation for the dismemberment and occupation of Yugoslavia in 1941. Thus Pope Pius XII recognized the NDH as soon as it was founded and gave it full support both internationally and in domestic policies.[24]

The fact is that the Vatican never recognized the World War II Croatian state, but through repetition this and other lies were accepted as truths by many people, both inside and outside the country.

The anti-Catholic campaign surged in the 1980s. It was driven by new writings as well as by reissues and translations. *Magnum crimen*, a rabidly anti-Catholic book first published in 1948, during the initial postwar communist terror, was reissued for the second time in 1986.[25] An even more virulent anti-Catholic diatribe, *Murderers in God's Name,* published in Paris in 1951 by a Serb émigré under the very French-sounding pseudonym Hervé Laurière, appeared in Serbian translation in 1987 with the original pseudonym and without any information that the author's real name was Branko Miljuš.[26]

The demonization of the Catholic Church was at the same time a demonization of the Croats, who, as Catholics, were seen as agents of a sinister force directed against "our peoples." In his two-volume work on the collapse of the Yugoslav monarchy published in 1982, the above-quoted army general and myth-historian Velimir Terzić described Croats as the main culprits for that collapse and the tragic events that followed.[27] And in 1986 Vasilije Krestić, a member of the

Serbian Academy of Sciences and Arts, asserted in his essay "On the Genesis of the Genocide of the Serbs in the NDH" that the Ustaša genocide was the realization of an idea "born in the remote past and developed for decades and centuries," which has a "rather broad base in certain segments of Croatian society."[28]

Actually, a vast majority of Croatians were so hostile toward the actions of the Ustaša regime that the commander of the German forces in Croatia, General Rudolf Lüters, complained that this hostility had a negative impact on the ability of the Wehrmacht to maintain order in the country. On March 16, 1943, in his confidential report to Field Marshal Alexander Löhr, commander in chief in southeast Europe, he stated,

> A radical change of the present situation could be achieved only by removing the present regime, which is supported by only some two percent of the population. The aversion of all segments of the population against the *Poglavnik* [the Ustaša leader] and the Ustašas gives additional strength to the insurgents, so that the pacification measures undertaken by German armed forces cannot lead to a lasting success.[29]

The high-end estimates of the number of Ustaša supporters are also quite low: "Even according to members of the Ustaši organization, the movement had at most about 40,000 "followers," or barely 6 percent of the population."[30]

Belgrade propagandists avoided mentioning such facts as carefully as they hid the extent of the Serbs' collaboration with the Nazis, including their participation in the Holocaust. Instead, they directed particular effort at portraying the Serbs as traditional friends and protectors of the Jews. Philip J. Cohen noted that this campaign started as soon as the communists came to power in Serbia: "Historical revisionism in Serbia began even before the end of the Second World War. Only days after the Partisan victory in Serbia, the Belgrade newspaper *Politika* . . . proclaimed Serbia's unbroken legacy of love for the Jews."[31]

Croats were the main target of demonization because Serbian nationalists in communist ranks knew that the essential step toward

the realization of Serbian hegemony in Yugoslavia consisted in limiting the power and prestige of the Croats, the second-largest nation
in the former Yugoslavia. Moreover, the Belgrade propagandists also
knew that the outside world was not interested in hearing about evil
Albanians, Muslims, Slovenians, and so forth, but was receptive to
the attractively simple story of good Serbs and bad Croats.

Internally, however, ethnic Albanians were always a major target
of defamation. False rumors about 300,000 Albanians from Albania
having settled in the Kosovo province after World War II were held
as proof that Tito's regime was conspiring to change the demographic picture of the province in favor of the Albanians, although
ethnic Albanians were victims of the worst persecutions by that
regime throughout the period when Ranković was at the helm of
the internal security apparatus, that is, until 1966. A new wave of
defamation and persecution began in 1981, following the ill-timed
Albanian demonstrations demanding the status of a republic for the
province of Kosovo. The abolition of the province's autonomy was
completed by 1989, the six hundredth anniversary of the Battle of
Kosovo. To justify the repression of the Albanians, various sources
accused them of terrorizing the Serbs. The 1986 Academy *Memorandum* voiced this accusation: "Not only are the last remnants of the
Serbian people leaving their land, constantly and at an unabated
rate, but . . . chased by violence and a physical, moral, and psychological terror, they are preparing for their final exodus." Actually,
census figures show that the number of Serbs in the province remained fairly constant (around 200,000) but their ratio kept diminishing because of the Albanians' high birthrate. Rapes of Serbian
women were also alleged to form part of the terror.[32] The resulting
hatred of Kosovo Albanians and fear of losing Kosovo were important catalysts for the rise of Serbian nationalism in the 1980s. Slobodan Milošević skillfully used it to expand his power in the second
half of the decade.

The fear of the "Muslim threat" was also used in the effort to
mobilize Serbs in a nationalist front. The Muslims of Bosnia-
Herzegovina were accused of working toward an Islamic state, although that idea was limited to a small group of intellectuals and

clerics. The future president, Alija Izetbegović, indirectly supported that idea in his *Islamic Declaration*.[33] Parts of the text were published in the 1970s, but the author did not experience any difficulties until 1983, when he was tried in Sarajevo together with other prominent Muslims and sentenced to a fourteen-year prison term. Serb nationalists used the trial to instill fear of the Islamic threat to the Serb population, although Izetbegović had little influence at the time. The war, started by the Serbs in 1992, made the idea of an Islamic Bosnia much more popular.

The falsehoods spread by the Belgrade propaganda machine did not benefit anybody. The intention to obtain higher war reparation payments by means of inflated numbers of Yugoslav war victims failed; the tensions among various Yugoslav nationalities, caused by this and other lies, made life in the common state more difficult and contributed to its violent disintegration.

The Fear of Vanishing

The Serbs' aggressiveness inspired fear in others, but the Serbs themselves were gripped by an intense fear, which was a source of their aggressiveness. This fear reflected the insecurity of a people dominated by a foreign civilization for five centuries, who enjoyed their own fully sovereign nation-state for only forty years between the Congress of Berlin in 1878 and the entry into the ill-fated Yugoslav union in 1918.

The fear of again being dominated by "others" was the fundamental reason for the Serbs' fierce opposition to Tito's attempt to turn Serbia from a dominant into a less unequal partner in the Yugoslav federation. The fear of being massacred again was intensified by huge exaggerations of Serbian victims during the Second World War and by the depiction of some of their neighbors as inherently genocidal. The fear of Slovenian and Croatian economic power and of the Albanian and Slavic Muslim birthrates also contributed to the Serbs' anxiety.[34]

Serbian fears were heightened by the Yugoslav Constitution of

1974, which gave greater power to the constituent republics and made the two "autonomous provinces" of Kosovo and Vojvodina truly autonomous. The reason for the changes was the aged Josip Broz Tito's intention to make Yugoslavia more stable after his departure by diminishing the imbalance of power between Serbia and the other republics, and making the Kosovo Albanians loyal citizens by giving them greater influence in the province. Tito correctly perceived that the ever-present dream of a Greater Serbia, coupled with Serbian dominance in federal administration and the armed forces, presented the gravest threat to Yugoslavia's future. But the 1974 reforms did not offer a solution because Tito, following his usual balancing tactics, matched the decentralization of the administrative structure and the party with a recentralization of the armed forces and an increase of military influence and status.[35] A seemingly monolithic army succeeded the no-longer monolithic party as the hopeful guarantor of the survival of the heterogeneous country whose incessantly changing charters (the communist Yugoslavia went through four constitutions in its forty-six-year history) and flawed institutions could not provide the needed cohesiveness. The result was that Tito simultaneously increased the Serbs' fears and made it more tempting for them to channel their fears into armed aggression.

Soon after the adoption of Yugoslavia's 1974 constitution, which reduced the power of Serbia, a poem was published that expressed the fear of Serbia's disappearance. Here are two stanzas from Tanasije Mladenović's "Triptych":

> Similar to an underground mole you rise, like a plant, out of the winter
> Sleep, awakened by the new sun. Ever and ever again with a new flash!
> Will you, as before, still be able to renew your strength, with a crash?
>
> Or will you, discouraged, exhausted, abandoned to the stream of time,
> Vanish among mountains and nations, and, in the last storm,

Blown to pieces by an apocalyptic force, sink into yourself, to
the bottom?![36]

Mladenović's poem caused a sensation because it was the first time
that apocalyptic nationalist anxiety appeared in print under the
communist regime. The fear of Serbia's demise became a prominent
theme of Serbian intellectual life in the 1980s. The fear is very much
present in Milorad Pavić's novel *Dictionary of the Khazars,* a work
that has achieved international success. Its subject, the Khazars,
formed a large state stretching from the Dnepr to the Volga Rivers
from the seventh to the tenth century, but they subsequently van-
ished, leaving hardly a trace. An Italian critic, among others, pointed
out that behind the plot of the novel "there lies, unhidden, the
Serbian anxiety, that of a small, besieged nation afraid of disappear-
ing. As if there were a conspiracy to eliminate it. Allegedly there is
an anti-Serbian racism in the same way there was, or is, anti-
Semitism. Pavić maintains that Serbophobia exists, and ... an-
nounces: 'This is why tomorrow we Serbs will have a holocaust.' "[37]
Pavić offers an explanation of why Serbia is weak and threatened:
"We have severed all the ties with our roots, with our civilization,
with the Greeks, with the Romanians, and during the communist
era with Russia, too, with the Orthodox Russia, with Ukraine, with
the Orthodox Ukraine, with Armenia."[38] He claims that a closer
alliance of "Byzantine" countries would be beneficial to Europe as
a whole: "Europe cannot renounce one of its two civilizations,"
which "have inherited the spirituality of the Eastern Roman Empire
and the spirituality of the Western Roman Empire."[39] However,
Pavić is aware that the result would be a "polarization" between
Eastern and Western Europe. His call for unity of Orthodox and
Byzantine countries is a variation on the old pan-Slavist idea, sub-
stituting religion and culture for race.

Analogous calls for "Byzantine" countries to close ranks have
been issued in Russia. In his article "Russia Is Looking for Allies,"
which announced the Conference of Spiritually Close Peoples, the
Russian intellectual and member of parliament Oleg Rumiantsev
stated that "geopolitically, the peoples of the post-Byzantine region

have always constituted a continent between the West and the East," and that "our coexistence with the Atlantic and Islamic civilizations will be beneficial only if there is mutual support of peoples and governments within the framework of our own world, acknowledging its individuality."[40]

In spite of the calls to form a united Orthodox bloc and a currently popular thesis that the postcommunist world will be marked by the clashes of civilizations, there is little reason to fear the emergence of unified cultural-religious blocs. The strong allegiance to the nation-state and its specific interests creates enormous obstacles to such unification. Orthodox church leaders usually consult with their governments before consulting with other Orthodox churches. The resulting divisions among Orthodox churches explain why no ecumenical council—a gathering of all Orthodox bishops— has been held since the seventh one in Nicaea in 787.

But even if an Orthodox bloc were feasible it would hardly be desirable. To ensure the welfare, and thereby the security, of Orthodox countries, Eastern Christians should join other Christian and non-Christian churches in an effort to emphasize common fundamental religious and ethical teachings. Stronger ties between the Orthodox and other churches would help the former loosen their traditional bondage to state and nation, which has been a great impediment both to the proper function of Orthodox churches and to the development of a free civil society.

There is also the question of how Byzantine the post-Byzantine world is. Byzantine civilization reached its peak from the ninth to the eleventh centuries, the time when the rest of Europe was poor and primitive, slowly emerging from the devastations inflicted by successive waves of barbarians who had destroyed the Western Roman Empire. But today, five and a half centuries after the disappearance of Byzantium, the Orthodox Church is the only specifically Byzantine institution still alive, and one of its salient features, subservience to state and nation, provides moral support to internal oppression and external aggressiveness.

The literature, music, and other arts produced in Orthodox Eastern Europe during the last two hundred years are not Byzantine.

Their motifs and themes may reflect local traditions, but stylistically they are an integral part of a largely secularized, universal, post-Western culture. This is certainly true of Pavić's works, which belong in the postmodernist movement. He obviously tries to emulate writers like Umberto Eco and Julio Cortázar, but denies it and asserts instead that his books "are a voice of this soil and this Byzantine civilization."[41]

Modern technology is making the world ever smaller and more homogeneous, but the reduction of differences between various entities does not necessarily reduce the mutual hostility. A consequence of the homogenization is the fear of losing one's identity and thus a passionate clinging to the remaining differences. A specific circumstance makes the identity issue particularly acute in the western Balkans, where Croats, Serbs, Montenegrins, and Slavic Muslims share basically one language. This situation has made the language an important political tool: the Serbs have claimed that all these nations speak the same language, with the aim of proving that they are all indeed one nation, and exerted great pressure in the monarchist and communist Yugoslavias to impose their own linguistic variant as the sÐtokavian standard. The others have resisted this pressure and clung to their own linguistic idiosyncrasies to protect their identity.[42]

The concern with Serbia's identity has been very much present in the mind and work of Dobrica Ćosić, the most celebrated contemporary Serbian novelist. In a 1978 speech at the Serbian Academy of Sciences and Arts, he stated that "the historical novel is a search for the lost individual and collective identity, a search for the times in which this identity could perhaps be found."[43] On another occasion he defined where it can be found: "Our spiritual being is integrated by religion and national mythology. Above all by the Kosovo myth and the great epic poetry."[44] Insofar as Matija Bećković's observation that "Myths are our religion"[45] is correct, the integration is based on mythology only.

Slobodan Milošević followed Ćosić's precept: he rallied the Serbian people around the Kosovo myth and Vid's Day cult, that is, around a cult of revenge and the promise of a new Serbian empire.

However, instead of creating an empire, he has dragged Serbia to a defeat that, unlike the one at Kosovo, could hardly be interpreted as a consequence of a moral stand. There is a symmetry here: a cult based on a military defeat over six hundred years ago culminating in a new defeat. Serbian textbooks, however, "blame the war on dark 'international forces' that 'conspired' to destroy Yugoslavia. Milosevic, the school texts say, heroically intervened to save the Serbs from annihilation."[46]

The Academy Memorandum

In the middle of the 1980s, a decade characterized by feverish re-countings of real and imagined past injustices and current threats to the Serbs, sixteen members of the Serbian Academy of Sciences and Arts formed a panel to write a compendium of Serbian fears and appeal to their compatriots to revolt against a supposed anti-Serb conspiracy.[47] The document they produced was leaked and published in September 1986.[48]

Because of the prestige of its authors, the *Memorandum* reinforced the conviction that the Serbs have been abused by their neighbors, who allegedly were plotting their destruction. It listed Serbian grievances based on distorted data and provided justification for the use of force to redress the supposed anti-Serbian discrimination in Yugoslavia. The *Memorandum,* a manifesto of Serbian nationalism, formed the ideological platform for the pan-Serbian policy of Slobodan Milošević. It became a program for action, launched when the disintegration of the communist order made many Serbs believe that they had a unique opportunity to transform federal Yugoslavia into Greater Serbia with the help of the Serb-dominated Yugoslav armed forces.

The *Memorandum* blamed decentralization for all the problems of communist Yugoslavia, including the economic problems. It was nostalgic for the hard-line, rigidly centralized period in the immediate postwar years, which replicated the Leninist Soviet system where all decisions were made at the center of power: "The initial

Yugoslav solution of the national question could be regarded as an exemplary model of a multinational federation where the principle of a unified state and state policy was successfully linked with the principle of political and cultural autonomy of the nations and national minorities."[49] The authors of the document lamented that five-year plans were abandoned and warned of "the danger that the political system may evolve in the direction of polycentrism."[50]

The *Memorandum* characterized the year 1965 as the "fatal turning point" that ended the best period in the history of communist Yugoslavia.[51] From the perspective of most non-Serb Yugoslavs it was exactly the opposite: the mid-sixties marked the beginning of significant economic and political liberalization, including curbs on the power of the federal bureaucracy in Belgrade. They also marked the beginning of a growing conflict between the northwestern republics, which were moving closer to pluralism and a market economy, and Serbia, where nationalists pushed in the opposite direction because only a rigidly centralized system could ensure Serbia's— and their—hegemony.

Essentially, the *Memorandum* presented a conspiracy theory, as the following excerpt illustrates:

> Under the impact of the ruling ideology, the cultural achievements of the Serbian people are being estranged from them, usurped or underestimated, neglected or permitted to decay, the language is repressed, and the Cyrillic script is gradually disappearing. . . . No other Yugoslav nationality's cultural and spiritual integrity is so rudely disputed as the Serbian is. No literary and artistic heritage is so routed, ransacked, and ravaged as the Serbian heritage. . . . While the Slovenian, Croatian, Macedonian, and Montenegrin literatures are being integrated today, only the Serbian one is being systematically disintegrated. . . . The Serbian culture has more unsuitable, banned, silenced, or undesirable writers and creative intellectuals than any other Yugoslav literature, many of them even being completely erased from literary memory.[52]

In the section titled "The Situation of Serbia and the Serbian People," the *Memorandum* asserted that the Serbs in Kosovo province were victims of a physical, political, legal, and cultural genocide, and that all over Yugoslavia they were victims of discrimination in spite of having sacrificed themselves for others: "Only [Serbia] made real sacrifices for the development of the three underdeveloped republics and the autonomous province of Kosovo, paying for its help to others with a lag in its own development."[53]

Another equally unsustainable grievance was that only Serbs had large minorities outside their own republic: "the worst trouble is that the Serbian people do not have their own state, while all the other [Yugoslav] peoples do."[54] The document is dominated by the idea that Serbs must undertake whatever action is necessary to bring all Serbs into one state as a defense against further attempts to annihilate them:

> The establishment of full national and cultural integrity of the Serbian people, regardless of which republic or province they live in, is their historical and democratic right. The achievement of equal status and independent development has a deeper sense for the Serbian people. In less than fifty years, during two successive generations, [it was] twice exposed to physical annihilation, forced assimilation, conversion, cultural genocide, ideological indoctrination, devaluation and rejection of its own tradition under an imposed guilt complex, [and] intellectually and politically disarmed.[55]

The authors of the text warned that "the existing depressive condition of the Serbian people . . . favors a revival and ever more drastic expression of the national sensitivity of the Serbian people and of reactions that can be incendiary, and even dangerous," if their demands are not met; at the same time they did their best to nurture such reactions by depicting Serbs as victims of a conspiracy.[56]

The driving force behind the *Memorandum* was the novelist Dobrica Ćosić, often called the "spiritual father of Serbia" because of his prestige and influence. He did not participate in the drafting of the document, but he was the earliest and strongest advocate of the theses contained in it.

Ćosić admired Josip Broz Tito as long as Tito retained the centralized system of the Soviet type, which gave great power to Serbia as the political and administrative center of the country. Ćosić liked

Tito's police chief Aleksandar Ranković even better. The purge of Ranković and the partial dismantling of the centralized police system were the main reasons for Ćosić's disappointment with Tito. His fondness for strong men who kept a centralized Yugoslavia together by the use of terror is reflected in his praise of the most important secret police chief after Ranković, Slobodan Penezić Krcun, former political commissar of the Second Proletarian Brigade and a "people's hero": "In politics I have probably never trusted and appreciated anybody as much as Krcun. This young man was the thinking elder of his generation. For all of us his age, he was the absolute authority in judging people and events."[57]

Ćosić's conviction of the Serbs' superiority over their neighbors is not shaken by his awareness of their faults:

> We have an aggressive, arrogant mentality, often an unbearable trait for a community. Our spontaneity can turn into vulgarity in our communication with peoples of other nationalities and languages. On our objective superiorities and traditional creative and liberal values we, Serbs, have established a supremacy over other Balkan and Yugoslav peoples. . . . Our capacity for observation and our willingness to recognize and properly appreciate values in somebody smaller and different from us are deficient. We also bear a lot of responsibility for Serbophobia because our civilizational level is unusually low. There is a lot of ignorance, disorder, and banality in our lives: the absence of civilized behavior is obvious, there is a lot of destruction, civic irresponsibility.[58]

Ćosić expressed the desire to see the rule of law established in Serbia: "I regard a consistent deideologization of the national and state policies, and a faster development of a modern state ruled by law as our most urgent task."[59] There is no reason to doubt Ćosić's sincerity in making such statements, but his propagation of nationalist myths undermined his expressed desire for order based on civility. There was an even greater discrepancy between Milovan Djilas's actions as a communist official and his later concern for human rights and justice during his dissident period. He, too, was equally genuine in both attitudes, and this is one more proof that a man can commit atrocities, or incite others to commit them, not because of a personality disorder but because of his belief in ideas that provoke and justify atrocities.

When hate-breeding myths are propagated by prestigious national institutions, it is even more difficult for individuals to resist them. Dostoevsky is an example of how even a genuinely pious man can be moved to a position contrary to his own better insights by a church traditionally subordinated to state and nation. His unsurpassed understanding of the evil in man did not prevent him from being an anti-Catholic and anti-Semitic bigot dreaming of a Holy Russia.

The drafters of the *Memorandum* and numerous other prominent Serbian artists and intellectuals who have painted an apocalyptic picture of the state of their nation and accepted violence against their neighbors as a solution are also generally normal men who acted abnormally when they combined the fear of their own annihilation with the expectation of a glorious future. They saw themselves as the nation's saviors who will, after destroying evil enemies, realize the old promise of a prosperous and glorious Second Serbian Empire as the dominant power in the Balkans.

The Church Identifies the Devils

The Serbian Orthodox metropolitan of Zagreb, Ljubljana, and Italy, Jovan (Pavlović), blamed the Serbian bishops' advisors from the ranks of the Serbian Academy of Sciences and Arts for the "disastrous policy" of the Serbian Orthodox Church, which had actively campaigned for a Greater Serbia: "With your proposals [for territorial and border issues] you have drawn the church even more into politics. You have made the proper work of the church more difficult. The flirting with the [nationalist] opposition has brought the church onto thin ice."[60]

This attempt to shift the responsibility for the church's nationalist zeal to the intellectuals is not well founded. Saint-Savaism, an ideology built on the fusion of church, state, and nation, is the most potent source of intolerance and occidentophobia in Serbian society. Miladin Životić, a recently deceased philosopher and leading Serbian democrat, maintained that the Serbian Orthodox Church and the Bosnian Serbs "share a common clerical-nationalist ideology that glorifies traditional, patriarchal society. 'This is a fundamentalist, anti-Western ideology,' said Zivotic. 'It's something that even Milosevic can't accept.' "[61]

As the main repository of Serbian nationalism, the Serbian Orthodox Church shared in nationalist excesses in Serbia, and after 1918 in Yugoslavia. It contributed to the failure of the first Yugoslavia by supporting Belgrade's efforts to establish Serbian hegemony instead of preaching tolerance and condemning violence. Svetozar Pribićević, an ethnic Serb politician from Croatia who had played an important role in the creation of the new state, wrote about the political engagement of the Orthodox Church in monarchist Yugoslavia:

> The episcopate of the Orthodox Church, with the patriarch at its head, has today become a militant instrument of the dictatorial regime. This results mainly from the fact that the church has become, so to speak, an integral part of the state's administrative machinery. The king appoints the patriarch and the bishops by decree, and decides on all church matters. . . . In return for the patriarch's devotion to the regime, the latter helps him build Orthodox churches in purely Catholic regions, with the aim of religious proselytism. . . . During the entire period since 1918 one has never heard from the patriarch's mouth a sermon on ecclesiastic and religious matters, man's relation to God, love of our neighbors, the needs of the human soul, moral conditions, or the purposes of life, but always [utterances] on matters of national and political character in the sense of imperialism and megalomania. He emphasizes the two-headed eagle, the powerful king, the blood shed on battlefields, war victims, in a word, whatever can serve the goals of an extreme nationalism, bellicose nationalism, so that, according to the ideas of the highest leader of the Serbian Church, the church should not let the barracks surpass it in nationalist propaganda.[62]

In the 1930s the church established a close relationship with the principal Serbian fascist movement, Zbor, and its leader, Dimitrije Ljotić:

> Ljotić enjoyed close relations with the Serbian Orthodox Church, in which he held an official position. As a member of the Patriarchal Council of the Serbian Orthodox Church in Belgrade, Ljotić established a close and long-lasting association with the highly influential Bishop Nikolaj Velimirović. Under Ljotić's influence, Bishop Velimirović's clerical organization *Bogomoljci* (Devotionalists) officially joined Zbor, and some of Velimirović's followers became Zbor functionaries.[63]

Not only was the Serbian Orthodox Church anti-Catholic and anti-Western, it was also virulently anti-Semitic. The anti-Semitic current in that church reached a high point in the writings of Bishop Velimirović, the main ideologue of militant Saint-Savaism, during the Second World War. Here is an excerpt from one of his addresses to the Serbian people:

> In the course of centuries those who crucified the Messiah, Lord Jesus Christ, the Son of God, have turned Europe into the main battlefield against God, for the devil. Europe is presently the main battlefield of the Jew and his father, the devil, against the heavenly Father and his only begotten Son, born of the Virgin, and against the Holy Ghost.
>
> . . . All modern European slogans have been made up by Jews, the crucifiers of Christ: democracy, strikes, socialism, atheism, tolerance of all religions, pacifism, universal revolution, capitalism, and communism. These are all inventions made by Jews, namely, by their father, the devil. All this has been done with the intention to humiliate Christ, to obliterate Him, and to place their Jewish Messiah on the Christ's throne, without being aware even today that he is Satan himself, their father, who has reined them in with his reins, and who whips them with his whip.
>
> . . . You should think about this, my Serbian brethren, and accordingly correct your thoughts, desires, and acts, so that you may not become Satan's children. May Christ help you. Amen.[64]

A *New York Times* reporter noted the widespread conviction that the Serbian Orthodox Church wants to save the world from the evils threatening it:

> "You know Tito was a Mason," said a 54-year-old Orthodox priest in St. Sava Cathedral one recent afternoon, "and so is the Pope and all the Catholic bishops. After Mahatma Gandhi was killed, Tito became the head of the Masons. And the toughest opponent of the Masonic order, which wants to rule the world, is the Serbian Orthodox church. We know Tito was secretly buried in the Vatican."[65]

Saint-Savaist idolization of the nation and hostility toward democracy and Western secular humanism explain why the Serbian Church gave enthusiastic support to the former communist technocrat Slobodan Milošević when he adopted Serbian nationalism to enlarge his power base. On Vid's Day 1989—the six hundredth anniversary of the Battle of Kosovo—when Milošević threatened the use of force against the perceived enemies of Serbia, the periodical *Glas crkve* (Voice of the Church) published a "Vid's Day Message," consisting of "A Proposal for the Serbian Church-National Program."[66] The proposal states that "for almost half a century Serbia had to endure economic subordination, underdevelopment, partitions, and political inferiority in the socialist Yugoslavia," thus echoing the main thesis of the Academy *Memorandum.* The document praises the new Serbian administration led by Milošević: "one must honestly recognize certain merits and commitment of the new Serbian leadership to the solution of the Serbian question. The new authorities were able correctly to use the great democratic energy and spiritual potential of the Serbian people, who have started to think independently and to again determine their fate."[67]

Serbian Orthodox churchmen joined the historians and novelists who nourished ethnic hatreds by writing about real and fictitious crimes committed against Serbs in the past and ignoring the crimes committed by the Serbs themselves. Bishop Atanasije Jevtić, for example, published a travelogue, *From Kosovo to Jadovno,* which portrays ethnic Albanians as rapists of "adolescent girls and old women (in villages and monasteries)."[68] He describes his pilgrimage to several places where Serbs were massacred during the Second World War, without ever mentioning the massacres committed by the Serbs at the same time.

A Dutch theologian finds a tension between the political and spiritual spheres in the lives of prominent Serbian Orthodox Church leaders throughout its history and today:

> It is also characteristic of the present patriarch, Pavle, who, before his election was very much honoured as a non-political spiritual authority, not only by the Orthodox but also by Muslims and Catholics in Kosovo and Croatia. After his elevation to patriarch on 1 December 1990, he tried sincerely to stimulate improvement in inter-confessional relations and reconciliation between the nations. At the same time, however, he became increasingly involved in politics through his official appearances on occasions like the *parastos* [memorial service] for the *četnik* leader of the Second World War, Draža Mihailović, and the controversial installation of the Serbian Bishop Lukijan in the new Serbian Orthodox eparchy of Dalj, only a few weeks after the massacre in Dalj in August 1991. A letter to Lord Carrington signed by the Patriarch is of central significance here.[69]

In the letter to the chairman of the peace conference, Patriarch Pavle restated standard Serbian nationalist slogans, such as the alleged murder of "more than 700,000 Serbs' by Croats during World War II and the artificiality of Croatia's borders "determined by the will of Josip Broz Tito"; depicted the ongoing brutal Serb military campaign in Croatia as a self-defense of Serb lives; asserted that ethnic Serbs in Croatia "must find themselves under the common roof with the present Serbia and all Serbian *krajinas*"; and drew the parallel between the fates of Serbs and Jews while echoing Hitler in his claim that all Serbs must live in one state.[70]

Such actions of the patriarch and the hierarchy of the Serbian Orthodox Church prompted a group of Paris-based Orthodox theologians and intellectuals to issue an appeal in late 1991 emphasizing the need "to break the chain of violence, of hatred, of death." The document reproaches Serbian bishops for inciting hatred:

The church you guide seems to contribute, unconsciously, without doubt, to these incitements to hatred. Simultaneously with some government propagandists—whose moral value is dubious—some church dignitaries are more and more often writing and preaching about the sufferings of the Serbs, the crimes of the Ustašas, the pits and caves where bodies of innocent victims were piled up. This type of "speluncar" considerations, as people ironically say, has even become a tirelessly repeated subject of the church press.[71]

Serbian bishops were not swayed by the appeal. They adamantly defended the wars against Croatia and Bosnia-Herzegovina, and repeatedly condemned what they term the "genocide" by Muslims and Croats against the Serbs in Bosnia and Croatia. They stopped supporting Milošević only after he distanced himself from the leaders of the Bosnian Serb Republic, having realized that his pursuit of a Greater Serbia had failed. A pastoral message issued by the Church Council of twenty bishops in mid-1992, when Milošević's drive for a Greater Serbia first ran into serious trouble (when the former Yugoslav republics gained international recognition and tougher sanctions were imposed on Serbia and Montenegro), called on President Milošević to resign but reiterated the bishops' allegiance to the idea that all Serbs should live in one state, and repeated the false nationalist claim that the borders between the republics of the former Yugoslavia were arbitrarily created by the communist authorities with the aim of dividing the Serbs: "The bishops repeated their support for unification of all Serbs in a single state and blamed Yugoslavia's Communists for dividing the Serbian population with republican borders that the European Community, the United States and the United Nations have in recent months recognized as international frontiers between Slovenia, Croatia, Bosnia and Herzegovina, and the new rump Yugoslavia consisting of Serbia and Montenegro."[72]

The Serbian church hierarchy not only refuses to acknowledge large-scale massacres committed by Serbs in Croatia and Bosnia but claims that there is an ongoing genocide against the Serbs. In April 1997, Patriarch Pavle blessed and signed a "Declaration against the Genocide of the Serbian People," which was sent to many international institutions. The declaration, also signed by four bishops, twenty-two members of the Academy of Sciences and Arts, and thirty-one additional prominent intellectuals and artists, is a solipsistic lament over the eternally suffering Serbia:

> The history of Serbian lands . . . is full of instances of genocide against the Serbs and of exoduses to which they were exposed. Processes of annihilation of Serbs in the most diverse and brutal ways have been continuous. Throughout their history they have faced the fiercest forms of genocides and exoduses that have jeopardized their existence, yet they have always been self-defenders of their own existence, spirituality, culture, and democratic convictions.[73]

The declaration defines the Serbs not only as self-defenders but also as defenders of Europe: "Since the early Middle Ages, the Serbs, together with their rulers and church dignitaries fighting the Turks, have been the last rampart in the defense of Europe from the Turkish invasion and the penetration of Islam."[74] There is no mention either of the Serbian role in the Turkish conquests or of the recent Serbian genocide against the Muslims, which, on the contrary, is obliquely justified as one of the "attempts to thwart expansionist trends whose root we can observe today in the shape of fundamentalism."[75]

The feeling that the world is passively watching genocidal actions by Serbia's enemies has generated threats against the world as a whole. A book issued by the influential publishing house Glas crkve (The Church's Voice) in 1988 threatens another world war if the world does not show a better understanding of Serbia's problems:

> Today it does not depend only on [the Serbian people] whether they will choose civilization or the abyss. But it should be clear to everybody once for all: if they are forced to precipitate themselves into an abyss, this people will, as on Vid's Day 74 years ago, drag down with itself the entire world, which is dangerously indifferent to the Serbian fate today.[76]

A Serbian scholar points out that "Even some church dignitaries have reconciled themselves to the idea that we Serbs 'do not need democracy,' that all the evil comes to us from democracy and basic human rights."[77] Some church thinkers have forwarded the thesis that myths are more truthful than historiography. An article about Vid's Day and the heavenly kingdom in a church publication advances such a view: "Historical science can change its truth with every new fact. Tradition does not need to change anything because it does not depend on facts, because it is an image of the divine Truth."[78]

Besides reminding their flock exclusively of the crimes committed by their neighbors, highly regarded authorities of the Serbian Orthodox Church harshly condemn Western Europe as a whole. The conclusion of the above-mentioned church-national program, for example, expresses the desire to find a place for the Serbian people in contemporary Europe but sets strict conditions for joining the latter, noting that "not long ago Europe learned statehood and democracy from Serbia":

> We do not want a Europe without God nor a pseudohumanist Europe where man, instead of God, is enthroned. We constantly keep in mind all the warnings issued by spiritual geniuses from Dostoevsky to Bishop Nikolai [Velimirović] and Father Justin [Popović] who fear for the future of such a de-Christianized Europe.
>
> We want to join a truly Christian Europe, where God and man will be together, where happiness and peace will be built as a model for all of mankind, not under the rule of a dull democracy or old theocracy but a creative and true *theodemocracy*.
>
> This is how we see the future of Serbia and Yugoslavia today.[79]

The Serbian theologian Archimandrite Dr. Justin Popović warned that Western Christianity was a betrayal of the faith: "The Second Vatican Council is a renaissance of all European humanisms, a renaissance of corpses."[80] Protestantism is no lesser an evil than Catholicism, for the Christian West as a whole is evil: "What then is Europe: The pope and Luther. . . . The European pope is human lust for power. The European Luther—the human determination to explain everything by intellect."[81] The ecumenical movement is consequently a threat to true Christianity:

> Ecumenism is the common name for pseudo-Christianities, for
> Western Europe's pseudochurches. All European humanisms, headed
> by papism, are in it with all their heart. All these pseudo-
> Christianities, all these pseudochurches are nothing but one heresy
> after another. . . . There is no essential difference here between pa-
> pism, Protestantism, ecumenism, and other sects, whose name is
> legion.[82]

Thus if a church union is to be Christian, it must recognize Orthodoxy as the one true church: "papist-Protestant ecumenism with its
pseudochurch and its pseudo-Christianity has no other way out of
its deaths and torments but a wholehearted repentance before God-
Man Lord Christ and His Orthodox Church. . . . Without repenting
and joining Christ's True Church it is unnatural and senseless to
talk about a union of "churches," a dialogue of love, an *intercom-
munio.*"[83]

These are not views of an arbitrarily chosen theologian. Archimandrite Popović, the author of a three-volume *Dogmatism of the
Orthodox Church* and a twelve-volume *Lives of the Saints,* is, besides
Bishop Nikolaj Velimirović, the most important twentieth-century
Serbian Orthodox theologian. He was the teacher of the aggressively
nationalist bishops who are presently playing the dominant role in
the Serbian Orthodox Church, and his book on ecumenism is the
only major Serbian work on the subject. Like Dostoevsky, whom he
greatly admired, Popović condemned the West and saw in Orthodoxy the power that could save the world, ignoring the wide gap
between the mystical orientation of Orthodox religious culture and
the frequent subordination of the Orthodox Church to secular
causes of dubious moral value.[84] Popović is venerated by many
Orthodox believers as a saint, and his tomb at the Ćelije Monastery
near Valjevo, where he had spent the last thirty-one years of his life,
has become a place of pilgrimage.[85]

The author of a well-researched book on the Serbian ecclesiology
of the nineteenth and twentieth centuries states that messianism is
even more pronounced in Bishop Velimirović's thought: "The core
of his reflections is that Christianity has been realized in its ideal
form in the Balkans, and that the Balkans, especially the Serbian

people, have been predestined for Orthodox Christianity more than other regions and peoples. This historical reference runs through the entire Serbian theology."[86]

The Serbs have long resisted establishing religious ties with Western Europe. Serbia was the only Eastern European Orthodox country that did not send representatives to the Council of Florence, which met in 1439 to solve dogmatic issues related to the unification of Eastern and Western Christendom and to develop a system of collective European security in the face of the Turkish threat to the continent. The Byzantine emperor and the ecumenical patriarch, who attended the meeting, sent a special envoy to persuade Despot Branković to do the same, but he preferred an alliance with the Turks, only twenty years before they conquered his small domain, the last vestige of the once powerful Serbian state. The council ended with the signing of the unification bull *Laetentur coeli* by the pope, the ecumenical patriarch, and representatives of Western and Eastern European churches. Only Bishop of Ephesus Markos Eugenikos refused to sign the bull. The Serbian Orthodox Church, like the Greek, canonized him, and celebrates Saint Marko of Ephesus on the first day of February.[87]

The 1931 Constitution of the Serbian Orthodox Church contained an article that stipulated that the church must work toward the rapprochement and unification of Christian churches, and some members of the Serbian Orthodox Church have been genuinely engaged in this endeavor.[88] However, that church's ecumenical activity was more noticeable at the international level than within Yugoslavia. Thus, the Serbian Orthodox delegation participated in joint prayers that opened and closed the Fifth World Conference of the Ecumenical Council of Churches in Nairobi in 1975, but Atanasije Jevtić, head of the Serbian Orthodox observers at the meeting of the Ecumenical Council of the Catholic Bishops' Conference in Yugoslavia, which was held in Zagreb at about the same time, declined a joint prayer. Moreover, the Serbian church was the last Orthodox church to join the Ecumenical Council of Churches and to send its observers to the Second Vatican Council. With the soaring of populism and nationalism in the late twentieth-century

Serbia, anti-ecumenists—many of them Justin Popović's pupils, known as Justinites—became even stronger and filled key positions in the church. Instead of standing against the rising religious and ethnic intolerance among the Serbs, they have contributed to it.

Fear Transformed into a Spider: Poisonous Best-Sellers

Numerous scholarly and theological treatises appeared in the 1980s depicting a morally inferior, conspiring, Serbophobic world as a threat to the very existence of the nation. These works played an important role in mobilizing Serbs for war. Poems, novels, and plays were even more effective in spreading the fear of annihilation. In fact, a single conceit, such as the poet Matija Bećković's characterization of contemporary Serbs as "remnants of a slaughtered people,"[89] can produce a greater impact than a voluminous treatise. The renowned filmmaker Dušan Makavejev testified to its electrifying effect: "When I first heard the statement about present-day Serbs as *remnants of a slaughtered people*, which has been repeated so many times by now, I was struck by a solemn awe, as if I had heard the truth about the people to whom I belong and about myself."[90]

A considerable number of Serb poets and writers of fiction took very active political roles in the campaign for a Greater Serbia, in which economists were conspicuous by their absence. Most prominent was the political engagement of the poet and psychiatrist Radovan Karadžić, the indicted war criminal who directed the Serb aggression in Bosnia-Herzegovina. Nikola Koljević, another high-ranking leader of Bosnian Serbs until his suicide in 1997, was a renowned authority on Shakespeare and also a poet. The Serb warlord in eastern Herzegovina, Božidar Vučurević, a former truck driver, writes in the style of folk poetry; and the poet Matija Bećković was the first to propose that ethnic Serbs in Croatia be given weapons.[91] The novelist Dobrica Ćosić became president of the new, truncated Yugoslavia in 1992. The second most popular Serbian novelist, Vuk Drašković, equally committed to the dream of a Greater Serbia, is the leader of one of the largest political parties in Serbia. The novelist Antonije Isaković was the leader of the group of intellectuals who wrote the *Memorandum*.

Radovan Karadžić, a psychiatrist by profession, is the author of several volumes of poetry, including one for children, most of which were published long before the war came to Bosnia. The most interesting aspect of his poems, which are of mediocre artistic quality, consists in the abundant imagery of death and destruction. Some of the terrifying images in the poem "Sarajevo," published in 1971, were transformed into reality by the author some twenty years later:

> I can hear the disaster actually marching
> transformed into a bug—when the moment arrives:
> it will crush the bug as a worn-out singer
> is crushed by the silence and transformed into a voice.
>
> The city is burning like a lump of incense,
> our conscience is twisting in the smoke, too.
> Empty clothes glide through the city. The stone,
> built into houses, is dying red. The plague!
>
> Calm. A troop of armored poplar trees
> in itself is marching upwards. Aggressor
> air circulates in our souls,
> —and now you"re a man, now an aerial creature.
>
> I know that all this is a preparation for wails:
> what does black metal in the garage hold in store?
> Look—fear transformed into a spider
> is searching for the answer in its computer.[92]

Besides the spider, the wolf is Karadžić's favorite animal. In the poem "One Half of the Morning Is Missing," the author, born in the mountains of Montenegro, seems to identify with it: "A tall, slender and strong wolf / descended from the mountain / he bit off one half of the morning / and in his heart / he took it to the mountain, to the wilderness. / Everything burst out crying afterwards."[93] The very titles of his poems or collections are often indicative of their mood: "The Morning Grenade," "Farewell, Assassins," "Hell," "Death," "A Vocabulary of Fear."

The dark tones and visions of destruction in many of Karadžić's poems make them—like the songs of the Kosovo cycle and Njegoš's *Mountain Wreath*—"songs of horror." Fear and the spider are their dominant concepts. In a short essay included in the volume containing the poem "Sarajevo," the literary critic Marko Vešović gave a very perceptive definition of "the basic premise of Karadžić's poetics: poetry is 'spiderism,' a criminal spidery activity against the world."[94] Two decades later, when Karadžić caught Sarajevo and all of Bosnia and Herzegovina in his deadly web, he proved that this definition fits his politics as well as his poetics.

Although Karadžić's poems are modern in style and very different from heroic folk songs, he occasionally accompanies himself on the *gusle*—the traditional instrument of folk singers—while reciting them. This incongruity becomes understandable if the traditional role of the folk singer as a carrier of national myths and tribal spirit in the Balkans is taken into account. Urbanization and much higher literacy have practically eliminated old-style singers in the course of the twentieth century, but the popularity of folk songs remains high and increases at times of upheavals and wars.

The Serbian sociologist Ivan Čolović called attention to the fact that "during World War II in Yugoslavia the Partisans and the Četniks fought fiercely to appropriate the best known folk songs, to recover them, to lay the egg of one's political propaganda in the nest of folklore."[95] Folk songs were also used in the 1990s wars, not only by the Serbs, and "apart from this, a sort of intra-party war is being waged, especially in Serbia, for the conquest of folklore texts, or, at least, folklore style."[96] Čolović also pointed out that in late 1992 Radio Pride in Belgrade started broadcasting exclusively folk songs twenty-four hours a day.

The Serbian twentieth-century fiction that has served the purpose of psychological mobilization for a war is marked by an intense preoccupation with history. Several prominent Serbian novelists have used their works to confirm nationalist myths through concrete characters and scenes, thereby complementing the historians' efforts to have their studies conform to the same myths. Fiction and history are closely connected in the work of Dobrica Ćosić, the most celebrated contemporary Serbian novelist. He has written a number of historical novels, the most prominent of which is *Vreme smrti* (A Time of Death), a four-part novel whose action takes place during World War I.[97] The substantial number of authentic or seemingly authentic historical documents in the novel has been further increased in the English-language edition,[98] with the apparent aim of making the reader experience the work as history rather than fiction. Most of the characters are well-known historical figures, national and international, but there is no protagonist; all the characters are only extras on the stage of history. The real protagonist is Serbia.

Not surprisingly, Ćosić's historical novels are not good literature. Even Alexander Solzhenitsyn, a much more gifted writer, has been unable to breathe life into the novels that present his view of Russian history. But Ćosić has failed not only as an artist: he has also failed to win over the few foreign readers patient enough to read his voluminous laments over Serbia, the eternal victim. He certainly did not persuade an American reviewer of his *Reach to Eternity:* "Pour Scotch, comb your hair, sleep: in some way everything you do has been influenced by Serbia; a semi-nation that reground the lens of all Western culture. *Reach* is remedial fiction. Besides: Serb, Slovene, Croat, louse, poverty, civil war, self-hate—by tacit projection Ćosić will give you a new, if grumbling, respect for Josip Broz Tito."[99]

Ćosić's earlier novel *Deobe* (Divisions), first published in 1963, pays more attention to individual destinies. It deals not with the confrontation between Serbia and the world but with the internal Serbian division between monarchist Četniks and communist-led Partisans during World War II. One notable aspect of the novel is its homage to the knife. The knife is the main topic of the prologue, which warns, "Left hand, look out! The right one, your sister, is holding a knife!"[100] In the central part of the novel the author lets a member of a British mission report on the role of the knife in Serbian history. Here is an excerpt from the fictional report:

Captain F. thinks that the cult of the knife has always reigned in the Balkans, that a large knife industry was developed there already in the early Middle Ages, that every region, every tribe, every family has its own shape of the knife, its own emblem on it, and that they distinguish and recognize one another by the knife. Among all the utensils, only the knife fully expresses the Serbs' racial and national qualities, and the entire personality. Captain F. also maintains that the Serbs have a great poetry whose motif and theme is the knife. Since the knife is also an obligatory requisite held and worn by all their saints and military and national chieftains, who are always canonized after their death, since, thus, the knife is the most frequent object next to the cross on the frescoes in all of their churches, it is not difficult to conclude that the knife had and still has a crucial significance in the spiritual life of the Serbs today.... The knife is the source of their energy.... I had several opportunities to observe the Četniks immediately after killing the enemy with a knife. Those were unforgettable images. These men displayed manifestations al- most identical to those sailors display in brothels in the moments immediately after the sex act.[101]

Later on in the novel there is a five-page "article" on the knife, which exalts the instrument as a holy object and a cornerstone of civilization, and concludes with the following words:

The creative nature of the knife has been especially manifested in the formation of man's moral consciousness, therefore of ethics, too, the most distinguished area of philosophy. Who can list all the virtues bestowed upon us by the knife? Is not one of the greatest, courage, a child of the knife? Then fidelity and honesty, its wisest products. And so many, innumerable civic virtues, a pride of today's humanity. Who would ensure the performance of civic and national duties, who would guard our common goods, cultural and economic insti- tutions, if it were not for the knife? Without it, what would happen to our Christian church and faith? Without the knife what would we need freedom for? What would we defend democracy with? If it were not for it, what would the state survive on?

It, the basis of the world, our strength, our future.

Kiss it, and pronounce its name softly.[102]

In the novel the knife is associated mostly with the Četniks, the Serbian nationalist militia, whom Ćosić painted as a largely negative force in comparison with the communist-led Partisans, because at the time he wrote *Deobe* he was still a fervent Titoist and preacher of the Marxist withering away of states and nations. But as he became disillusioned with communism (which also wielded the "knife" very skillfully but did not glorify it) and embraced nationalist ideology, the old cult of the knife became respectable again.

The cult of the knife in modern Serbian fiction has a principal source in the cult of the heroic ancestor Miloš Obilić, who used the knife to kill the Ottoman sultan at Kosovo in 1389. In the novels of the 1980s the knife (literally, or as a metaphor for any instrument of killing) fulfilled a double purpose: the selective and wildly exaggerated recital of the use of the knife against the Serbs inflamed the hatred against their neighbors, and, at the same time, prepared the Serbian minds for the use of the knife against the demonized enemy. This double purpose is particularly obvious in the novel by the Bosnian Serb writer Vuk Drašković, appropriately titled *Nož* (The Knife), the most popular of the "gospels of hatred" published by Serbian writers since the late 1970s. While there is some sarcasm and self-deprecation in Ćosić's writings about the knife, Drašković is in deadly earnest.

The action of his best-selling novel takes place in Bosnia during World War II, and the highlights of its plot are sadistic killings of Serbs by Muslims, such as the following episode in which all the killers have distinctly Muslim names:

> [Kemal] stood up suddenly, with a wild expression in his eyes that kept shedding tears, turned like a liver-fluke-infected sheep, pulled the knife out of the sheath, jumped on Ljubica, grabbed her by the hair, and threw her down next to Hussein.
>
> With one swing, as if he were cutting a leg of lamb, he cut off her left breast, she screamed, the blood spattered onto his forehead and cheeks. He cut off her nose, pulled the tongue out of the mouth, and cut it off. He stuck the tip of the knife into her eye, circled it a few

times, and pushed the steel under the bloody ball that was moving under his fingers. After pulling the eye out he threw it on the copper tray in front of Father Nikifor. Then he slaughtered Ljubica!

Holding Anđa by the hair and pulling her head back, with a skilled movement Zulfikar swung the blade; the head remained in his hands, eyes wide open, the mouth ajar as if about to say something.

Fazli proceeded differently: he bent down, listened to Kosa's heart, aimed precisely between the ribs, thrust with all his strength, twisted the knife, played with it, made circles.

Kemal kept crying, looking around him, threatening, and repeating, "You'll pay dearly for Hussein, my dear Nikifor!"

Suddenly he stopped, wiped his tears with the sleeve of his military overcoat, spat at Ljubica, took the cut-off breast and put it on the piping-hot range. Bloody raw meat sizzled, and he, laughing, went to Bratomir. Without aiming or preparing he stuck the knife into his throat, grabbed a glass from the table, filled it to the brim with blood, and let Bratomir's head go. He laughed so loudly that Fazli had to cover his ears. Kemal filled another glass with wine and shoved it in front of Nikifor: "Here, my dear, let me fulfil your wish to clink glasses and drink with me!"

He drained the glassful of blood at a gulp, smacked his lips, and exclaimed, "Merry Christmas, my dear."[103]

Echoing both Njegoš's *Mountain Wreath,* which ends with the blessing of a gun, and the exaltation of the knife in Ćosić's *Deobe,* Drašković's *Knife* ends with a "Saga of the Knife." It fills the last six pages of the book. "Our people have a device," it begins, "that we handle better than anybody else in the world, and a word we pronounce most beautifully. This device, not complicated at all, and this word, not a bit remarkable, are our seal, our sign, our first mark in history."[104]

Drašković ignores the fact that during the Second World War all sides in the conflict used the knife effectively, and that Muslims and Serbs suffered about the same relative losses. His saga, like the novel as a whole, is very selective. Serbs kill only when they are pushed to act in reaction to what is done to them. All the sadistic wielders of the knife are Catholics and Muslims:

Water was a KNIFE, too: the Ustašas cooked children in it, and the tar was a KNIFE: they poured it on open wounds, and the soil was a KNIFE: it was thrown over live people, and rats were a KNIFE: mice eating the human intestines was an Ustaša invention, and the Franciscan cloak was a KNIFE: many were strangled with it, and the Qur'an was a KNIFE: everything was done with Allah's blessing.[105]

A London experience related by Dušan Makavejev illustrates the popularity of Drašković's work: "During the Serbian book celebration at Collet's on Charing Cross Road, our books were on sale. I was delighted to see books by Kiš, Selenić, and Pavić in the window. 'How are they selling?' I asked. . . . Unfortunately nothing had been sold except for one that went in a flash, titled *The Knife*. 'Written by a certain Drašković.' "[106]

The novels that form part of Vojislav Lubarda's trilogy—*Transfiguration*, *Repentance*, and *Ascension*—also have Bosnia as the place of action, and hatred as their main theme.[107] The author, a Bosnian Serb, traces in these novels the relationship between a Serb village, Izgor, and a Muslim town, Čaršija, in eastern Bosnia, from 1715 to 1945. The author operates with standard nationalist clichés: Serbs are innocent victims of others. If they commit cruelties it is only because they were driven to it by the actions of others. Most often they forgive the crimes committed against them, and suffer a repetition of the crimes as a result of their forgiving nature. All the Austrian, Croatian, and Hungarian officers are bribe takers, cowards, and turncoats, skillful only at abusing the goodness of the Serbs.

Not all of Lubarda's Serbian characters are obsessed with the desire for revenge. A few occasionally advocate tolerance, but they are exceptions. The dominant tone is that the time for forgiving is over and retaliation has to take place. This is the essence of "Grandma Milica's doctrine"—a curse and a call for revenge repeated, with variations, by her and other characters like a musical theme throughout the novel (together with additional curses):

We will repay them. . . . One day, god and our Saint John the Baptist willing, the time of retaliation will come: men and women, old and young will attack, on horses, with pitchforks and hoes, with scythes, they will stab and cut, trample and set on fire, they will burn all of Čaršija so that no seed of theirs will remain. This, my child, will be the long-awaited revenge for our Izgor, which they set on fire so many times. For my Jovo, too; he did not trample even a worm, yet the enemies took him ... to a willow tree, may a willow grow through their bones. All of their terror will get into their throats once it starts being repaid: we will repay ours, the Vukovićs theirs, the Vidrićs theirs, the Gazivodas theirs. And others will do it, too. My god, when one fine day all of them get together and move, all of Izgor, all of Glasinac, and the people from the Drina, when they start from all sides, no trace will remain of Čaršija.[108]

Lubarda's novel deals mainly with the hatred between the Serb village and the Muslim town but depicts a lot of hatred within the Muslim community also. The cruel local potentate Sacir Bey has many enemies among fellow Muslims, but the hatred felt by his Christian victims produces the most savage curse in the novel:

Oh, Sacir Bey, we piss on your face and your Turkish faith. You feed on our blood and you will pay for it with your blood. You and all these Turkish heathens who enjoy our suffering. You *bey*, human excrement, may you see the heads of your sons hang without being able to help them. May your offspring and any memory of yours vanish without trace. May your ninth generation still pay for it. May millet sprout from your eyes. And you other Turks, may you pray without having anybody to pray to, as we don't have. We shit into the mouth of this Allah of yours who is watching all this. He is worse than a dog because even a dog would feel pity.[109]

Grandma Milica's words depict an apocalyptic time of chaos and revenge—the transfiguration that will take place at the pivotal moment in the history of the area:

Nobody will trust anybody. And nothing will be sacred. People will be possessed by frenzy and universal rage. It will last long. Maybe ten years, and maybe longer. In their insatiability and frenzy they will start exterminating one another. Hatred will blind the people so badly that fathers will not trust their sons. Human heads will be cheap because only killers will be revered. And denouncers. Only after the crop, and stock, and meadows, and they themselves are ravaged, and after they completely destroy one another, will human order and law rule again.[110]

The dominant mood of Lubarda's trilogy is the anticipation of this quasi-eschatological time of chaos, out of which a new order will arise. The author's eschatological intent is manifested in the titles he gave the three novels: *Transfiguration, Repentance, Ascension.* The instrument of salvation in his nationalist eschatology is the knife. Like Ćosić and Drašković, Lubarda describes the knife as an object of solemn reverence and affection. The following is a description of what happens when Serb peasants meet:

> as soon as several, even as few as ten, of them gather, by some invisible command they immediately form a barrier athwart the road, stop, start singing, and, oh miracle, start dancing the *kolo.* One must not approach them then; they see neither themselves nor others, do not hear, and if they see or hear anything, they know only one answer—the knife.
>
> This is a long and pointed haiduk knife with a little curve at the tip, which becomes magically swift and powerful in the hands of young men from Glasinac and Izgor: they kiss it and coddle it, sometimes they prattle to it as if it were a girl, adorn it with song, throw it high up in the air and catch it with their bare fingers, depending on what their intention is, and sometimes—this is the utmost expression of affection—they carry it in their teeth the same as a delighted girl carries a love flower.[111]

Lubarda justifies this hatred and call to revenge by maintaining that Bosnia has always been a land of hatred. "Bosnia was and has remained the bottom of darkness where bad contests with worse, and all the Satans of this world dart out," says one of his characters.[112] In order to support the thesis, Lubarda begins his novel *Gordo posrtanje* (Proud Stumbling) with a quotation from Ivo Andrić's "Letter from 1920," which contains the statement "Bosnia is a land of hatred."[113] Lubarda uses the prestige of the Nobel-laureate Andrić to boost his thesis without informing the reader that the "letter" is in fact not a letter but a short story, written not in 1920 but shortly after the Second World War, when most of Europe was consumed by hatred.

The description of Bosnia as a land of hatred is used by a fictional character in Andrić's short story as a justification for his decision to leave it, but a real personal letter Andrić wrote shortly after Yugoslavia was created displays an intense love for Bosnia and nostalgia for its past: "I'm sad when I think how our old, strange Bosnia is dying out every day, and there's nobody to record and preserve the dark beauty of the former life ... I'm sad when I think that a verse dies with every old woman and a story with every friar. I'd better not even talk about today's Bosnia."[114]

The presence of various religions and cultures in one territory offers dangerous opportunities to instigators of communal strife. Religious differences have erupted in hatred and civil wars even in much more homogeneous societies than the Bosnian. Yet, throughout the four centuries of Turkish rule in Bosnia and Herzegovina there were no civil or religious wars there, while several such wars devastated large parts of Western Europe. There was no strife under Austro-Hungarian rule either, when religious tolerance continued, equality under the law and a modern administration were introduced, and the process of industrialization started. The old tolerance largely reasserted itself even after the mutual killings of World War II, as evidenced by the extremely high ratio of mixed marriages (27 percent) in the period preceding the latest war. Thus the thesis that Bosnia is a land cursed by hatred is a myth propagated mainly by those who wanted hatred to thrive in order to establish an "ethnically cleansed" Serbian Orthodox Bosnia and by the outsiders who refused to interfere with the deadly process.

Lubarda's *Proud Stumbling,* first published in 1970, preceded by about ten years the flood of novels that spread fear and hatred among the Serbs. Vuk Drašković, in the handwritten dedication of the copy of his novel *The Prayer* he sent to Lubarda, thanked him for the inspiration:

While I was writing *The Knife* and both *Prayers*, and even *The Judge*, I could not shake off myself, out of myself, the excitement, the desperation and the desire, a horrible and immense desire to transform my pen into a sword . . . an excitement that has haunted me since the day when I read *Proud Stumbling*. I thank you for it.[115]

A man who became the commander of Drašković's brutal paramilitary organization Serbian Guard provided an illustration of the effectiveness of his boss's literary sword: "I beat up many Muslims and Croatians on vacation in Cavtat because of his *Nož*. Reading that book, I would see red, I would get up, select the biggest fellow on the beach, and smash his teeth."[116]

Serb writers have been no less busy depicting Croatia as another land of hatred, and Croats as bloodthirsty demons. In Drašković's two-volume novel *Molitva* (The Prayer), most killers are Croats, and one of the most repugnant characters is a Catholic priest. In the concluding part of that novel, a character expresses an idea that could serve as a motto to all of Drašković's novels: "there are not only individual martyrs but also nations-martyrs. Those that are always found guilty by somebody and, apparently, bear the Golgotha as their eternal sentence. Christ was crucified for three hours only, but some nations never descend from the cross."[117] Drašković has not changed his approach to writing even after the debacle to which he had contributed. His more recent novel, *Noć đenerala,* repeats the formula used in his hatred-stirring novels that preceded the war.

In the course of the 1980s a Herzegovinian Serb novelist, Neđo Šipovac, published a cycle of three novels whose action takes place during the early phase of World War II in Bosnia-Herzegovina.[118] They depict the sinister minds of their Croatian and other Catholic characters. Still another Herzegovinian Serb, Jovan Radulović, wrote a play, *Golubnjača*, whose title denotes a pit in Croatia where bodies of massacred Serbs were thrown. First published in 1981, this well-written play deals with a legitimate subject for a literary work, but given the circumstance that nobody was writing at the time about the pits into which Croatian and Muslim corpses were thrown, such one-sided coverage of past horrors fomented the cult of revenge among the Serbs.[119]

By the late 1980s the Serbs' intoxication with self-pity and hatred became so widespread that even the novelist Slobodan Selenić, who had frequently been critical of Serbian mores, was swept away by it. Stating that Milošević restored his pride, he joined the campaign of fear and hatred with his novel *Timor mortis* (Fear of Death—a telling title) in 1989, which barrages the reader with accounts of the eternal Croatian hatred of the Serbs and graphic descriptions of sadistic murders. The Partisans, that is, members of the communist-led Yugoslav World War II resistance movement, are also shown as sadistic savages. The book ends with the death of a teenage Serbian prostitute after "Partisans" ram a pole into her vagina as a punishment for having had a German lover.

No other nation in the former Yugoslavia produced literary works containing similar grisly accounts and magnifications of old sufferings. This was done exclusively by Serbian literati, and to great effect, as proved by the fact that most of the above-mentioned works became best-sellers. A Serbian sociologist described the role played by the Serbian intelligentsia, "particularly the one assembled around the Academy of Sciences and Arts, that is, the institutionalized intelligentsia" in this process:

This elite of the Serbian intelligentsia was the first to start talking . . . of the *genocidal* character of the Croatian people. . . . It was their duty to explain to their compatriots who have never had direct contact with the Croatian people how much the latter are . . . murderous and incurably dangerous. The somber, dreadful, and traumatizing past of the two peoples began to "emerge in full light." Proofs appeared daily, served in homes at dinner time, every evening. After half a century bones began to be pulled out of the earth. The academicians, these chosen people dedicated to a cause, patriots, "fathers of the nation," have marched like necrophiles toward mass graves, while the people whose trauma and distress began to be manipulated stood by as public and victim. Historians explained what had happened; they told the "real truth" about the events that had been "hidden and hushed up" until then. Psychoanalysts explained why, thanks to the specific character of certain peoples, things had to happen that way. Poets added a few poems about the calvary of their own people, regarded as heavenly, and the atmosphere of hatred—which became a way of life—started from there.[120]

The Highlanders as Scapegoats

The traditional propensity to violence of the people in some undeveloped, mountainous areas of the former Yugoslavia contributed to the brutality of the country's disintegration, but it was only one ingredient in the process. The genesis of a war is usually a very complex phenomenon, involving both domestic and international actors, so it does not seem credible to single out one particular group of people, small in number and with little influence over affairs of state, as the main culprit for a war. Nevertheless, highlander bashing has become a popular sport in Serbia. It consists in blaming Dinaric people—Serbian, Croatian, and Muslim—for the war. This thesis conveniently makes most Serbs, especially the Belgrade elite, seem innocent victims of primitive outsiders. Miloš Vasić, the editor of the Belgrade magazine *Vreme*, uses such a simplistic approach to a very complex situation, as an American journalist reports:

> "This war is definitely anthropological," he told me, sitting in *Vreme*'s grim and busy offices. "We always divided our population more by altitude than by language or ethnic group."
>
> "First, there is the mountain cattleman approach. The other is the farmers' approach. The cattlemen perceive the world in terms of space for their herds; the farmers in terms of time for their crops. That is why the "wild mountain men" with no sense of humor are the driving force of this war. And that is why Sarajevo and Mostar were so savagely destroyed. These cities are a different civilization to guys frustrated by not being able to settle in them."[121]

There are several problems with this thesis. One is that the population of the sparsely inhabited mountainous areas engaged in cattle raising is insignificant both in number and in influence. Several persons from the Dinaric area, such as the Montenegrin-born Radovan Karadžić, played a prominent role in the war, but they were not mountain cattlemen. Karadžić is a psychiatrist and an admirer of Walt Whitman who took a course on creative writing at Columbia University in New York City. His former deputy and subsequent rival, Biljana Plavšić, an expert in plant diseases, spent fourteen months as a Fulbright scholar in New York in the early 1970s.[122] All the other members of the Bosnian Serb leadership are highly educated too, and several of them were university professors before they brought the war to Bosnia. It has often been pointed out that the parents of Slobodan Milošević (who was born and raised in Serbia) were Montenegrins, implying that his ancestry explains his behavior. Yet the behavior of this former banker and communist party boss is very different from that of primitive highlanders. He has shown an excellent understanding of Western leaders and, most of the time, a virtuosity in exploiting their weaknesses. There is both racism and social snobbery in making Dinaric people the scapegoats.

Neither is it true that cities alone have been singled out for destruction. Villages have been as mercilessly destroyed in the war for a Greater Serbia. By far the most devastated city, Vukovar in Pannonian Croatia, far from the Dinaric Mountains, was totally destroyed because the attackers were unable to conquer it without demolishing it (thus disappointing the orchestrators of the war, who had intended to replace Vukovar's slaughtered and expelled citizens with Serbs). But neither cities nor villages as such were marked for destruction. What were deliberately marked for destruction, besides human targets, were monuments of cultural identity—churches, mosques, libraries, museums, archives, cemeteries—testimonies of the historical presence of a different people. This is why that war has been characterized as "culturecide" and "memorycide." It has certainly been neither a peasants' revolt nor a postindustrialist utopian campaign for a return to the presumed virtues of an agricultural society.

There is a substantial analogy between the role of Dinaric Serbs in the 1990s wars and that of Croatian Dinaric highlanders in the Second World War. The latter's participation in the Ustaša regime and its crimes was much higher than their ratio in the population.

But the role of the Ustašas in prewar Croatian political life was so marginal that they could not have come to power through their own efforts. They unleashed their criminal activity for the sake of a Greater Croatia—"ethnically cleansed" of Orthodox Serbs—only after Benito Mussolini persuaded Adolf Hitler to put them in power, knowing that the Ustaša regime would repay the favor by surrendering a large portion of Croatian territory to Italy. As for the strong negative impact of Croatian Dinaric highlanders, primarily from western Herzegovina, in Croatian politics and economy of the 1990s, it would not have been possible if President Franjo Tudjman (who himself is not from a Dinaric area) had not supported them in return for their support of his nationalist policies and authoritarian rule.

Regarding the above-quoted reference to "altitude," the urban underground played a larger role in the Serbian aggression than did the Balkan highlands. Urban criminals, such as Željko Ražnatović "Arkan" and Dragan Vasiljković, better known as "Captain Dragan," particularly excelled in brutality. Ražnatović had spent three years in a Belgrade jail by the age of twenty, before becoming an international hit man for the Yugoslav communist regime. He is one of Interpol's twelve most wanted fugitives, with seven arrest warrants. The small-time criminal Vasiljković, also known to the Australian police as Daniel Snedden, migrated to Australia as a young boy in the 1960s and grew up in Melbourne to become a thug involved in escort agency protection and the usual rackets that operate in association with drugs and prostitution. Both of them—with the help of the Yugoslav army and Serbian authorities—organized paramilitary units that committed large-scale atrocities in Croatia and Bosnia-Herzegovina.

These people are modern upholders of the haiduk tradition, which, although extinct in its original form, has found a new habitat in the international urban crime world. Their glorification is strongly reminiscent of the celebration of the deeds of the haiduks. In both cases, criminal activity has been interpreted as patriotism and heroism in a noble fight against foreign enemies.

Ražnatović's wedding in Belgrade in 1995 was a big media event, attended by high dignitaries of the Serbian Orthodox Church. Ljuba Magaš-Zemunac, a murderer and rapist active in Frankfurt, Germany, is another urban criminal glorified by some as a hero. Killed by a fellow Serb in 1986, he died too soon to participate in the aggression against Croatia and Bosnia-Herzegovina, but he is perceived as a defender of the people and a victim of the nation's enemy. Here is the epitaph on his tomb at a Belgrade cemetery:[123]

> He had a warm heart for small people
> He carried a sharp sword in a world without justice
> He punished insatiable dragons
> His ways led him to Robin Hood.
>
> He saved people in difficulties
> Gave away a lot of his blood
> Everything became knightly with him
> Born to be a leader, he remained the first.
>
> He had a deep contempt for cowards
> He knew the secret that binds people together
> He fell bullet-riddled in a German trap
> With dignity he lay down in his land.

Such criminals—whether from the highlands, cities, or anywhere else—have been a mere tool of the organizers of the war for a Greater Serbia, while most of the leaders have not bloodied their hands directly.

Herzegovinian Serb and Montenegrin highlanders, active in the 1991 attack on the city of Dubrovnik, had attacked the same city in 1814. On that occasion also they shelled the city and looted, killed, burned, and raped in the surrounding area, while the Russian fleet protected them. They attacked Dubrovnik not because it was a city but because it was a city whose culture they detested and whose wealth they wanted to loot. They would not have been able to mount either attack without outside support. In 1814 it was the Russian support; in 1991–92 it was the support of the pan-Serbian war machine. The Russian support was due not to a presumed Orthodox solidarity but to Russia's long-standing interest in gaining access to naval facilities on the Mediterranean Sea.[124]

It must be kept in mind that even the most violence-prone part of the Dinaric highlands, Montenegro, produces people who put their humanity above any nationalist and ideological madness, such as the attorney Jovan Barović, who defended many victims of the Yugoslav communist regime and died in a mysterious car accident in 1979. Another member of the same clan, Admiral Vladimir Barović, disobeyed the order to shell a Croatian coastal city in 1991 and allegedly committed suicide, but was probably killed for his refusal to follow the pan-Serbian war plan. And all "balkanizationalists" who think that bigger is better, and that separation is the mother of violence, should notice that the people who fight for the rule of law in their native Montenegro are almost invariably also fighters for its autonomy or even independence. Moreover, there is the coincidence that Njegoš, who glorified genocide as a way to an Orthodox theocracy, was a fervent promoter of the thesis that Montenegrins are Serbs.[125]

Thus, the main culprits for the explosion of Serbian violence in the late twentieth-century Balkan wars were no primitive cattlemen but highly educated, sophisticated, and powerful people: novelists, poets, literary critics, psychiatrists, and other intellectuals and artists who used a Western ideology to convince fellow Serbs that their moral superiority is menaced by a worldwide conspiracy;[126] leaders of the Serbian Orthodox Church who want all the territories under its jurisdiction to become a part of the Serbian state; political leaders who fanned and used nationalist passions to increase their power; and well-paid generals who believed that the tremendous arsenal amassed by the Yugoslav People's Army would preserve their privileges and ensure their control of all of the former Yugoslavia. Those in positions of power and influence are responsible for the outbreak of the war. Violent highlanders and urban criminals, as well as ordinary citizens who suddenly became killers, were their tools; they were given weapons and opportunity to loot, rape, and kill in order to realize the ambitions of the elite.[127]

However, it was not an exclusively one-directional influence. The Serbian elite could not have succeeded in mobilizing the support of large masses of the population for the war had the latter not been already under the influence of old national myths. Milošević, a skillful populist politician, switched from Marxism to nationalism in 1986 because he correctly sensed the intensity of the popular desire to make Serbia the greatest power in the region again after six and a half centuries. The bellicosity of both the elite and the ordinary people was stimulated by the apparently rational expectation, shared by many foreign analysts, that the Serbs' huge military advantage would easily turn the old dream into reality.

Whatever the mechanism of the escalation of Serbian aggressiveness, the world could have prevented the war had it been aware of the falsity of the myths on which the war campaign was based. Instead, the world acted as an accomplice. For nearly two centuries a considerable segment of Western intelligentsia had eagerly accepted Serbian myths, thus increasing their destructive effect in the home country. By adopting the myth of an innocent, suffering Serbia, and often misrepresenting facts in an effort to give it substance, the world unwittingly reinforced the Serbs' view of themselves as eternal victims and fed their desire for avenging real and imaginary past injustices.

6

The Outsiders' Myth-Calculations

The Acceptance of Heavenly Serbia

Serbian myths were first received and amplified in the West, as outlined above, during the Romanticist period. The second wave of Western glorification of Serbia started during the First World War, when that country, having precipitated the war, shared the same enemy as Britain, France, and subsequently the United States. As usual in wartime, the enemy was demonized, and the enemy of the enemy glorified. The Kosovo myth, in particular, served to propagate the image of Serbia as a country committed to freedom and morality, as an American expert on Kosovo, Thomas A. Emmert, notes:

> During the war Serbia was the "darling" of both the English and French publics, which interpreted her determination to fight and secure her freedom as an expression of the Kosovo spirit. In 1916 a nation-wide tribute to Serbia was arranged in Britain to celebrate the anniversary of Kosovo. . . . R. W. Seton-Watson, who helped organize the celebration, prepared an address on Serbia. . . . Entitled "Serbia: Yesterday, Today, and Tomorrow," the address was read aloud . . . in almost twelve thousand schools. . . . In his brief remarks Seton-Watson characterized the battle of Kosovo as one of the decisive events in the history of Southeast Europe.[1]

The Reverend R. G. D. Laffan's series of lectures delivered in Salonika and published after the war as *Guardians of the Gate* is a classic in the genre of beatification of Serbia. According to Laffan, Serbia is, "indeed, one of the gateways of civilized Europe,"[2] while "the Serbs are physically the "thoroughbreds" of the Balkans,"[3] and "magnificent specimens of humanity." They are characterized as possessing "spiritual glory" too. The Serbian peasant-soldier, for example, combines "the heart of a child with the strength and technical skill of a man."[4] The contributor of the foreword to Laffan's lectures, Vice-Admiral E. T. Troubridge, was made equally dizzy by the moral height of Serbia: "Serbia has indeed well and bravely answered the great question He asked: 'What shall it profit a man if he gain the whole world and lose his own soul?' "[5]

The adoption of the myth of Kosovo was no less enthusiastic in the United States, where the anniversary of Kosovo was recognized as a day of special commemoration in June 1918, five months before the end of the war. The meaning of Kosovo became the subject of innumerable sermons, lectures, and addresses throughout the United States. "In a special service in New York City's Cathedral of St. John the Divine, the Reverend Howard C. Robbins compared Serbs to the people of Israel and observed that Serbia 'voices its suffering through patience far longer than Israel's and it voices a hope that has kept burning through five centuries.' "[6]

A former assistant attorney general of the United States, James M. Beck, spoke as another true believer in a Heavenly Serbia at the Kosovo commemoration held at the Waldorf-Astoria on the evening of June 17, 1918:

> It is true that we commemorate a defeat, but military defeats are . . . often moral victories. If Serbia is now temporarily defeated, she has triumphed at the great bar of public opinion, and she stands in the eye of the nations as justified in her quarrel. Serbia was not only the innocent, precipitating cause of this world war, but it is the greatest martyr, and I am inclined to think in many respects its greatest hero.[7]

An interesting aspect of the widespread enthusiasm for Serbia's innocence was its suddenness, which was noted by the historian Edward Crankshaw:

The legend of "gallant little Serbia" (or Servia, as they used to call it), which sprang to life as soon as England found herself at war with Germany and Austria-Hungary in August 1914, at once obscured the fact that for the previous decade Serbia had been regarded generally as a thorough-going nuisance, a nest of violent barbarians whose megalomania would sooner or later meet the punishment it deserved. There had been several occasions when the rest of Europe fully expected to see Austria lash out and wipe Serbia off the map.[8]

The Kosovo cult was also celebrated by many other south Slavs, including Croats, who, discontent with their status in the Habsburg monarchy, embraced the idea of the Yugoslav union and ignored the aspects of the Serbian heritage that were going to make that union much worse than the one from which they wanted to escape. A prominent Croatian artist, raised in the Dinaric patriarchal-heroic culture, went so far as to design a Vid's Day Temple as a national shrine to be built in Kosovo.[9]

Balkanization or Scandinavianization

The myth of Heavenly Serbia became much less appealing, and less frequently invoked, once the south Slavic union was established under Serbian hegemony following World War I. But, however disappointing the new state, it was still regarded as beneficial to the powers that facilitated its creation, and they used another myth to justify its existence and the efforts to prop it up. The balkanization myth provided the most frequently invoked rationale for the preservation of Yugoslavia, as it did for the preservation of any political entity threatened with partition.

The concept of balkanization implies that any breakup of a political unit leads to disorder and violence. According to *Webster's New World Dictionary*, for example, to balkanize means "to break up into small, mutually hostile political units, as the Balkans after World War I."[10] Similar definitions can be found in dictionaries of other languages.[11]

Yet if it were true that partition of a political entity necessarily leads to conflicts, how could one explain the fact that elsewhere in Europe another group of countries, similar in number of entities and population size, have achieved a level of freedom, prosperity, and international cooperation matched hardly anywhere else in the world? The multiplication of sovereign Scandinavian states from two in 1905 to five in 1944[12] not only has not led to conflicts but has eliminated earlier frictions in the area, such as those between Norway and Sweden or Denmark and Iceland while they were united in one state.[13] Thus one could introduce the concept of scandinavian-ization to designate a process leading to peace and prosperity through fragmentation of larger political entities. Such a concept would make no less—and no more—sense than the concept of balkanization, which is a good comment on the value of sociopoli-tical theories condensed into one word. The truth is that there is no correlation between the size and number of states in an area and the intensity and frequency of conflicts between them. The peaceful separation of Czechs and Slovaks in 1993 is a recent proof that separation and violence are not necessarily connected.

The concept of balkanization in the above-mentioned sense be-gan to be widely used during the Balkan Wars (1912–1913), that is, at the time when many Europeans west of the Balkans were still convinced that the progress of civilization had made them immune to the savagery of war. The term attained popularity very quickly and has become a part of the universal vocabulary. There are several reasons for the swift acceptance of the concept. One is the fear of change, that is, of possible complications that may arise out of the change of borders and the emergence of a new state. The change of the status quo is generally supported only when it is expected to increase one's own power. Even when the right to self-determination is respected in principle and there is sympathy for the plight of a group of people oppressed by another within the borders of a state, the sympathy usually does not lead to the support of other peoples' fight for freedom and independence.

The predisposition in favor of the global status quo receives an important boost from the fear that the breakup of a foreign country may encourage secessionists in one's own. Many countries contain territories with strong secessionist trends. Scotland, Ulster, South Tyrol, Corsica, Catalonia, and the Basque lands are prominent examples of such territories in Europe. Even when there are no secessionist threats, as in the United States today, concern with national unity may contribute to hostility to any fragmentation anywhere: "America's anxiety over the fragmentation of foreign states and societies arises from our sense that American society is fragmenting, culturally and ethnically."[14]

The concept of balkanization condemns any striving for autonomy or independence by associating it with strife and backwardness. It is used as a conceptual scarecrow to justify the preservation of the status quo even when the central power is so corrupt and brutal that secession is the only way for the oppressed community to preserve itself (and thereby sometimes lead to a more stable situation).

Hostility to small nations can also be a result of the conviction that they are an obstacle to the inexorable progress of history toward its fulfilment. This is how the cofounder of Marxism, Friedrich Engels, expressed it: "By the same right under which France took Flanders, Lorraine and Alsace and will sooner or later take Belgium —by that same right Germany takes over Schleswig; it is the right of civilisation as against barbarism, of progress as against stability. . . . it is the right of historical evolution."[15] There is little interest in such amalgamations in Western Europe today, but the hostility of a large segment of Western intelligentsia toward the efforts of various ex-Yugoslav nationalities to avoid their assimilation by Serbia was based on the same belief that physical integration is the key to a better future. Such a belief is as strong on the right as on the left of the political spectrum.

The Imaginary Bulwark

Both the myth of the Heavenly Serbia and the balkanization myth helped to justify the creation of a Serb-dominated multinational state in the Balkans in 1918, but a more specific political reason for that action was the belief that the Serbs, in return for the large increase of the territory under their control, would remain a forever grateful ally of those who made the expansion possible. The first step in the buildup of a Greater Serbia was taken in 1913: Kosovo, a landlocked area between Albania, Macedonia, Montenegro, and Serbia proper, inhabited primarily by Albanians, was given to Serbia. The effects of that fateful gift are still haunting the world, as an American scholar expounds:

> But for the intervention of Britain, France, and Russia in 1913, Kosovo would have been assigned to Albania at the time that country was accorded diplomatic recognition. But Albania, which declared its independence from Ottoman Turkey only in 1912, was seen as a client of Austria-Hungary and Italy, and the other Great Powers wanted to keep the friends of their rivals small. Britain, France, and Russia therefore appointed a Conference of Ambassadors which, on July 29, 1913, recognized Albania within reduced borders. Kosovo and part of Metohija (including Prizren), despite their majority-Albanian population, were handed over to Serbia, a friend of France and Russia, while Montenegro (another friend of Russia's), received Pec, Djakovica, and Istok. It was, thus, a Great Power veto of Kosovo's right of national self-determination that sowed the seed for all the problems that developed subsequently.[16]

Less than two years after permitting the transfer of a territory containing almost half of the total Albanian population to Serbia, the same powers contemplated an even more drastic reduction of Albania, by giving one part to Italy and the remainder, except for a small central section, to Montenegro, Serbia, and Greece. Britain, France, and Russia disclosed their intention in a secret pact with Italy concluded in London on April 26, 1915. Its purpose was to draw Italy into the war on their side by generous territorial promises. Article 7 of the agreement summarizes the promised territories inhabited primarily by Austrians, Slovenians, and Croatians, and contemplates a possible butchering of Albania:

> Having obtained Trentino and Istria by Article IV, Dalmatia and the Adriatic Islands by Article V, and also the Gulf of Valona [Vlorë],

Italy undertakes, in the event of a small autonomous and neutralized state being formed in Albania, not to oppose the possible desire of France, Great Britain and Russia to partition the northern and southern districts of Albania between Montenegro, Serbia, and Greece.[17]

The partition of Croatia was not hypothetical. As the note to Article 5 states, it was to retain only a relatively small part of an ethnically and historically Croatian coastland. Most of the Croatian littoral was assigned to Italy, Montenegro, and Serbia. The note defines the area the two Orthodox countries would receive:

to the south of the Adriatic, where Serbia and Montenegro are interested, the whole coast from Cape Planka [Ploča] to the river Drin, with very important ports of Spalato [Split], Ragusa [Dubrovnik], Cattaro [Kotor] . . . as also the islands of Grande and Piccola Zirona [Veliki and Mali Drvenik], Buja [Čiovo], Solta [Šolta], Brazza [Brač], Cikljan [Jakljan], and Calamotta [Koločep].[18]

The 1915 London Pact defines only the changes in coastal areas of the eastern Adriatic. It does not deal with substantial inland Croatian territories that the Entente powers also intended to give to Serbia but that are not contiguous to the territories promised to Italy. There is no mention of Bosnia and Herzegovina either, but the fact that the southern Croatian coast was assigned to Serbia and Montenegro clearly implies that the territory separating that part of Croatia from Serbia—that is, Bosnia and Herzegovina—was also to be given to the Balkan ally.

The Entente powers' plan for the creation of a Greater Serbia was not an expression of love for the Serbs. Britain broke off diplomatic relations with Serbia for three years after the 1903 regicide in Belgrade. Nor was Russia's cultural and religious bond with Montenegro and Serbia the primary reason for its strong interest in extending Serbia's borders to the shores of the Adriatic Sea, and for giving the Bay of Cattaro to Montenegro. Russia pursued the old goal of acquiring access to warm sea. Those three powers thought that Greater Serbia, as their permanent ally against the revisionists claiming lost territories, would constitute a bulwark against German influence in southeastern Europe.

Later in the war, when the decision was made to add all south Slavic areas of the Austro-Hungarian monarchy to Serbia, the new country was still thought of as an expanded Serbia. There was no inclination, as the English historian Robert W. Seton-Watson (1879–1951) once put it, to allow the "strong wine of Serbia to be dissolved in the weak water of Yugoslavia."[19] On the contrary, it was expected that the other nationalities would dissolve, as a University of Chicago professor wrote in 1922: "Apparently Bosnia, Dalmatia, Croatia and the other historical entities composing the new state are earmarked for disappearance."[20]

The new Serb-ruled country was intended by the Entente powers as a link in an anti-German and anti-Soviet *cordon sanitaire* stretching from Greece to Czechoslovakia. Three new, or newly expanded, states in this bloc—Yugoslavia, Romania, and Czechoslovakia—formed a coalition named the Little Entente. However, Yugoslavia did not act toward Germany as expected. Leaders of the new country took its borders for granted and pursued policies intended to expand them even more. Showing a severe lack of judgment, Yugoslav authorities sympathized with the Nazi attempts to annex Austria because a revival of the Habsburg monarchy was their worst nightmare, and they believed that German annexation of Austria would offer them an opportunity to annex some adjacent areas of that country. This is why the Yugoslav government widely tolerated the activities of national-socialist organizations against Austria staged from northwestern Yugoslavia in 1933 and 1934, and after the failed Nazi coup in Vienna in the summer of 1934 gave asylum to about 2,500 Nazis fleeing Austria.[21]

Economic interests were another reason for good relations between Belgrade and Berlin. The Austrian historian Arnold Suppan notes that "the leading politicians of the Third Reich—and first of all ... Göring—strived foremost to gain the sympathies of pan-Serbian circles, so they could pursue the policy of economic expansion through Belgrade."[22] However, Yugoslav-German economic relations were flourishing even before the Nazi era, and the money France poured into its intended ally often ended up in Germany's pocket, as a well-informed French observer, Henri Pozzi, noted:

In Belgrade to-day, Germans are everywhere. French is *never* spoken. Not a merchant, not one waiter out of ten understands, much less speaks, French. Nine out of ten speak and understand German. . . .

I will give but a single example of German prowess in the Balkan Babylon. Almost 250 million francs were loaned by France to Belgrade in 1931. Of this sum a little more than half was used by the Yugoslavs to buy long-range observation "planes from the German Junker works. The rest went to pay for bombing "planes furnished by the [German] Dornier establishment in Italy.[23]

The same author pointed out one of the reasons for Yugoslavia's uncooperative attitude toward its mentor: "The Pan-Serb circles do not love France. How could it be otherwise? Their atavisms, their education, their political ideals, their principles of government, their ambitions for the future, their intellectual and moral formation, all are entirely opposed to those of France."[24] Pozzi was not the only Frenchman who realized the weaknesses of the official French policy toward Yugoslavia. At the time when the new country had barely been created, Charles Rivet foresaw that Pan-Serbism would lead to its failure:

A Greater Serbia might be endured, it will never be freely accepted by the Yugoslavs. For this reason, it is unable to assure to the new state the strength, the internal force which can only be acquired in a union of equals. A Greater Serbia is bound to incite separatisms. To Belgrade's imperialism Zagreb would respond with a Croatism which would lead to a conflict that cannot end but with a rupture.

A Greater Serbia is a threat because we would create a power which would, in its turn, rely on a sharpened sword and a powder barrel to become a Balkanic Prussia. It would develop an already existing danger, Serbian militarism, a danger not only to its neighbors but also to the internal life of the country.[25]

The policy of forcible assimilation of the majority non-Serb population of Yugoslavia, which intensified in 1929, contributed to the development of extremist movements in Yugoslavia. Terrorist nationalist groups sprang up in Croatia and Macedonia, but the most massive Yugoslav Fascist movement—Dimitrije Ljotić's Zbor—developed in Serbia. The government of Prime Minister Milan Stojadinović not only established excellent relations with Fascist Italy but openly imitated it. And as the Nazis put the industrial machine into high gear, Germany's economic dominance in Yugoslavia became even stronger. By 1938 Yugoslavia's trade with Germany accounted for 53 percent of exports and 65 percent of imports.[26] This was not the only Yugoslav policy with which the Nazis were satisfied: "On October 5, 1940, six months before the Nazi invasion of Yugoslavia, the Yugoslav Royal Government issued two anti-Jewish decrees. One prohibited Jews from the production and distribution of food; the other restricted the enrollment of Jews at universities and high schools. . . . Notably, this legislation was not implemented in Croatia."[27]

Such events help to explain why Yugoslavia (in spite of being a creature of the hated Versailles settlement), and the Serbs in particular, enjoyed considerable sympathies in the Nazi camp, as a former Nazi intelligence officer reports:

> Chief of the Press Section of the German Foreign Ministry Dr. Paul . . . Schmidt published a number of pro-Yugoslav articles in the German Press, his primary object being to awaken a sympathetic interest in Hitler and the other leaders for Yugoslavia and, in particular, for the Serbs. He lauded the centuries-old and heroic struggle of the valiant Serbian people against the Turkish oppressor, the military virtues of the warlike Serbs, their chivalrous characteristics and so on, and succeeded in making quite a plausible cause for a moral relationship which he professed to see between Germans and Serbs. By this means he greatly strengthened the pro-Serb feeling which already existed among the German leaders. Hitler himself repeatedly declared that he regarded an alliance with the brave and warlike Serbs as an object particularly worth striving for.
>
> The Croats, on the other hand, had no really influential man in Berlin to plead their cause.[28]

Instead of admitting the failures of their Yugoslav policy, Britain and France ignored them and took every opportunity to sustain the myth of the good, friendly Yugoslavia, or Serbia. One opportunity was offered by the Belgrade coup d'état of March 27, 1941.

Two days earlier, Yugoslav Regent Prince Pavle and the government reluctantly signed the Tripartite Pact in Vienna as the only way to spare Yugoslavia from the war.[29] Any other alternative was worse. But British S.O.E. intelligence agents—taking advantage of nationalist Serbs' resentment against the government, which had made concessions to the Croats by allowing a high degree of autonomy to Croatia in 1939—had already persuaded a group of air force officers in Belgrade to stage a coup d'état without making any commitments of aid to the new government.[30] An Englishman employed at the time at the royal court in Belgrade stated, on the basis of personal communication from an S.O.E. officer and the documents that had been released, that "there would certainly have been no *coup d'état* if the British had not planned it," noting that "the conspirators were for the most part irresponsible Serb officers, who had little sympathy for the Croats and Slovenes, and whose object, apart from personal ambition, was to conduct a policy which was exclusively in the Serb interest."[31]

The coup was successfully staged in the early hours of March 27, and was enthusiastically welcomed by Winston Churchill in isolated and besieged England. "Early this morning the Yugoslav nation found its soul," he said at a meeting the same day, reviving the myth of the Serbs/Yugoslavs as heroic allies: "This patriotic movement arises from the wrath of a valiant and warlike race at the betrayal of their country."[32] But just three days later the new government realized that its options were as limited as those of the government it had overthrown, and informed the German military attaché and the German envoy in Belgrade of its decision to accept all international obligations of the former government, including the accession to the Tripartite Pact. The instant disappearance of the newly found Yugoslav soul was ignored in Britain, while Hitler issued a directive ordering the invasion of Yugoslavia, a few hours after he had received the news of the revolt.

The German attack on Yugoslavia gave rise to still another myth: that the twelve-day Yugoslav Blitzkrieg caused a fateful delay in Hitler's invasion of the Soviet Union by exposing his forces too soon to the Russian winter. William L. Shirer was one of the propagators of the myth that depicts the Serb-led Yugoslavia as David who defeated the Nazi Goliath: "This postponement of the attack on Russia in order that the Nazi warlord might vent his personal spite against a small Balkan country which dared to defy him was probably the most catastrophic single decision in Hitler's career."[33] However, a non-mythical assessment of the German attack on the Soviet Union does not even mention the events in Yugoslavia among the factors causing the delay of Operation Barbarossa:

> The assault by the 153 divisions succeeded. It had been delayed at least twice and opinions differ among scholars as to whether the postponements were caused by the German intervention in Greece or for other reasons—a late thaw was probably a prime cause—but Brauchitsch's troops were able to pierce the Soviet frontier positions and conduct their operations according to plan.[34]

In the early stage of the war, the pan-Serb Četnik movement, led by the royalist Colonel Draža Mihailović, was celebrated in the West for waging a heroic struggle against the Axis forces. Actually, the Četniks' program, outlined in a document titled "Homogeneous Serbia," was "to create a Serbia that would bring together all Serbs and all lands where Serbs live."[35] Although the Četniks counted on the Allied victory to bring them to power in a restored monarchist Yugoslavia, they avoided clashes with German and Italian military units, and frequently collaborated with them against their own domestic rivals. For this reason, in 1943 Britain and the United States stopped giving aid to the Četniks and switched their support to the Partisans. This decision was influenced by the British military observers' unrealistic assessment of the communist-led multinational Partisan resistance movement's contribution to the anti-Axis effort. However, the Partisans, who also fought primarily against their domestic rivals, with the aim of establishing communist rule at the end of the war, formed a pan-Yugoslav movement with a greater potential for inflicting losses to German forces and their collaborators.

Subsequently, the Allied propaganda glorified the Partisans as uncritically as they had glorified the Četniks, but one thing remained constant through this change: the old image of the Serbs as a noble and faithful ally. Dating from World War I, it proved stronger than the facts refuting it, as the British reporter Jonathan Sunley notes:

> [M]ost portraits of the [Partisan] movement still depicted it as a kind of crusade headed by Serbs seeking to redeem their fallen brothers, the Croats and Slovenes. What characterizes the three best-known memoirs written by British soldiers who served with the Partisans—*Eastern Approaches* (1949) by Fitzroy Maclean, *Partisan Picture* (1946) by Basil Davidson, and *The Embattled Mountain* (1971) by Bill Deakin—is precisely the absence of any recognition of just how much the Partisan movement relied on diverse national efforts, it being the rule of all guerrilla movements that they can survive only where the population supports them with recruits, supplies and intelligence. In late 1943, the Partisan forces numbered some 300,000 fighters, arranged in twenty-six divisions: of these, two were located in Serbia, one in Montenegro, seven in Bosnia-Herzegovina, eleven in Croatia and five in Slovenia.[36]

In 1944, however, when Serbia was liberated from German occupation, Partisan units began to be transformed into the Yugoslav army. Many Serbs, including the Četniks taking advantage of an amnesty, joined. Serbian dominance of the armed forces was thereby established and remained a feature of the Yugoslav military establishment until its end.

The liberation of Yugoslavia, or, more exactly, the replacement of fascist with communist totalitarianism, was accompanied by large-scale massacres of war prisoners. Britain, at whose initiative the communists received the aid that helped them come to power, supplied them with about twenty-five thousand victims—military and civilian anti-Tito refugees who had sought asylum in the British zone in Austria and were forcibly extradited.[37] To make the operation of "clearing the decks" (as Field Marshall Alexander referred to it) smoother, officials told the prisoners that they were going to be transported to Italy; instead the trains took them to Tito's killing fields. A still larger group of victims of the brutal retaliation consisted of those who were forcibly prevented from crossing into Austria. Even some victims of the Nazi terror did not escape the

Yugoslav communist terror. In the so-called Dachau Trials, held in Yugoslavia in 1948 and 1949, thirty-four surviving inmates of the Dachau and Buchenwald concentration camps were accused of having collaborated with the Gestapo because, according to the prosecution, only such collaboration could explain their survival. Eleven were sentenced to death, and the others to long prison terms.[38]

The brutality of Tito's regime in its early phase was ignored in the West, partly because of the West's complicity in its rise to power, and also because old myths die hard. Still, because of its aggressive foreign policy, which included shooting down unarmed American planes in Yugoslav airspace and aiding the communist rebellion in northern Greece, Yugoslavia lost most of the sympathies it had won during the war.[39] But when Stalin condemned Tito and the Yugoslav leadership in 1948, the myth of a heroic Yugoslavia suddenly revived. The West did not care that Tito used Stalin's methods against Stalin's real and suspected supporters in Yugoslavia; it was interested only in maintaining the split in the communist camp by helping Yugoslavia survive Soviet pressure. As a result of spontaneous sympathy for a small country threatened by a totalitarian giant, and the leftist intelligentsia's urge to find a "nice" communist country, Yugoslavia was granted the "heavenly" status again: an innocent David who courageously defied both the Nazi and Soviet Goliaths. Heavenly Yugoslavia was at the same time Heavenly Serbia because the world, on the basis of old glorifications of the Serbs and with the help of the Serb-dominated Belgrade propaganda machine, cultivated the image of the Serbs as the freedom-loving guardians of Yugoslavia.

Expecting that Serbs would further British interests, Winston Churchill wanted them to attain the same dominant role in Yugoslavia they had played before the Second World War. His note to Foreign Secretary Anthony Eden of December 8, 1943, demonstrates that he worked toward such a solution: "My unchanging objective is to get Tito to let the King come out and share his luck with him and thus unite Yugoslavia and bring in the old Serb core."[40] Fifty years later the same pro-Serbian stance remained strong in British politics. The right-wing activist David Hart stated in the *Spectator* that "[t]here are, in fact, several respectable arguments that Britain's national interest would be best served, if we have to act at all, by helping the Serbs," because "[c]reating a Muslim enclave would involve at least 100,000 ground troops, many aircraft and some ships," whereas a "strong Orthodox Serbia would undoubtedly act as a bulwark against any Islamic incursion into western Europe."[41] Less than a year after making these statements, Hart became an advisor to Britain's minister of defense. As for the de facto creation of a Muslim enclave, it did not require any effort by the international community but was a result of its passivity. Another commentator writing in the same magazine explained why one should not be sentimental about Bosnian victims of Serbian expansionism: "They [the Bosnians] are Balkan, and even the Ottoman Empire at the height of its voluptuous power wished it had never tried to conquer these tricky, duplicitous people."[42]

Some very important people, who could have prevented the war had their view of reality not been obfuscated by myths, shared the belief that a Yugoslavia ruled by Serbs is good for Britain's and France's strategic goals, and that Serbs are superior to their rivals. For example, French president François Mitterrand took both the myth of ancient hatreds and the myth of the Heavenly Serbia seriously, as another well-known Frenchman, the philosopher Alain Finkielkraut, relates:

> Invited by journalists of the *Frankfurter Allgemeine Zeitung* to clarify the French position on the war in Croatia, President François Mitterrand stated the following thoughts: "What I know is that the history of Serbia and Croatia has been full of such dramas for a long time, especially during the Second World War, when numerous Serbs died in Croatian camps. As you know, Croatia formed part of the Nazi bloc, Serbia did not. After Tito's death, the latent conflict between Serbs and Croats had to explode. That's where we are now. I do not think that Serbia wants to wage war to seize Croatia but to obtain a shifting of borders and a form of direct or indirect control over Serb minorities in Croatia."
>
> Reading this declaration and noticing that it did not irritate the

political leaders either of the majority or of an opposition that is otherwise so prompt to sound the mort for the chief of state, I experienced a sense of shame. After the destruction of Vukovar, and before Osijek's, with hundreds of thousands of Croatians in exodus, the man who speaks in my name, the man who decides the policy of my country repeats point by point, and without anybody refuting it, the aggressor's deceitful and racist propaganda.[43]

The ignorance of historical facts displayed in this instance by Mitterrand is shared by other politicians who think of themselves as great strategists when they reduce historical complexities to simplistic black-and-white schemes. Their indifference to facts is matched by their indifference toward the fate of the peoples affected by their uninformed decisions.

Indifference Makes a Difference

In his significant study of small Central and Eastern European nations, the Hungarian historian István Bibó pointed out that "in Eastern Europe, the same as in Western Europe, the number of nations has changed very little in the last one thousand years. In Eastern Europe, let us say six hundred years ago (around 1300–1350), there existed the Polish, Hungarian, Czech, Serbian, Croatian, Lithuanian, and Greek nations."[44] But the ethnic nations that emerged, or reemerged, as political nations in the twentieth century—Albanian, Estonian, Latvian, Slovak, and Slovenian—are no less old. Although submerged in various empires for centuries, they constituted communities aware of the bonds that tied them together.

The long duration of nations is an important fact that should be taken into account whenever there is an opportunity to make changes in political geography. The modern idea of progress has advanced the belief that nation-states are relics of the past that will fade away on the way to the ultimate unity of mankind at the utopian end of history. In the real world, however, there are no signs of such fading. This makes it important to provide each nation with a suitable territorial framework that reduces both internal and external frictions. One way of achieving this is to make an ethnic nation as coextensive with a sovereign state as possible, without substantial minorities but also without resorting to population transfers, not to mention more drastic measures, to make a nation fit a state.

However, when powerful countries are given the opportunity to change international borders, instead of being guided by such principles they often rearrange the map of the world the way they think will contribute to their own security and power, or simply accept the factual demarcation regardless of its randomness. They arbitrarily enlarge some nations, shrink others, throw several heterogeneous nations into one state, separate one nation into two states, create nationless states, and leave large nations stateless. Major wars in the second half of the twentieth century—in Korea, Vietnam, the former Yugoslavia—are the consequences of such solutions. Arbitrary border drawing has aggravated the formation of viable states in a large part of Africa. And the failure to provide the Kurds with a country of their own has resulted in a constant low-level warfare and genocides that are devastating not only for the Kurds themselves but also for the nations that persecute them.[45]

Arbitrary nation engineering may occasionally produce some short-term benefit to the power engaged in it, but the conflicts and wars that almost inevitably result from ignoring others' vital interests far outweigh any possible benefits. Indifference to the fate of other nations is a widespread phenomenon, not limited to big powers. It was evident in the relations between various entities within the former Yugoslavia. For example, when Slobodan Milošević presented his plan to abolish the autonomy of the province of Kosovo in 1989, the leaders of all the Yugoslav republics gave their consent in the expectation that this would satisfy Serbian appetites. Not surprisingly, they were faced with the threat to their own autonomy two or three years later.

The indifference of bureaucrats and politicians guided by public opinion polls rather than by knowledge and principles is more responsible for the world community's failure in the former Yugoslavia than any presumed conspiracies. British pro-Serbian policy, for example, was primarily a result of a political vacuum caused by indifference and failure to use reliable information, as the sociologist Daniele Conversi notes in his study of the British stand toward the war in the Balkans:

> British politics had been moving in a vacuum that was filled by the Serbs, who controlled the most sophisticated propaganda machine in the Balkans, which they had inherited from the Yugoslav state (Croatian propaganda has been much more ineffective, due to internal divisions and lack of expertise; Bosnian propaganda was virtually nonexistent during the whole initial phase of the war).[46]

When an issue is approached with indifference, decisions are more easily corrupted by extraneous influences, including money.[47] Another important reason that indifference leads to poor decisions is that it is inevitably accompanied by ignorance. The history of Bosnia offers a fine illustration of the pernicious consequences of indifference and ignorance on policymaking. This Balkan country with three major religions and cultures would seem to have been destined to perpetual infighting. Nevertheless, during four centuries of Ottoman rule there were no interethnic or religious wars in Bosnia, while several fierce religious wars raged in Western Europe. The Habsburg rule also preserved peace in Bosnia and launched rapid industrialization and modernization. The country became a killing field for the first time when Nazi Germany and Fascist Italy invaded, and the Ustašas and Četniks unleashed their murderous campaigns. Even under a communist dictator there was peace in Bosnia-Herzegovina, and painful memories faded.

The second conflagration in Bosnia-Herzegovina in this century was also prompted by outsiders—in this case, Slobodan Milošević and his partners in the campaign for a Greater Serbia. The international situation was incomparably more favorable this time than in 1941. Instead of aggressive totalitarian nations on Yugoslavia's borders, there were the European Community (on the verge of becoming the European Union), NATO, and the United Nations, organizations set up to ensure that certain things would never happen again. And yet they have happened, on a smaller scale but with unsurpassed brutality.

There is no mystery in this paradox. In the Ottoman and Habsburg empires as well as in Tito's Yugoslavia, policies relating to Bosnia were made by people well acquainted with the area and highly motivated to preserve order, because it was a part of their dominion.[48] But during the war in Bosnia-Herzegovina in the 1990s, crucial decisions affecting it were made in distant centers by people with little knowledge of the area and considerable indifference to the suffering of the local population. Distance seemed to make them immune to the consequences of their lack of commitment to the preservation of order.[49]

Germany is usually regarded as the main driving power behind the efforts to recognize the two former Yugoslav republics that were the first targets of Serbian aggression, and it is frequently accused of having been guided by a long-standing hostility toward Yugoslavia. In his excellent work on the breakup of that country, the Oxford University historian Mark Almond points out how wrong this interpretation is:

> Contrary to the view that Helmut Kohl and Hans-Dietrich Genscher deliberately set out to foster the collapse of Yugoslavia, all the evidence points to their desire to preserve it. It was German public opinion which forced Bonn out of the consensus followed by the rest of the EC. Upset by pictures of violence in its former holiday haunts, the German public put pressure on the Bonn establishment to support the right to self-determination in Slovenia and Croatia to which their government had only paid lip-service. In all the fateful months leading up to the crisis the German government loyally endorsed every EC communiqué which misread the situation in Yugoslavia.[50]

However, after German public opinion prompted the politicians to act, a general familiarity with the area—on the part of ordinary citizens and businessmen as well as politicians and reporters[51]—and the closeness to the theater of events contributed to the vigor with which German foreign policy opposed the indifference of other major powers toward brutal Serbian aggression in the course of

1991.[52] Paradoxically, Germany's Nazi past may have played a role in the formation of German public opinion regarding the events in Yugoslavia at a time when the distinction between the aggressor and the victim was very clear. A people with a sense of guilt about their ancestors' passivity and complicity in the Nazi era may have found it harder to passively watch a genocide than did the peoples whose ancestors fought totalitarian regimes. But as the war in the former Yugoslavia continued, and assumed aspects of a civil war, Germany joined its Atlantic partners in the pattern of weakness and appeasement that was repeated in Bosnia-Herzegovina and Kosovo.

The only Western statesman in office who persistently warned of the possible outbreak of violence in Yugoslavia and the danger of inactivity was Alois Mock, the foreign minister of Austria, a neighboring country that had ruled over parts of the former Yugoslavia for centuries. Unfortunately, the EC's leaders ignored his warnings. The Vatican, center of a religious institution present on the eastern shore of the Adriatic Sea for nearly two thousand years, showed an equally good grasp of the situation. It was among the first to support Croatia's and Slovenia's right to self-determination by recognizing them as sovereign states, while it had refused to recognize the World War II Croatian state.

However, proximity by itself is no guarantee of good diplomacy. If it stimulates desires to unduly extend one's influence or territory, or if it breeds fears and hatreds, it can have negative consequences. But the post-Habsburg Austria has no imperial ambitions, and the Catholic Church, especially since Vatican II, has been guided by sincere efforts to establish better relations with Orthodox countries.[53]

It should be clear in retrospect that the measure first proposed by Austria's foreign minister—a firm stand against the attempts to transform the former Yugoslavia into a Greater Serbia by force—could have prevented the war, and, inversely, that the assurance given to the Serbs that their victims would not receive any international help precipitated it. The renowned American strategist Albert Wohlstetter pointed out the connection between this promise and the launching of the war:

The West invited Serbia's genocidal war when it made clear to the Serbs that it would not let the former Yugoslavian republics acquire the arms needed to defend themselves. In Bosnia in particular, the war was not a spontaneous eruption of "ancient hatreds" on all sides, but a heavily armed Serbian aggression against a recognized, sovereign member of the U.N.[54]

No credit was given to those who advocated an approach that could have prevented the war; instead, the opposite happened: the invention of the myth that the allegedly premature recognition of Slovenia and Croatia encouraged these two nations to secede from Yugoslavia, which in turn led to the armed conflict. A related myth blames Slovenia and Croatia for the war because they refused to accept Serbia's terms, although their acceptance would have constituted political suicide for the two nations.[55]

The assertion that the recognition of the two most developed Yugoslav republics was responsible for the war is remarkable for being a diametrical inversion of the truth, easily detectable by a brief glance at the chronology of events.[56] The Yugoslav People's Army provoked the war in Slovenia on June 27, 1991, and four weeks later launched a full-scale attack on Croatia. Pressured by Germany and several other countries, the EC recognized Croatia and Slovenia on January 15, 1992, that is, more than five months after the start of the war allegedly caused by the recognition.

The recognition, in fact, led to the end of the war in Croatia. More precisely, the mere announcement of recognition did it. On December 23, 1991, Germany announced that it would recognize Slovenia and Croatia and offer economic aid to Croatia. Eleven days later, that is, even before the recognition became effective, Croats, rebel Serbs, and Yugoslav officials accepted the Vance Plan, which included a cease-fire. Unlike the fourteen previous cease-fires, which had lasted only a few days or even hours, this one was lasting.

An analogous coincidence marked the beginning of military action. The first of the 1990s wars for a Greater Serbia started six days after U.S. Secretary of State James A. Baker III announced in Belgrade that the United States would not recognize any Yugoslav republics that opted for independence.[57] These two sequences only confirm what could be expected by elementary logic: one does not prevent wars by assuring the potential aggressor that his victims would not receive any support.

The myth of German responsibility for the war through the recognition of Croatia and Slovenia is not necessarily an expression of anti-Germanism. The myth has many followers in Germany itself, who believe that the dissolution of Yugoslavia was an act contrary to the progress of history and that a progressive, socialist Serbia was provoked by its reactionary western neighbors.[58] It should also be noted that, in Austria, Alois Mock faced strong internal opposition to his advocacy of recognition of the two Yugoslav republics.

The international community's further complicity in Serbian aggression consisted in the imposition of the arms embargo against all Yugoslav republics when the expected swift Serbian victory did not materialize. The embargo was an aid to the aggressor because Serbs had all the weapons they needed, having access to the arsenal of the Yugoslav federal army (the fourth largest in Europe), while their victims had only a limited supply of small arms. The European Community imposed the embargo on July 5, 1991, eight days after the start of the twelve-day war against Slovenia, when the unexpected humiliating defeat of the Yugoslav federal army became obvious. And on September 25—about two months after the start of an all-out attack on Croatia by local Serbs, paramilitary forces from Serbia, and the Serb-led Yugoslav federal army—when the initial Serbian advances began to stall, the UN Security Council voted unanimously to impose a total arms embargo against Yugoslavia (Resolution 713). The embargo had been requested by the Serb-dominated government in Belgrade.

The UN arms embargo was similar to the one the League of Nations imposed on Spain when it was under attack from General Franco and his allies, Mussolini and Hitler. The dominant attitude in both cases has been indifference: the conflict is not worth the engagement of democratic powers, and the sooner it ends the better, even if German, Italian, or Serbian Fascists determine the end. Indifference to the suffering of others may have increased in the meantime due to the unparalleled power of bureaucracies in today's world. The sociologist James J. Sadkovich speaks of an era of new barbarism, which he defines as a form of bureaucratic indifference.[59]

Having failed to prevent the outbreak of the war, the international community could have impeded its spread by letting the Croats defeat the aggressor instead of restraining them with the arms embargo and other measures. By December 1991 the newly organized Croatian military units stopped the Serbian advance and even reversed it in some areas, particularly in western Slavonia. If they had been allowed to regain all the occupied territories (at a time when Russia was too preoccupied with its own internal problems to cause any complications), it could have dealt a decisive blow to pan-Serbian ambitions and prevented the tragedy in Bosnia. It was common knowledge at the time that, if unimpeded, the next stage of the campaign to bring all Serbs into one state would bring the war to Bosnia-Herzegovina, and that there it would be even bloodier. As an American reporter wrote in January 1992, "It has become a cliché of Yugoslavia's collapse that the war in Croatia, where about 10,000 people have been killed and more than 600,000 made homeless, is but a prelude for the unspeakable butchery that could come in Bosnia-Hercegovina."[60]

Instead of preventing further wars for a Greater Serbia at no cost to the international community, international mediators led by Cyrus Vance forced Croatia to accept an unfair cease-fire and helped the Serbs retain control over almost a third of Croatia, which they had brutally "cleansed" of non-Serbs. The international forces sent to Croatia under the label of UNPROFOR—United Nations Protection Forces—protected the Serbian conquests from Croatian counterattacks, and freed Serb forces in Croatia for action in Bosnia—the next stage of Milošević's campaign for a Greater Serbia. Thus the UN forces became accomplices in the Serbian war effort.

The extension of the arms embargo, at Vance's request, was still another way of helping the Serbs continue their genocidal campaign. The embargo was immoral from the beginning, but with the international recognition of the former Yugoslav republics it became illegal as well, because it was contrary to the United Nations Charter, whose Article 51 defines the right of individual and collective self-defense as "inherent."

Fig-Leaf Myths

The involvement of the international community led not to peace but to a new phase of the war, even more brutal than the preceding one. The UN troops observed the atrocities without trying to prevent or stop them—Srebrenica being the most horrible example—and the entire world joined by watching the televised genocide in their homes. Such a situation created the need to justify the passivity of the people who knew—and saw—what was happening. The myth of ancient hatreds was one of the fig leafs created in response to this need. It portrayed all the parties in the conflict as incorrigible brutes who have been at each other's throats for centuries, so that they did not deserve to be helped. It became one of the most repeated clichés in the coverage of the war. Lawrence Eagleburger expressed it forcefully:

> I have said this 38,000 times and I have to say this to the people of this country as well. This tragedy is not something that can be settled from outside and it's about damn well time that everybody understood that. Until the Bosnians, Serbs and Croats decide to stop killing each other, there is nothing the outside world can do about it.[61]

Like the other myths that thrived in the chaotic and bloody breakup of the former Yugoslavia, the myth of old hatreds was very distant from reality. The reality was that the various religious communities in Bosnia-Herzegovina, unlike those in Western Europe, had never engaged in mutual slaughter until the occupation of Yugoslavia by the Nazis and Fascists in 1941. And the worst destruction of Sarajevo prior to the 1990s was the work of the famous Habsburg commander Prince Eugen of Savoy, during the last Christian crusade against the Ottomans in 1697. These facts have been largely ignored, and ignorance provided a fertile ground for myths. One of the most enthusiastic propagators of the thesis of ancient hatreds, the writer

Robert D. Kaplan, pushed it so far that, in his view, Balkan hatreds were the source of Nazi hatred, as he explains in his *Balkan Ghosts: A Journey through History:* "Nazism, for instance, can claim Balkan origins. Among the flophouses of Vienna, a breeding ground of ethnic resentments close to the southern Slavic world, Hitler learned how to hate so infectiously."[62]

Ironically, the book Kaplan took for his model, Rebecca West's very popular and influential account of her visit to Yugoslavia, *Black Lamb and Grey Falcon: A Journey through Yugoslavia,* was inspired by hatred. Her view of Yugoslavia was essentially that of her Serbian guides, and her adoption of their prejudices was influenced by British rather than Balkan realities, as a biographer notes: "Rebecca was not keen on the Croats, because they reminded her of the Catholic Irish. She identified passionately with the Serbs."[63] She even took their messianism seriously: "If it were not for a small number of [men like her Serbian *cicerones*] the eastern half of Europe (and perhaps the other half as well) would have been Islamized, the tradition of liberty would have died for ever under the Habsburgs, the Romanoffs, and the Ottoman Empire, and Bolshevism would have become anarchy and not a system which may yet be turned to many uses."[64]

Black Lamb and Grey Falcon was published in Serbian for the first time in 1989, in a translation by Nikola Koljević, one of the leaders of Serb genocide in Bosnia-Herzegovina. It was a part of the avalanche of publications in the decade preceding the war that predisposed Serbs for military action by spreading the idea that they were a superior people, thwarted by their evil neighbors.[65]

Rebecca West's, and the West's, apparent love for "Heavenly" Serbia was to a large extent based on shared hatreds. Had it been inspired by genuine affection for the Serbs, it would have facilitated a sound knowledge of Serbia. Instead, the propagation of Serbian myths by hosts of Western writers, scholars, reporters, analysts, and politicians resulted in monumental ignorance, which contributed to the outbreak of the war and did enormous harm to Serbia, among others.

The alleged artificiality of Bosnia is another popular fig-leaf myth, created to conceal or justify the international community's failures in its intervention in that country. Like most fig-leaf myths, this one is also remote from reality. Unlike Yugoslavia, which existed for about seventy years, Bosnia has had an uninterrupted existence as a political entity since the tenth century, except for the 1929–45 period. It is a remarkable endurance for an "artificial" entity.

Nevertheless, the same powers that allowed the war to break out, in the expectation that Serbian military power would prevent the partition of Yugoslavia, were eager to partition Bosnia-Herzegovina. This willingness was first manifested in the plan drafted in late October 1993 by the international mediators Cyrus Vance and David Owen. The Vance-Owen Plan as well as the subsequent Owen-Stoltenberg Plan accepted the results of Serbian conquest and ethnic cleansing, and assigned to the aggressor a far larger territory than to the more numerous Muslims. Pro-Serb sympathies and the line of least resistance cooperated in this decision: Bosnia was de facto partitioned by the warring parties.

Canadian Major General Lewis MacKenzie, former head of the UN forces in Bosnia-Herzegovina, acknowledged in his testimony before the U.S. Congress in May 1993 that there was no justice in the solution, but he found nothing wrong with it: "Now obviously the critics will say this rewards force and sets a bad example. I can only say to them, read your history. Force has been rewarded since the first caveman picked up a club, occupied his neighbor's cave, and ran off with his wife."[66] General MacKenzie apparently did not realize that such acceptance of the law of the jungle rendered the presence of the international forces he commanded superfluous. In a BBC documentary, another commander of the same forces, British Lieutenant General Michael Rose, equally candidly admitted his indifference to what was going on around him in Bosnia. He gave the following justification for his refusal to use air attacks to stop Serb attacks on the civilian population: "We are not here to protect or defend anything other than ourselves or our convoys."[67]

Before the Vance-Owen Plan for the partition of Bosnia-Herzegovina, Muslims and Croats were allies in the fight against the Serbs. But when the mediators showed their willingness to partition the country and made the idea particularly attractive to the Croats by offering them a larger part of Bosnia-Herzegovina than they had expected, a war broke out between the two former allies, each one trying to secure as much land as possible before the partition would be finalized. Herzegovinian Croats and Croatian president Franjo Tudjman had been inclined to the partition of Bosnia and the annexation of the ethnically Croatian territories to Croatia from the beginning, but these inclinations turned deadly only after they had been blessed by international mediators.[68] As Noel Malcolm states,

> It is probably fair to say that Tudjman's own position was that of a rational opportunist. If he were given clear signs by the outside world that they would not allow the defeat and carve-up of Bosnia, then he would go along with that policy; but if the world was prepared to let the Serbs seize territory and hold it, then he would wish to have his slice of the cake, too.[69]

In addition to the war between Croats and Muslims, a war between two Muslim factions erupted at about the same time. The army organized by the Muslims in the Bihać enclave in northwestern Bosnia, whose civilian leader was Fikret Abdić, clashed with the predominantly Muslim army under the command of President Alija Izetbegović in Sarajevo. The "peace mediator" David Owen also contributed to this sub-war by encouraging Abdić's political ambitions in order to weaken the position of Izetbegović and make the government in Sarajevo accept the partition of Bosnia-Herzegovina according to his and Vance's plan.

After belated action by the United States stopped the war in Bosnia-Herzegovina and led to the efforts to reestablish unity, the partition of Bosnia—justified by the myth of its artificiality—has been advocated by Henry Kissinger, among others.

The myth of brave Serb warriors who allegedly saved Europe from Islam and mounted a heroic anti-Nazi resistance has also served as a justification for the prolonged refusal of the international community to take military action against an extremely brutal aggressor. Serbs may be good, brave soldiers when they defend their own country, but they, like most people, are less willing to risk their lives to subjugate others. Any coward can shoot with heavy cannons or sniper's rifles at defenseless citizens. International officers and soldiers serving in the former Yugoslavia under the flag of the United Nations also acted cowardly, because of their indifference toward the people caught in the conflict (some of them even sympathized with the aggressor).

Prolonged appeasement of a brutal aggressor had a corrosive effect on international institutions that were created to prevent the sort of things they passively witnessed in the former Yugoslavia. Bosnian Serbs' contempt for these institutions, which culminated in their capture of UN soldiers, discredited the powers and institutions—the United Nations, the North Atlantic Treaty Organization, the European Union, the United States—that proved themselves impotent in dealing with a ragtag army, good only at killing defenseless civilians. The facetious reading of the NATO acronym, "No Action Talk Only," was very appropriate for a long time. If NATO had not eventually acted to stop the genocide, it would have negated the reason for its existence.

Although less strong than in Europe, the opposition to the use of force was widespread in the United States as well. In the Pentagon, for example, General Colin Powell, chairman of the Joint Chiefs of Staff, discouraged military action by conjuring up the mythical image of the "invincible Serbian warrior" and exaggerating the size of military force needed to stop Serbian attacks. The United States finally decided to act because its own credibility as a superpower and the credibility of NATO and its other international instruments for keeping order in the world were jeopardized. A show of force quickly brought the Serbs to the negotiating table, which proved that proposals for tough action against them were right from the beginning. But the Dayton Accords are tainted: they rewarded Bosnian Serbs, who represented only 31.4 percent of the population of Bosnia-Herzegovina before the war and the genocide that they started, with 49 percent of its territory. Peace without justice is unstable. The same indifference that allowed the war to break out resulted in a settlement that may lead to a new war, unless costly international military involvement continues.

Conclusion

The campaign for a Greater Serbia, which intensified around 1980 and led to the war ten years later, should not make us forget that many Serbs want to live in peace with their neighbors and build an orderly and tolerant society. Even under the communist regime Serbia produced some able and honest politicians, opposed to nationalist adventures, who worked to make the regime less oppressive. They assumed the highest positions in the republic after Tito purged pan-Serb hard-liners in the mid-1960s, and were removed in his purge of liberals in 1972. Three-month-long mass demonstrations against President Milošević, organized by students and the opposition coalition Together after he refused to honor the results of the November 1996 elections, expressed, among other things, a yearning for the rule of law.

Unfortunately, the demonstrations also revealed severe obstacles to the achievement of a democratic order in Serbia in the near future. Nationalism was the dominant mood of the protests against the man who used nationalism to gain power and lead the country into war.[1] The carnival atmosphere of the protests reflected an unwillingness to recognize the horrors the drive for a Greater Serbia had recently created. Many demonstrators acted as if Milošević had been responsible for everything, and as if his removal from office would exorcize the evil and restore Serbia's innocence. Some protesters carried emblems, such as Njegoš's portraits, that expressed their acceptance of massacres in the struggle for a homogeneous nation and showed that they were angry with Milošević not because he had started the war but because he did not win it.

The two principal politicians who placed themselves in the lead-

ership of the wave of discontent—Zoran Đinđić and Vuk Drašković—did not offer a real alternative to Milošević's policies. They
did not deplore the nationalist obsession with a Greater Serbia (in
which they themselves rivaled Milošević), nor did they denounce
the myths that prevent many Serbs from coming to terms with their
past. Drašković's persistence in his militant nationalism, including calls for a new war, made him, in fact, a worse alternative
to Milošević. Vesna Pešić, the third member of the short-lived
anti-Milošević coalition Together, was decidedly less nationalistic,
but as the leader of a small civic organization she has little political
power.

The elections that preceded the protests revealed a strong support
of extremist policies: one of the most rabid nationalists, Četnik
leader Vojislav Šešelj, whose paramilitary units had excelled in
atrocities in Croatia and Bosnia, won 18 percent of the votes, and
was elected mayor of the city of Zemun, adjacent to Belgrade. In
the October 1997 elections he won even more votes and became a
serious contender for the presidency of Serbia.[2]

Those Serbian intellectuals who bravely defy the popular myths
and offer a realistic assessment of their country's past and present
cannot exert significant public influence because they are restricted
to a few media with a very limited audience. Their efforts are
thwarted not only by Milošević (who successfully uses his virtual
monopoly over mass media to reinforce the old myth of the Serbs
as innocent victims of an international conspiracy and to hide the
failure of his policies), but also by other prominent intellectuals and
artists who see Serbs only as victims. In October 1997, sixty of them
issued a second "Declaration for the Dismissal of Legal Proceedings
against Radovan Karadžić at the Hague Tribunal" (the first one was
issued in June 1996), criticizing the demands for the extradition of
the indicted war criminal:

> The enemies of the Serbs are particularly disturbed by the deep bond
> between Dr. Karadžić and the Serbian people, and especially by his
> connection with high-class intellectuals—Serbs and their friends in
> the world. Dr. Karadžić succeeded in directing all his efforts against

chauvinism and local patriotism, but also against the false protectors of the Serbs and other citizens who live in this area.[3]

A further obstacle to a healthier political climate is the present hierarchy of the Serbian Orthodox Church; the people who should represent the moral conscience of the nation and condemn the crimes committed in the attempt to create a Greater Serbia are instead ardent nationalists and inciters of xenophobia.

Thus many Serbs' genuine striving for an end to the vicious circle of violence and for the establishment of the rule of law has been foiled by national institutions and their leaders. External circumstances are also impeding the formation of a strong political force free from populist demagoguery. Foremost among them is the volatile situation in Bosnia-Herzegovina. The uncertainty about its future as a unified country encourages nationalists in every camp. Croatian and Serbian nationalists keep hoping to annex parts of it, while Muslim nationalists count on a new war to gain more territory than the Dayton Accords assigned to them. But even if the situation in Bosnia keeps stabilizing, continuous efforts to make Kosovo an integral part of Serbia may sustain illiberal facets of Serbian political culture.

Disunity among influential powers is another external obstacle to peace in the area. This was particularly obvious in the early 1990s, when Britain, France, and Russia backed Serbia, while Germany and Austria strived to protect the nations threatened by the Serbian expansionist drive. The division, similar to the one in 1914, made Europe unable to solve a problem in its own backyard and once more made it dependent on the United States. This particular discord has subsided since, but a widespread lack of determination to undertake whatever needs to be done remains a further obstacle to a durable peace in the Balkans.

Like most wars, the recent wars for a Greater Serbia are a complex phenomenon, caused by numerous internal and external influences. Every party that contributed to it should recognize its share in the tragedy, instead of blaming others exclusively and cultivating the myth of its own innocence. The writer, former dissident, and president of the Czech Republic Václav Havel has pointed out that Western democracies are not innocent either:

> Let events in the former Yugoslavia stand as a warning: this is not just a Balkan predicament. The inability of Europe and the United States to intervene effectively in defense of the basic values of civilization that are being so drastically destroyed in the Balkans (and, what is more, in an area that was always an integral part of Europe) tells us something about the democratic world as well.[4]

The Yugoslav debacle has confirmed what could have been learned from other recent conflicts in various parts of the world: national self-interest cannot be advanced by means of strategies that ignore the welfare and security of other nations. Instead of treating entire nations as chips in a poker game, their legitimate aspirations must be taken into account if the pursuit of one's own interests is to be successful. It is arrogant and naive to believe that those nations will accept the role assigned to them if it harms them or leads to their obliteration. The decisions to put several nations under the Serbian yoke early in the twentieth century and to let the Serbs attack them at the end of the century for not accepting the reimposition of the yoke are examples of such amoral political engineering that ends up harming everybody, including the nation that is apparently favored.

In the contemporary world any local conflict reverberates everywhere, and the threat of nuclear devastation makes peace and order more important than ever. The stability necessary in such a world cannot be improved with blind adherence to the status quo. Neither can it be achieved with interventions after conflicts break out. No country or group of countries possesses sufficient resources to maintain order everywhere, and the reluctance of democratic countries to intervene in foreign conflicts is aggravated by the paralysis— caused by the lack of consensus—of the international bodies that are supposed to legitimize the interventions.

A more efficient method of reducing the number and intensity of conflicts in the world consists in avoiding the creation of unstable situations that breed conflicts. The drawing of borders that split one nation into two or more states, put several nations into one state, or leave a nation stateless has been mentioned above as a generator of several twentieth-century wars. Any pursuit of short-term benefits that creates long-term tensions also breeds international conflicts, and so does too narrow a definition of self-interest. Still another major cause of foreign-policy failures is the coddling of brutal politicians and regimes with the aim of turning them into allies, even if they engage in genocidal activities. Respect for the rights of every individual citizen has always been the basis for a free and orderly society; specific conditions of the modern world also make international order impossible unless there is respect for the legitimate rights of every community that forms part of it.

This makes it imperative to avoid the trap made by the intertwined phenomena of indifference and ignorance. Decisions must be based on an informed, realistic assessment of every concrete situation. The British thinker Isaiah Berlin emphasized that political decisions should be made on the basis of understanding "a particular situation in its full uniqueness, the particular men and events and dangers, the particular hopes and fears which are actively at work in a particular place at a particular time."[5] An American writer has similarly emphasized the need for a thorough understanding of the complexities of our world, an understanding that merges knowledge and ethics:

> We need to embrace, in the place of mere realism, a more robust and complex view of the world, what we might call meta-realism, which recognizes a context more intricate and subtle than we had hoped would be necessary, that also takes into account some values, beliefs, wishes, and hopes that are completely unrealistic. This meta-realism might finally be indistinguishable from the elusive and contradictory tenets of ethics, which are, finally, no more nor less than the accumulated practical folk wisdom of millennia of human experience.[6]

Abstract formulas frequently mask the absence of adequate knowledge of complex situations. Some of the simplistic rules that have been mechanically applied to the disintegration of the communist

Yugoslavia with disastrous consequences are the preservation of the status quo, the prevention of balkanization, and the artificiality of Bosnia-Herzegovina. They can make an ignorant politician temporarily appear statesmanlike, but they constitute an evasion of reality and aggravate problems instead of solving them. Bloody totalitarian adventures have all been based on seductively simple formulas.

Myths and lies are used to justify uninformed policies and hide the ignorance and amorality of their makers. If the latter believe in the myths they use, as they often do, myths become even more dangerous than if they are used cynically. Some of the myths that have contributed to the brutal disintegration of the former Yugoslavia are still taken for truths by many people all over the world. If unchallenged, they will lead to new failures. For example, the balkanization fallacy, which served as a justification for the creation of Yugoslavia and for letting the Serbs prevent its dissolution with the force of arms, makes many Europeans confident that political integration can prevent future conflicts among members of the European Union, although the former Yugoslavia offered living proof that the creation of a supranational entity cannot by itself provide protection against destructive lies, fears, and hatreds, and can even contribute to their growth. Accordingly, EU bureaucrats have been happily creating an ever more uniform Europe, but they have been less able to prevent old fears from producing new lies that corrode European unity, such as the blatant falsehood about the German responsibility for the eruption of the wars for a Greater Serbia. This does not necessarily mean that a United Europe is a bad idea, but only that it is dangerous to expect too much from a political framework while ignoring the ultimate threat to European unity: fears and lies that breed distrust and hatred.

Another moral of the story of Serbia is that a tribalistic cataloguing of nations into good and evil, heavenly and demonic is dangerous because it distorts perception of reality. We must recognize, without falling into the trap of moral and cultural relativism, that nations—unlike regimes—are too complex to fit any black-and-white schemes. The Turks' relative tolerance of other religious and ethnic communities in the Ottoman Empire has been referred to earlier, but the Turks committed the first modern genocide with the massacres of Armenians during the First World War. Their original tolerance was not genetically determined; it was based on a genuinely religious spirit and the need to maintain order in their empire.[7] With the dissolution of the empire and the emergence of nationalism as a pseudoreligion, genocidal massacres became an instrument for the achievement of a homogeneous nation-state.

This study has emphasized the role of nationalist and millenarian myths in modern collective crimes, but it would be a mistake to condemn all myths as bad. By means of simple images and stories, myths can offer marvelous insights into important aspects of the human condition. Classical Greek myths—those of Sisyphus and Prometheus, for example—and myths that form the basis of higher religions fall into this category. They teach humility by showing man as a fragile creature in a universe he cannot understand or dominate.

The difference between beneficial and harmful myths derives from what they convey of man's possibilities. Modern myths that have inspired genocides are based on the Enlightenment idea that man is by nature good and able to solve all problems with the help of his intellect. This concept provides the basis for the glorification of particular persons, classes, races, or nations as saviors who will eliminate the evil from history. Such a lofty end legitimizes the use of any means to achieve it. Therefore, it is of vital importance to recognize the validity of the religious concept of Original Sin, which teaches that the capacity for evil is present in every human being. For this reason, evil cannot be eliminated from history. The only way to lighten the burden of history consists in the pursuit of truth and justice, and in compassion toward every fellow human being.

Let the tragic events in the former Yugoslavia remind us that in the small, interdependent modern world, everyone is to some degree responsible for the actions of others anywhere; that indifference to the suffering of others abets evil and brings it closer to home; and that the only pragmatic international policy is one that combines ethics, knowledge, and strength.

Notes

NOTES TO THE INTRODUCTION

1. Vladimir Dvorniković, "Psihogeneza epskog deseterca," *Prilozi proučavanju narodne poezije* 3, no. 2, quoted by Braun, *Kosovo*, 96.

2. Elias, *The Germans*, 4.

3. George F. Kennan, introduction to *The Other Balkan Wars* (Washington, D.C.: Carnegie Endowment for International Peace, 1993), 4–5.

4. The volume titled *The Authoritarian Personality* (New York: Harper, 1950), written by a group of scholars headed by Theodor W. Adorno, contains the classic presentation of this approach.

5. Adolf Eichmann, head of the Gestapo's Jewish section, is a good example. "A half-dozen psychiatrists certified Eichmann as 'normal,' and [Hannah Arendt] did not judge him especially driven by anti-Semitism. His prime motivations included a sense of duty, a willingness to obey authority, and a bureaucrat's drive for advancement." Kressel, *Mass Hate*, 9. Eichmann is no exception: "After reviewing three major studies of the Nuremberg Rorschachs with great care, Gerald Borofsky and Don Brand of Harvard Medical School concluded in 1980 that 'the results to date are such that no major differences between the psychological functioning of the [Nazi war criminals] and the psychological functioning of other comparison groups have yet been demonstrated.'" Kressel, *Mass Hate*, 159.

6. Radovan Samardžić, "Za carstvo nebesko," in Đuretić, *Kosovska bitka 1389*, 12.

7. Aleksandar Petrov, "Kosovo—sveta priča srpskog naroda," in Đilas, *Srpsko pitanje*, 46.

8. "Od Golgote do pobede," *Jugoslovenske novine* (Belgrade) 1, no. 1 (October 8, 1936): 1.

9. Jevtić, *Sveti Sava*, 300–301.

10. Eric Hobsbawm, "The New Threat to History," *New York Review of Books*, December 16, 1993, 63.

11. Popović-Obradović, "Zablude o 'zlatnom dobu,' " 14.

12. Popović, Vidovdan i časni krst, 152.

NOTES TO CHAPTER 1

1. About these texts, see Trifunović, Srpski srednjovekovni spisi.

2. Karadžić, Srpske narodne pjesme, vol. 2, no. 45, vv. 11–26.

3. Ibid., vv. 42–44.

4. Đorđe J. Janić, "Dan opredeljivanja—Vidovdan," Pravoslavlje (Belgrade), July 1, 1995, 3.

5. Historical research has reached the conclusion that Vuk Branković, traditionally accused of treason in the Kosovo Battle, fought loyally in the Christian army, but the presence of a traitor enhanced the analogy with the Last Supper and provided an additional explanation for the Turkish victory.

6. Popović, Filosofske urvine, 192.

7. In the oldest sources his name is spelled Kobila, Kobilić, or Kobilović.

8. Milan Đ. Milićević, Kraljevina Srbija: Novi krajevi (Belgrade, 1884), 28.

9. Low, The Ballads of Marko Kraljević, 106. The translator uses the language of English chivalric poetry, which is very different from the language of the original songs. Most folk singers, as well as their audience, were illiterate; they used simple, everyday language in their songs.

10. Ibid., 42, 44.

11. Koljević, The Epic in the Making, 182ff.

12. "Prince Marko and the Eagle," in Noyes and Bacon, Heroic Ballads of Servia, 130–31.

13. "Marko Kraljević i soko," in Karadžić, Srpske narodne pjesme, vol. 2, no. 54, vv. 28–29.

14. Gavrilo, "U čemu je značaj 27. marta?" in Memoari patrijarha srpskog Gavrila (Belgrade: Sfairos, 1990), 270.

15. René Guerdan, Byzance (Paris: Perrin, 1973), 231.

16. Brodsky, Less Than One, 411.

17. The existence of national churches in England and some Scandinavian countries is not comparable to the situation in Eastern Orthodox countries, among other reasons because national churches in the former were established after the institutions and patterns of thought and behavior characteristic of Western societies had been formed.

18. George Schöpflin, "The Political Traditions of Eastern Europe," in Graubard, Eastern Europe, 61.

19. Alain Ducellier (1976), 138. The Russian intellectual Gleb Yakunin formulates in similar words the main tenet of a theology of history that has very concrete political consequences:

Eastern Orthodoxy always leaned towards fatalism and passivity. That God *permitted* something to happen was taken to mean that He *willed* it to happen. And the Orthodox mind often succumbed to the temptation to see everything that happened in the world and in history—both the good and the evil—as taking place by "the will of God" and with "the Lord's most blessed desire." Yakunin, "Moscow Patriarchate," 13.

20. Mango, *Byzantium*, 151.

21. Jevtić, *Sveti Sava*, 323.

22. Ibid., 242.

23. There are no strict rules for canonization in the Serbian Orthodox Church; consequently, no single authoritative list of saints exists. The present account is based on the data in *Srpska pravoslavna crkva 1219–1969* (Belgrade: Sveti arhijerejski sinod Srpske pravoslavne crkve, 1969), 391–92, which lists fifty-eight individual Serbian saints and a group of nine saints under the collective name of Sinaites.

24. *Despot* is a Byzantine title used by a number of Serbian rulers, mostly Turkish vassals, after 1402.

25. Cerović, *Svjetlosti i sjenke jedne tradicije*, 151.

26. Petrovich, *A History of Modern Serbia*, 1: 10.

27. Popović, *Vidovdan i časni krst*, 48.

28. Čajkanović, *O srpskom vrhovnom bogu*, 7. Vladimir Ćorović's anthology of popular songs and stories about Saint Sava, "Sve narodne pesme i priče o Svetom Savi," has been reissued in *Sveti Sava*, ed. Veljko Topalović and Branislav Brkić (Belgrade: Vrhunci civilizacije, 1989), 130–245.

29. Pedro Ramet, "Factionalism in Church-State Interactions," *Slavic Review*, summer 1985, 301.

30. Slavoljub Kačarević, "Bogovi su među nama," *Intervju* (Belgrade), March 28, 1986, 39.

31. Marian Zdziechowski, "Avstroslavizm i Rossiia," *Moskovskii ezhenedel'nik*, May 16, 1909, 42–43.

32. Soloviev, *Russia and the Universal Church*, 71.

33. Nikolić, *Kamena knjiga predaka*, 270.

34. Yakunin, "Moscow Patriarchate," 8–9.

35. Mićunović, *Moscow Diary*, 25.

36. Velimirović, *Nacionalizam svetoga Save*, 27–28. Bishop Velimirović's

admiration of national socialism was not an isolated phenomenon in the Orthodox Church. The noted social critic Walter Laqueur mentions the intense anti-Semitism of the Russian Orthodox Church Abroad, formed by émigrés from the Soviet Union, whose most authoritative bishops' synod resided in the city of Sremski Karlovci in Yugoslavia up to the end of the Second World War: "World Jewry, they announced at their second *sobor* in 1938, was engaged in subverting the Christian world by organizing the narcotics trade. The synod accused the Catholic church of rapprochement with Judaism, and the German Catholic church (!) of defending the Jews from Hitler and for protesting against anti-Semitism." Laqueur, *Black Hundred*, 225.

37. Žarko Gavrilović, "Svetosavlje na žeravici razmeđa istoka i zapada," *Glas crkve*, 14, no. 2 (1986): 32.

38. Danilo Medan, "Konture svetosavske ideologije i njen značaj u prošlosti i sadašnjosti," *Svetosavlje*, no. 6 (1937): 88.

39. Velimirović, *Kosovo i Vidovdan*, 95.

40. Popović, *Filosofske urvine*, 194.

41. Velimirović, *Dva vidovdanska govora* (Kragujevac, 1939), 14.

42. Velimirović, *Iznad greha i smrti* (Belgrade, 1914), 12.

43. Milomir M. Stanišić, *Nikolaj* (West Lafayette: Stanišić, 1977), 70.

NOTES TO CHAPTER 2

1. Popović, *Vidovdan i časni krst*, 49.

2. *Pamiętniki Janczara czyli Kronika turecka*. The book was quite popular in the sixteenth and seventeenth centuries, and was published several times in Polish and Czech.

3. Mihailović, *Janičarove uspomene*, 94–95. Injustice weakens a society. The arrogance of feudal lords, which led to peasant revolts, made Hungary and Croatia less able to resist the Turkish advance. These revolts were brutally suppressed. A red-hot crown was placed on the head of György Dósza, the leader of the Hungarian peasant revolt of 1514, and a comrade of his was impaled (Matija Gubec, the leader of the largest Croatian peasant revolt, was similarly "crowned" in 1573). The Hungarian kingdom was defeated by the Turks in 1526.

4. Patriarch Kallistos anathematized Tsar Dušan in 1350, and excommunicated him from the community of Eastern Orthodox churches.

5. Bojović, "Historiographie dynastique et idéologie politique," 38–39.

6. Vladimir Ćorović, "Boj na Kosovu," in Đurić, *Kosovski boj,* 191. Dejanović was killed fighting for the Ottomans in the same 1395 Battle of Rovine in which King Marko lost his life.

7. For a survey of early reports on the battle, see Radovan Samardžić, "History and Legend in the Kosovo Tradition," in Srejović, *Bitka na Kosovu,* 115–19; and Emmert, *Serbian Golgotha,* 54–60.

8. *Cambridge Medieval History,* 4: 561.

9. Tuchman, *A Distant Mirror,* 560.

10. *Cambridge Medieval History,* 4: 562. After the death of Sultan Bayezid I, Despot Stefan Lazarević became a vassal of Hungarian King Sigismund, but this did not lead to a lasting political association between the Serbs and the Hungarians.

11. See Constantine the Philosopher, *Život despota Stefana Lazarevića,* in *Stara srpska književnost,* vol. 3 (Novi Sad: Matica srpska, 1970), 203.

12. *Cambridge Medieval History,* 4: 572–73.

13. Ibid., 573.

14. Ranke, *History of Servia,* 84. There is one more explanation for the popularity of a Serbian ruler who served the Turks: many Serbs served in the Ottoman army. These Christian soldiers, called martologues, could identify with a hero who served the same master as they did. Prince Marko appears as a relentless fighter against Turks and protector of his people only in the songs created at the time of rebellion against Turkish rule after 1815, a period of nationalist revival of heroic folk poetry.

15. Stanojević, *Istorija srpskog naroda,* 240.

16. The Bulgarians, who were less cooperative than the Serbs, had to wait until 1870 for the restoration of the autocephalous Bulgarian Orthodox Church.

17. It is not clear whether Patriarch Makarije was the grand vizier's brother or cousin.

18. The Balkan Vlachs were also called Morovlachs (Black Vlachs) and, by contraction, Morlaks.

NOTES TO CHAPTER 3

1. See "Maina," in Gesemann, *Heroische Lebensform,* 278–306.

2. The Croats of Herzegovina and the Muslims of Sandžak display characteristic Dinaric traits such as clannishness and a propensity to violence.

3. On Dinaric and Balkanic highlander culture, see Cvijić *La péninsule balcanique;* Gesemann, *Heroische Lebensform;* Tomasic, *Personality and Culture;* Kaser, *Hirten, Kämpfer, Stammeshelden;* and Žanić, *Prevarena povijest.*

4. The blood feud survived longest among the Montenegrins and Albanians. The Kosovo Albanians abandoned the custom very recently.

5. "There is considerable evidence that Montenegrin lineages shifted in a very fluid manner not only between the Catholic and Muslim faiths but between Montenegrin and Albanian identity. It seems that, given the uncertainty over who held power in the region, the retention of a foot in more than one confessional or linguistic camp was often regarded as a kind of collective insurance policy." "History of Montenegro: Under the Prince-Bishops," *Encyclopedia Britannica,* 1996.

6. Djilas, *Land without Justice,* 77.

7. Boehm, *Montenegrin Social Organization and Values,* 66. The word *brastvo* (the standard spelling is *bratstvo*) means *clan.*

8. See Brković, *Glosarij,* 158.

9. Đorđević, *Naš narodni život,* 149. The word *podušje* (the root—*duša*—means *soul*) seems to refer to the meal honoring the slain elder.

10. Tomasic, *Personality and Culture,* 24.

11. Djilas, *Land without Justice,* 313.

12. Medaković, *Život i običai Crnogoraca,* 17.

13. The Serbian and Croatian word *hajduk* was borrowed from the Hungarian, where the term *hajdúk* designated soldiers who had been recruited from among marauders and robbers.

14. Ranke, *A History of Servia,* 279–80.

15. Koljević, *The Epic in the Making,* 228.

16. Karadžić, *Srpske narodne pjesme,* vol. 3, no. 7, vv. 28–30.

17. Ibid., vv. 280–87.

18. Ibid., vv. 314–16.

19. Koljević, *The Epic in the Making,* 232.

20. The character of Old (Starina) Novak is based on two famous fifteenth-century haiduks of that name. A legend pinpoints a cave in the Romanija Mountain above Sarajevo as his hiding place.

21. Song no. 110 in Vladimir Bovan's manuscript collection. See Vladimir Bovan, "Preobražaj istorijskog hajduka Novaka u pesnički lik Starine Novaka," in *Starina Novak i njegovo doba,* ed. Radovan Samardžić (Belgrade: SANU, 1988), 143.

22. "Novak i Radivoje prodaju Gruicu," in Karadžić, *Srpske narodne pjesme,* vol. 3, no. 2, vv. 142–45.

23. The year 1516 is frequently regarded as the beginning of the Montenegrin bishops' assumption of the role of heads of state, but the historian Ilarion Ruvarac proved a century ago that Montenegro was under Turkish rule in the sixteenth and seventeenth centuries, and subsequent research has confirmed his findings. Moreover, the secular power of the bishops of Cetinje was challenged by the power of Montenegrin clans for a long time.

24. Through most of its history Montenegro (or Zeta, as it was previously called) was politically separate from Serbia, and the feeling of a separate nationhood is still strong there. But religious and linguistic bonds make the two countries culturally similar, and Serbs regard Njegoš's work as an integral and important part of Serbian literature.

25. The subtitle is present in many subsequent editions but has been omitted from all editions since the end of World War II. The omission reflects the efforts to deny that the massacre had ever taken place, although Njegoš himself believed in its historicity. Pavle Popović presents the arguments for the factuality of the event in his study *O Gorskom vijencu,* 2d ed. (Belgrade, 1923), 209–10. Before Njegoš, the "Montenegrin Vespers" appeared as the subject of the Montenegrin folk song "Serbian Christmas Eve around 1702," and as the concluding episode of his teacher Sima Milutinović's drama "Dika crnogorska."

26. Njegoš, *Gorski vijenac,* vv. 671–75.

27. Ibid., v. 95. The first recorded use of the word "cleanse" (*čistiti*) to denote the extermination of unwanted segments of the population dates from the time of the First Serbian Uprising against the Turks (1804–13).

28. Ibid., vv. 175–78.

29. Ibid., vv. 2575–76.

30. Ibid., vv. 2581–82.

31. Ibid., vv. 2585, 2596–2606.

32. Ibid., vv. 2614–17.

33. Ibid., vv. 2619–21.

34. Ibid., vv. 2712–13, 2722–24.

35. Ibid., vv. 2729–32. Jovan N. Striković, a neuropsychiatrist, has written a book titled *Njegoš's Manifesto: Abbot Stefan's Laughter,* where he states that "Njegoš's laughter assigned to Abbot Stefan has entered the treasury of mankind's eternal values." *Njegošev manifest: Smeh igumana Stefana* (Belgrade: Partizanska knjiga, 1981), 26.

36. Njegoš, *Gorski vijenac,* vv. 131–32.

37. Ibid., vv. 2797–2802.

38. The idea of rebirth is enhanced by the abbot's comment that Christmas and New Year should be celebrated at the beginning of the spring.

39. Njegoš, *Gorski vijenac*, 660–62.

40. The characters express the author's views. "Having once attended the opera in Venice, [Njegoš] suddenly refused to do it again, finding that such performances are not suitable for a bishop because they 'cannot have a good effect on human hearts used to seriousness, instead of to what can be called shame and disgrace.'" Pavel Apollonovich Rovinskii, *Rovinski o Njegošu* (Cetinje, 1967), 133 (first published in Russian in 1889).

41. Njegoš, *Gorski vijenac*, 1517–20.

42. See Djilas, *Njegoš*, 205.

43. Njegoš, *Gorski vijenac*, 1490.

44. Velimirović, *Religija Njegoševa*, 166.

45. Njegoš, *Lažni car Šćepan Mali* (1851) vv. 1879–80.

46. Dvorniković, *Karakterologija Jugoslovena*, 970.

47. Quoted in ibid.

48. Njegoš, *Gorski vijenac*, vv. 2499–2502.

49. Nikolaj Velimirović states that the Manichean view of the human soul imprisoned in the body is more pronounced in Njegoš's poem *Luča mikrokozma*: "Body is a 'dark ruler' that enslaves the divine spark of the human mind; it is 'muddy,' and therefore 'opaque'—'mortality's opaque curtain'—which hides the heavens from the human view; it is the shackle of the soul, 'a burdensome physical shackle,' under whose yoke the soul groans," *Religija Njegoševa*, 79.

The God that creates an evil world is himself tainted with evil. Thus in a folk song a fairy predicts that Prince Marko will not die from a human hand but "from God, the old executioner." "Smrt Marka Kraljevića," in Karadžić, *Srpske narodne pjesme*, vol. 2, no. 74, v. 42.

50. Njegoš, *Gorski vijenac*, v. 301.

51. Ibid., vv. 585–86.

52. Ibid., vv. 866–67.

53. Ibid., vv. 631–32.

54. Stanzas 44 and 45. Translated by Enikő Molnár Basa.

55. Pavao Ritter Vitezović, *Odiljenje sigetsko*, in *Zrinski, Frankopan, Vitezović: Izabrana djela* (Zagreb: Matica hrvatska), 1976, 424.

56. Ibid., 420–21.

57. Andrija Kačić-Miošić, *Razgovor ugodni naroda slovinskoga* (Zagreb: Matica hrvatska, 1967), 261.

58. In an essay dealing with epic poems by a prominent twentieth-century Montenegrin Serb poet, Matija Bećković, the critic Ljubomir Simović makes the following comment: "In the poem 'Aleksa Marinkov's Grandson' the poet says that 'Montenegro has no other women—/ but sisters,' and female personalities in his poetry, as well as in this [tribal] language, are never lovers but exclusively 'homekeepers,' self-denying sisters and grieving mothers." "Epske poeme Matije Bećkovića," in Bećković (1976), 261.

59. Matija Bećković, who grew up in the tribe of Rovci in a remote area of the Dinaric highlands, says with reference to the people from his village, "The faithful of a tribe do not speak their own thoughts but the tribe's thoughts." Bećković, *Reče mi jedan čoek,* 166.

60. Daniel Rancour-Laferriere argues, however, that there is a masochistic trait in Tatiana's lasting devotion to Onegin, "the master of her fate." See *The Slave Soul of Russia* (New York: New York University Press, 1995), 86–89.

61. Serbian literature also contains works that expose the futility of violence. One of them is the novel *Gorski car* (The mountain tsar) in which the author, Svetolik Ranković (1863–99), shows the loneliness and self-destructiveness caused by violence in the life of a haiduk. But this well-written work, very different from the popular haiduk legends, has not attracted the attention it deserves. On the other hand, Janko Veselinović's *Hajduk Stanko* (1896)—which portrays the haiduk as a romantic hero—is one of the most popular Serbian novels.

62. However, even the Russian believers who rebel against the subordination to the state are not necessarily free of another deviation from religious universalism: the folk-worship. Nicholas Berdiaev made the following observation:

> The religious and the "people's" elements are so mixed up in Russian consciousness that it is difficult to distinguish them, and in their formal religion they are often almost identified. The people believe in a "Russian Christ," who is the national god, a peasant god with their own characteristics—it is a pagan tendency in the very bosom of Orthodoxy. This narrow and exclusive religious nationalism, foreign to Western Christianity and purely negative in its attitude towards Catholicism, is completely out of accord with the universalist spirit of Christ. *Dostoevsky,* 184–85.

63. Popović, *Vidovdan i časni krst,* 99.

64. Milorad Ekmečić, "Profiles of Societies in the Second Half of the

Nineteenth Century," in Ekmečić et al., *History of Yugoslavia* (New York: McGraw-Hill, 1974), 372.

65. Djilas relates the following experience from his elementary school days, when he used to read *The Mountain Wreath* to local peasants: "One could stop reciting at any verse, and someone else would take it up and continue. Sometimes people would interrupt the narrator to interpret passages, ardently and long. . . . These people hardly knew the Bible. For them *The Mountain Wreath* might have served as such a book." *Land without Justice*, 130.

66. Ibid., 206.

67. Ibid., 188.

68. Ibid., 208–9.

69. It is indicative of Djilas's fascination with Njegoš that he had published three studies of the poet before his extensive *Njegoš: Poet, Prince, Bishop*. In the first three writings Djilas argues against nationalist interpretations of Njegoš; in the last one he joins them.

70. Djilas, *Njegoš*, 426.

71. Dedijer, *Veliki buntovnik Milovan Đilas*, 43. Dedijer offers an additional detail about Djilas's fondness for *The Mountain Wreath*: "During the war Djilas told me that this was the book he always carried with him, not Marx's works" (156).

72. Djilas, *Wartime*, 283.

73. See Dedijer, *Veliki buntovnik Milovan Đilas*, 263–71.

74. Richard West, "The Newest Class," *Harper's*, September 1981, 24.

75. Djilas, *Njegoš*, 244.

76. George Urban, "A Conversation with Milovan Djilas," *Encounter*, December 1979, 24.

77. Djilas, *Njegoš*, 319.

78. Ibid.

79. Ivo Andrić, "Njegoševska čovečnost," in *Sabrana djela Ive Andrića*, vol. 13 (Sarajevo: Svjetlost, 1976), 51.

80. Velimirović, *Religija Njegoševa*, 181.

81. It has been translated into some languages, such as German and English, more than once.

82. Rizvić, *Kroz "Gorski vijenac,"* 11–12. In spite of his restraint, Rizvić's study was attacked by most Yugoslav literary critics, angry that he found any fault with Njegoš, an untouchable cultural icon.

83. Ibid., 12.

84. The analogies between the two works are very superficial. One of

Schiller's characters suggests that the enemy be struck on Christmas Day, but the reason for the suggestion, which was rejected, was the ease of entering the castle on the day when visitors bring presents to the bailiff.

There are two assassinations in Schiller's play (one reported, one witnessed on the scene) but, although the victims are foreign oppressors, one assassination is strongly condemned, and there is a lot of uneasiness about the other: Tell puts his crossbow away, never to use it again, and his wife shudders at the thoughts of touching the hand that launched the deadly arrow.

85. *Time*, April 22, 1966, 92.

86. John Simon, "The Shepherd Prince," *Book Week*, May 29, 1966, 11.

87. *Choice* (Chicago) 3, no. 9 (November 1966): 841.

88. Anthony West, "The Case for Headhunting," *New Yorker*, July 30, 1966, 82.

89. Albert B. Lord, "Father of Serbian Literature," *Saturday Review*, April 30, 1966, 29–30. Lord is best known for his study of south Slavic and Albanian oral poetry, *The Singer of Tales* (Cambridge: Harvard University Press, 1960).

NOTES TO CHAPTER 4

1. For more information about the myth of the Great Migration and the fallacies that support it, see Malcolm, *Kosovo*, 139–62. The condensation of a long process into a single event is a favorite myth-historical device. Mythical accounts of the Battle of Kosovo in 1389, for example, condense the almost nine-decade-long process of the subjugation of Serbia into a single battle. The myth of the Great Migration has something else in common with the Kosovo myth: the pattern of a brave stand against the infidels followed by a great national catastrophe. Noel Malcolm, for his part, sees the Great Migration myth as the central section of a three-part theological parallel between Serbia and Christ. The first phase consists of the parallel between the Battle of Kosovo and the crucifixion of Christ; "the second phase, corresponding to Christ's death and burial, is the withdrawal of the Serbian people from Kosovo in the [Great Migration], and the third phase, corresponding to the resurrection, is the reconquest of Kosovo by Serbian forces in 1912." *Kosovo*, 140.

2. Quoted in M. Pavić, foreword to Obradović, *Pismo Haralampiju*, 32–33. There is a connection between antiwesternism and hard-line policies in Serbia. The linguist Radoslav Katičić pointed out that "In the era of the

campaign against Serbian liberalism, in the early 1970s, one spokesman in a communist party forum said that it must be finally accepted that there is no Baroque in Serbian cultural history. This is an obvious untruth. There was no Baroque in Serbia but it was present among the Serbs in Hungary and Slavonia." *Globus* (Zagreb), August 9, 1996, 50.

3. The ecumenical patriarch in Istanbul, Antim V, also asked for a prohibition of Obradović's works. See Đurić, foreword, 41.

4. Ibid., 19.

5. Milorad Pavić, "Die serbische Vorromantik und Herder," in Potthoff, *Vuk Karadžić*, 182.

6. Đurić, foreword, 7.

7. The historian Stanoje Stanojević defines him thus: "St. Sava is the founder of Serbian literature and the originator of Serbian nationalism, which has become the main quality and the most distinguished trait of our national being, and the substance of our national life." *Sveti Sava*, 123.

8. Obradović, *Pismo Haralampiju*, 58.

9. Ibid., 45.

10. Obradović, *Izabrani spisi*, 363–64. *Mezimac* was first published in Buda in 1818.

11. Jovan Rajić, *Istorija raznih slavenskih narodov, najpače Bolgar, Horvatov i Serbov* (Vienna, 1794–95).

12. Djilas, *Njegoš*, 318–19.

13. M. Popović, *Vidovdan i časni krst*, 112.

14. Štokavian dialects, which cover most of Croatia and Serbia, and all of Bosnia-Herzegovina and Montenegro, form the basis of the standard languages in all these countries. The other two major central south Slavic dialects—čakavian and kajkavian—are spoken in Croatia only. The names of these dialects are based on their renderings of the word *what: što, ča,* and *kaj.*

15. Bonazza, "Bartholomäus Kopitar," 293. Bonazza points out that Kopitar was the coauthor of the Serbian-German-Latin dictionary of 1818, although Karadžić is listed as its sole author. Karadžić could not have written it by himself because he did not know Latin, and his German was insufficient at the time the dictionary was written (291–92).

16. Pavel Šafařík, *Slavianskiia drevnosti,* trans. O. Bodianskii (Moscow, 1848), 274. Dobrovský and Šafařík thought that the name *Spors* (Σπόροι)—the Slavs' original name according to the sixth-century Byzantine historian Prokopios—was a corruption of the name *Serbs.* See also Dobrovský, *Geschichte der Böhmischen Sprache und ältern Literatur* (Prague, 1818), 9–10.

17. See Karadžić (1849), 119. The chapter titled "Srbi svi i svuda" (Serbs All and Everywhere), 113–34, offers a concise statement of Karadžić's linguistically based Pan-Serbism.

18. See Kaspar Zeuss, *Die Deutschen und die Nachbarstämme* (Munich, 1837), 58, 67.

19. See Lubor Niederle, "Ueber die Σπόροι des Prokopios," *Archiv für slavische Philologie* 23 (1901): 130–33.

20. See Miodrag Vukić, "Vuk Karadžić zwischen Grimm und Goethe: Eine Skizze ihrer Wechselwirkung und Freundschaft," in Potthoff *Vuk Karadžić*, 134–48.

21. "Asanaginica" was not a Serbian heroic song, but a lyrical ballad about a woman who dies of grief after being separated from her children. Goethe became acquainted with it through Alberto Fortis's account of his travels on the eastern shore of the Adriatic Sea. Fortis's *Un viaggio in Dalmazia*, published in Venice in 1774, contained the ballad both in the original language and the Italian translation. The book was promptly translated into major European languages (the French and English translations appeared in 1778, the latter without the ballad) and made Morlaks very popular "noble savages." Fortis labeled the poem Morlakian (Karadžić called it Serbian), though Croatian folk singers from the Biokovo area were the source of all its versions. Prosper Merimée, Gerard de Nerval, Walter Scott, Alexander Pushkin, and Adam Mickiewicz also translated it.

22. *Goethes Werke*, section 2, vol. 41 (Weimar: Böhlau, 1903), 466.

23. Some "Illyrians" expected that Slovenes might become a part of the Croatian nation, but such an idea has been absent from Croatian political thought since the mid-nineteenth century.

24. The Croat Matija Ban, who settled in Serbia in 1844, is commonly regarded as being the first to use the term "Yugoslav," in a poem in 1835.

25. In his work *Croatia rediviva* (Zagreb, 1700), Pavao Ritter Vitezović expressed a desire for all south Slavs to unite under the Croatian name, but this was an isolated case, long before the advent of modern nationalism.

26. Banac, *The National Question in Yugoslavia*, 108. Although Starčević was a nationalist, he envisioned Croatia as ethnically and culturally pluralist because his concept of the Croatian nation was based primarily on what he regarded as the traditional territory of the Croatian state.

27. About the two approaches and their relation to Yugoslavism, see ibid., 108–11.

28. Jelavich, *South Slav Nationalisms*, 137.

29. Ibid., 243.

30. Ibid., 175.

31. Numerous examples of such identification by Serbian Orthodox clergy are contained in Hadrovics, *Le peuple serbe,* 112–18.

32. The only significant territorial change of the two entities consisted in the enlargement of Bosnia, mainly at the expense of Croatia, under Turkish rule.

33. Karadžić, *Kovčežić,* 119. The historian Josef Konstantin Jireček deals with titles of Serbian kings in *Istorija Srba,* vol. 3 (Belgrade: Geca Kon, 1923), 3–5. According to him, "At the time of the Nemanjić dynasty, the shortest royal title is "Serbian king" or "king of all Serbian land' " (4).

34. Konstantinović, *Filosofija palanke,* 238 n.

35. Popović, *Vidovdan i časni krst,* 144.

36. *Vid* in south Slavic appears to be a variant of the form *Vit* found in east and west Slavic. Some linguists reconstruct the word as meaning "lord." See Moszyński, *Die vorchristliche Religion der Slaven,* 61–63.

37. *The First Nine Books of the Danish History of Saxo Grammaticus,* trans. Oliver Elton (London, 1894), 393–95.

38. Ibid., 397.

39. "Pjesma domaćinu od bolje ruke," in Karadžić, *Srpske narodne pjesme,* vol. 1, no. 164, vv. 1–3.

40. Đurić, *Kosovski boj,* 21.

41. The military saints cannot, however, claim an exclusive prerogative to military deeds: "the Virgin Mary, the apostle Andrew, and some other saints were also active as military protectors of the Byz[antines]." *The Oxford Dictionary of Byzantium* (New York: Oxford University Press, 1991), 1374.

42. In Catholic Slavic countries the name Vid (Vit) can also denote St. Vitus. The Catholic Church used the identical name to suppress the cult of the pagan god, but there is no St. Vitus in the Serbian or any other Orthodox church.

43. According to Vuk Karadžić, the first Serbian calendar appeared in 1766. See *Dela Vuka Karadžića* (Belgrade: Prosveta, 1969), 240.

44. For a more detailed account of the gradual transformation of Vid's Day into a national and church holiday, see Popović, *Vidovdan i časni krst,* 137–41.

45. Miodrag Popović finds a moral victory of paganism over Christianity in one of the oldest folk songs containing the myth of Heavenly Serbia, "The Prince's Supper," in which Obilić is falsely accused by Prince Lazar as a traitor. See *Vidovdan i časni krst,* 99–110.

46. Ibid., 150.

Some prominent twentieth-century Serbian writers did not celebrate the war god. Rastko Petrović's novel, *Dan šesti* (The sixth day), completed in 1934, depicts the chaos and misery of the withdrawal of Serbian forces through Albania in 1915, in which he participated. Because of its gloomy depiction of that military campaign, the novel could not be published in the monarchist Yugoslavia. His contemporary, Miloš Crnjanski (1893–1977), forcefully expressed a nihilistic disillusionment with the cult of war and death in *Vid's Day Songs*, written around 1920. He begins "Hymn," the first poem in the cycle, with the statement, "We have nothing. Neither God nor master. / Blood is our God." *Sabrane pesme*, 11. "The Toast," like most poems in the same cycle, contains a sarcastic expression of the spirit of necrophilia implicit in the Vid's Day cult:

> *Long live the cemetery!*
> *It alone is beautiful, clean and faithful.*
> *Long live rocks and ruins!*
> *Let what blooms high up be cursed.*
>
> *We are for death! (13)*

47. Ranke, *History of Servia*, 203. Karađorđe's behavior made Ranke comment that "His character much resembles that of the heroes celebrated in the national songs of Servia" (207). However, Ranke was not a hostile observer. He wrote of the Serbs and Serbia with sympathy, which is why this work has been published in Serbian translation more than once.

48. Ibid., 206.

49. Dragoslav Janković, "Vođi i učesnici prvog ustanka," in Minčeta and Vučinić, *Srbi i demokratija*, 9.

50. Petrovich, *A History of Modern Serbia*, 1: 213–14.

51. *New York Times*, June 14, 1903, 11. The leader of the assassination plot was Dragutin Dimitrijević Apis, a colonel of the Serbian general staff and president of the terrorist organization Black Hand. Eleven years later he organized the assassination of the heir to the Austro-Hungarian throne in Sarajevo. The Orthodox metropolitan of Belgrade condoned the 1903 killings.

52. Nikola Stojanović, "Srbi i Hrvati," *Srpski književni glasnik* 4 (1902): 1149–59. The magazine that published the article "at the time undoubtedly represented the meeting place and mouthpiece of the intellectual elite of the young Serbian middle class, its most liberal and educated segment."

Marko Ristić, *Politička književnost* (Zagreb: Naprijed, 1958), 187. The article was promptly reprinted by a Serbian newspaper in Zagreb, and led to anti-Serbian demonstrations there.

53. Njegoš, *Gorski vijenac*, v. 132.

54. Popović-Obradović, "Zablude o "zlatnom dobu,' " 15. Another Serbian analyst had written in 1928, "We have not had a real and true parliamentarism either before, in the Kingdom of Serbia, or today, in the Kingdom of Serbs, Croats and Slovenes, although ever since the 1888 Constitution we have lived, and still do, in the illusion that we indeed have it." Fedor Nikić, "Da li smo imali i da li danas imamo parlamentarizam," in Minčeta and Vučinić, *Srbi i demokratija*, 133.

55. The document was largely unknown until it was published in its entirety for the first time by Milenko Vukićević in 1906. See "Program spoljne politike Srbije na koncu 1844. godine," *Delo* 38 (1906): 321–36.

56. Hehn, "The Origins of Modern Pan-Serbism," 159.

57. Archives Czartoryski 5404, in *Spomenik Srpske kraljevske akademije*, vol. 91 (Belgrade, 1939), 105–15.

58. František A. Zach, "Plan," in *Spomenik Srpske kraljevske akademije*, vol. 91, 75–102.

59. Hehn, "The Origins of Modern Pan-Serbism," 163.

60. Ibid., 158.

61. Ibid., 159. The most prominent nineteenth-century Serbian socialist, Svetozar Marković (1846–75), was opposed to Garašanin's idea of a unitary Greater Serbia. Marković realized that the attempt to bring all Serbs into one nation-state would lead to a conflict with analogous attempts by other nations. Instead he advocated a federation of Serb lands within a wider federation that would include Bulgaria and "could very easily expand into a federation of the peoples on the Balkan Peninsula and even further," across the Sava and Danube Rivers. However, like Garašanin and other proponents of a Greater Serbia, he regarded Bosnia, Herzegovina, Montenegro, and some Habsburg-ruled south Slavic territories as Serb lands. Bosnia, for example, in his view was "the land where the Serbian people are divided into three religions." *Sabrani spisi*, vol. 4 (Belgrade: Kultura, 1965), 422.

62. Todor Ilić, quoted by Dedijer, *The Road to Sarajevo*, 347. Friedrich Heer devotes a chapter titled "Franz Ferdinand, Gavrilo Princip, Adolf Hitler" to the similarities between the beliefs of the young revolutionaries of the Young Bosnia movement and those of Hitler in *Der Glaube des Adolf Hitler: Anatomie einer politischen Religiosität* (Munich: Bechtle, 1968), 171–

79. Hitler also was ecstatic about the murder, because Ferdinand's intention to make Austro-Slavs equal partners in the Austro-Hungarian monarchy would have made it even less Germanic and more stable:

> When the news of the murder of Archduke Francis Ferdinand arrived in Munich . . . I was at first seized with worry that the bullets may have been shot from the pistols of German students, who, out of indignation at the heir apparent's continuous work of Slavization, wanted to free the German people from this internal enemy. . . . But when, soon afterward, I heard the names of the supposed assassins, and moreover read that they had been identified as Serbs, a light shudder began to run through me at this vengeance of inscrutable destiny. The greatest friend of the Slavs had fallen beneath the bullets of Slavic fanatics. *Mein Kampf*, trans. Ralph Manheim (Boston: Houghton Mifflin, 1943), 158–59.

63. Quoted by Zvonimir Kulundžić in *Atentat na Stjepana Radića* (Zagreb: Stvarnost, 1967), 207.

64. The assassin was treated very lightly. Officials changed the penal law before his trial in order to spare him from capital punishment. In his report to the secretary of state, the American ambassador characterized the trial as disgusting. Two collaborators and instigators were freed, while Račić served his sentence living in the villa of the director of the penitentiary and enjoying freedom of movement.

65. Intellectual and political leaders were prime targets. The internationally renowned historian Milan Šufflay was killed in 1931. His assassination drew protests from Albert Einstein, Thomas Mann, and others. See "Einstein Accuses Yugoslavian Rulers in Savant's Murder," *New York Times,* May 6, 1931, A1. Another prominent historian, Ivo Pilar, who published *Die südslawische Frage und der Weltkrieg* in 1918 under the pseudonym Südland, was found dead in 1933, soon after the authorities had identified him as the author. The official who led the Croatian Peasant Party after its other leaders had been killed or jailed, Josip Predavec, was assassinated the same year.

66. "Iseljavanje Arnauta," in Čović, *Izvori velikosrpske agresije,* 111. Čubrilović's lecture, given in Belgrade in 1937, was published for the first time in 1988.

67. *Documents diplomatiques français, 1932–1939,* series 1, vol. 7 (Paris: Imprimerie nationale, 1979), 650.

68. "Ustaše," *Enciklopedija Jugoslavije* (Zagreb: Leksikografski zavod, 1971).

69. Svetozar Pribićević (1875–1936), leader of the Serb Autonomous Party since 1903, cofounder of the Croato-Serbian Coalition in 1905, and an architect of the unitary state in 1918, entered a coalition with the Croatian Peasant Party in 1927 to fight Belgrade centralist policies.

70. See *Ekonomska politika* (Belgrade), January 27, 1969, 12, for federal officials; and *Statistički godišnjak Jugoslavije, 1973* (Belgrade: Savezni zavod za statistiku), 351, for the general population data of the 1971 census.

71. *Frankfurter Allgemeine Zeitung*, August 24, 1983, 3.

72. "In most of the contested Serbian constituencies for the Federal Chamber, one of the candidates represented the Partisan (and Party) 'old guard,' typically a much decorated hero of the Partisan war; his opponent tended to be a man of the reformed and 'liberalized,' post-Rankovic Party machine. It was the old Partisans, the 'wild' and unwanted candidates labeled as communist 'conservatives,' who won over the younger 'official' Party-sponsored men." Dennison I. Rusinow, *American Universities Field Staff Reports*, Southeast Europe Series, vol. 16, no. 6, 2.

73. Vernon V. Aspaturian, "Conceptualizing Eurocommunism: Some Preliminary Observations," in *Eurocommunism Between East and West* (Bloomington: Indiana University Press, 1980), 14.

NOTES TO CHAPTER 5

1. Vladeta Vučković describes the event in an article titled "Sahrana jednog mita" (The Burial of a Myth), *Naša reč* (N. Harrow, Middlesex), no. 368 (October 1985): 2.

2. *Žrtve rata 1941–1945* (Belgrade: Muzej žrtava genocida and Savezni zavod za statistiku, 1997), 16 vols.

3. Myers and Campbell, *The Population of Yugoslavia*, 23.

4. Kočović, *Žrtve drugog svetskog rata*, 123, 125; Žerjavić, *Population Losses in Yugoslavia*, 154.

5. Žerjavić, *Population Losses in Yugoslavia*, 156.

6. The difference between Kočović's and Žerjavić's estimates is by far the largest in the case of Montenegrin losses: twenty thousand versus fifty thousand. Kočović arrived at a much higher figure because he assumed a high population growth in Montenegro in 1931–41, and an even higher one in 1941–48.

7. Kočović, *Žrtve drugog svetskog rata*, 124–25.

8. Ibid., 65; Žerjavić, *Population Losses in Yugoslavia*, 151.

9. Kočović, *Žrtve drugog svetskog rata*, 70; Žerjavić, *Population Losses in*

Yugoslavia, 150. Žerjavić, who became acquainted with Kočović's study as he was finishing his own study, points out the reasons for some discrepancies between the two on 165–68.

10. The massacre is named after the Austrian town where British forces extradited Croatian soldiers and civilians, who had sought refuge in that country, to the Yugoslav authorities. The term also refers to those victims who were not able to enter Austria and were captured by the Yugoslav army.

11. *Enciklopedija Leksikografskog zavoda*, vol. 3 (Zagreb, 1958), 648–49.

12. Ibid., vol. 4 (1959), 322.

13. *Intervju* (Belgrade), August 5, 1983, 9.

14. Bulatović, *Koncentracioni logor Jasenovac*, 413. An analysis of the numbers of victims of the Ustaša concentration camps is offered by Mirko Peršen (who was an inmate in one of them) in the chapter "Bilanca smrti," in *Ustaški logori*, 313–29.

15. Vuk Drašković, *Odgovori* (Belgrade: Glas, 1987), 102. The American writer Brian Hall observed similar play with the number of victims at a World War II German concentration camp in Belgrade. Unlike the Jasenovac camp records, many of which were destroyed, the meticulously kept records of executions at the Belgrade camp, known as Banjica, have been preserved. A record made shortly before the camp was closed, whose photocopy is exhibited in the museum at the site of the camp, refers to the victim number 23,233. Hall noticed that a "wooden plaque carved by survivors of the camp claimed a total of forty thousand dead. By the time my brochure for Belgrade's museums was printed in 1989, the number was eighty thousand." *The Impossible Country*, 106.

16. Žerjavić, *Population Losses in Yugoslavia*, 89.

17. Ibid., 91.

18. Kočović, *Žrtve drugog svetskog rata u Jugoslaviji* 2d ed. (Sarajevo: Svjetlost, 1990), xviii.

19. Data presented at the conference titled "Jasenovac: 'Dark Secret' of the Holocaust, 1941–1945, in the Former Yugoslavia" at CUNY's Kingsborough Community College, October 30–31, 1997. In his three-volume study of the Jasenovac concentration camp, *Koncentracioni logor Jasenovac 1941–1945: Dokumenta* (Belgrade: Narodna knjiga and Spomen-područje Jasenovac, 1986, 1987), Miletić listed the names of about thirty-thousand victims.

20. Nevertheless, as if the realistic numbers were not horrible enough, many Serbs continue using proven falsehoods, even in international scholarly publications. For example, Miloš Vasić cites "some 500,000–700,000

dead" in the Ustaša extermination camps in "The Yugoslav Army and the Post-Yugoslav Armies," in *Yugoslavia and After*, ed. David A. Dyker and Ivan Vejvoda (London: Longman, 1996), 122.

21. Ramet, "The Catholic Church in Yugoslavia," 189.

22. Alexander, *The Triple Myth*, 2. See also Ramet, "The Catholic Church in Yugoslavia," 181–86. In her book *Balkan Babel* Ramet notes that, contrary to the Yugoslav communist regime's portrayal of "the Catholic Church's role during Word War II monochromatically as the advocacy of Croatian independence and Ustasha rule, a rather substantial number of Catholic clergymen actually cooperated with or fought on the side of the partisans" (136–37).

23. Terzić, *Jugoslavija u aprilskom ratu 1941*, 63.

24. Ibid., 65.

25. Viktor Novak, *Magnum crimen: Pola vijeka klerikalizma u Hrvatskoj* (Belgrade: Nova knjiga, 1986).

26. *Assassins au nom de Dieu* (Paris: La Vigie, 1951); *Ubice u ime božje* (Belgrade: Višnjić, 1987).

27. Velimir Terzić, *Slom Kraljevine Jugoslavije 1941: Uzroci i posledice poraza* (Belgrade: Narodna knjiga, 1982).

28. Vasilije Krestić, "O genezi genocida nad Srbima u NDH," *Književne novine* (Belgrade), September 15, 1986, 5.

29. Report no. 1504/43, published as Document no. 38, in *Zbornik dokumenata i podataka o Narodnooslobodilačkom ratu naroda Jugoslavije*, vol. 12, book 3, *Dokumenti nemačkog Rajha 1943* (Belgrade: Institute for Military History, 1978), 172.

30. Milazzo, *The Chetnik Movement*, 10.

31. Cohen, *Serbia's Secret War*, 113.

32. Regarding the alleged "nationalist" rapes, the report by an independent commission, formed by Srdja Popović, Dejan Janča, and Tanja Petovar, stated that rapes and other crimes against human dignity and morality were significantly higher within each Kosovo ethnic group than in contacts between members of different groups, but noted that "If each 'interethnic' crime is interpreted as a *political act* and as an expression of nationalist hatred, and if it is given huge publicity, a single such event suffices to scare the entire population of Kosovo." *Kosovski čvor: Drešiti ili seći* (Belgrade: Hronos, 1990), 47.

33. Alija Izetbegović, *Islamska deklaracija* (Sarajevo: Bosna, 1990). This "program for the Islamization of Muslims and Muslim peoples" (1), written in 1970, states that an "Islamic order can be established only in the coun-

tries where Muslims constitute the majority of the population" (37), but at the time Izetbegović wrote it he could expect that the Muslims' high birthrate would make them a majority in Bosnia within a few decades. He also stated that "There is no peace or coexistence between the 'Islamic faith' and non-Islamic social and political institutions" (22), and set "a general rule: the Islamic movement must and may undertake the takeover of power as soon as it is morally and numerically so strong that it can not only overthrow the existing non-Islamic authority but also build a new Islamic one" (43). The author thinks that the goal of "the creation of a large Islamic federation from Morocco to Indonesia, from tropical Africa to Central Asia" (48) is realistic (3), and repeatedly scorns Turkey for having adopted secularism: "Turkey as an Islamic state ruled the world; Turkey as a European plagiarism is a third-rate country" (4).

34. In 1961 Serbs constituted 42.8 percent of the population of Bosnia-Herzegovina, Muslims 25.6 percent. By 1991 the ratio of Muslims increased to 43.7 percent while that of Serbs dropped to 31.4. The resentment of the high Muslim birthrate resulted in an additional oppression of raped Muslim women in the 1990s war: some of them were forced to carry their pregnancies to term and bear their captors' "Serbian babies." Raped Croatian women, whose birthrate is low, were less frequently subjected to this treatment.

35. The 1974 Constitution subordinated territorial defense forces (organized by political authorities in the various republics) to the army, and assigned one seat in the newly formed ten-member state presidency to the representative of the armed forces (the other members being one representative from each of the six federal republics and two autonomous provinces, and Tito). The army was promptly dubbed the "seventh republic." At the same time, a general became minister of internal affairs, for the first time since 1946, and twenty-one generals and other high-ranking officers took over key party posts. See Gow, *Legitimacy and the Military*, 59–61.

36. "Triptihon," *Književne novine*, April 1, 1977, 6.

37. Bernardo Valli, "Dobrica Ćosić: Serbia mia, tragico romanzo," *La Repubblica* (Rome), August 10, 1991, 29.

38. *Intervju*, December 13, 1991, 8. The Armenian Church is not Orthodox, but Pavić apparently regards Armenia as a part of the Byzantine world.

39. Ibid.

40. *Nezavisimaia gazeta* (Moscow), April 29, 1993, 5.

41. *Intervju*, December 13, 1991, 8. The adjective "Byzantine" fits Pavić's work better if it is used in a pejorative sense. The following characterization

of Pavić's writing can be taken as a manifestation of such Byzantinism: "The trick is to say something that can't be contradicted and at the same time eludes any paraphrasable meaning, and it is a trick that Pavić never tires of." Thomas M. Dish, "Two Sides of the Story," *Book World*, July 11, 1993, 5.

42. "Serbo-Croatian" can be regarded as one language in the sense that various štokavian dialects are for the most part mutually understandable, but specific linguistic traditions in Bosnia, Croatia, and Serbia have shaped the common štokavian stock into three distinct literary languages, and Montenegrin may emerge as a fourth.

43. Ćosić, *Srpsko pitanje*, 19.

44. Đukić, *Čovek u svom vremenu*, 209.

45. Bećković, *Reče mi jedan čoek*, 166.

46. Chris Hedges, "Election Aside, Milosevic Plans to Rule Yugoslavia," *New York Times*, November 4, 1996, A10.

47. The panel was headed first by the academy president, Dušan Kanazir, and subsequently by its vice president, Antonije Isaković. One member of the panel was the long-lived Vasa Čubrilović, a participant in the 1914 plot to assassinate the heir to the Austro-Hungarian throne, and the author of a 1938 plan for the expulsion of the Kosovo Albanians.

48. It was first published, unofficially, in a limited edition in Belgrade in September 1986. Because of great interest it has been republished several times since.

49. *Memorandum*, 278.

50. Ibid., 258, 263.

51. Ibid., 275.

52. Ibid., 294.

53. Ibid., 284.

54. Ibid., 298.

55. Ibid., 297.

56. Ibid., 298.

57. Đukić, *Čovek u svom vremenu*, 138.

58. Ibid., 308.

59. Interview in *Politika* (Belgrade), July 27, 1991, 7.

60. Anne Herbst. "Serbische Bischöfe gegen Patriarchen," *G2W* (Zollikon-Zurich), no. 3 (1996): 14.

61. "Serb Orthodox Church Accused of Fanning Bosnia Strife," *Los Angeles Times*, August 12, 1995, B5.

62. Pribićević, *La dictature du roi Alexandre*, 245–46. Pribićević contrib-

uted to the creation of a unitary Yugoslavia but, disappointed with the abuse of centralism, became one of the leading advocates of federalism.

63. Cohen, *Serbia's Secret War*, 15. About the support the Serbian church gave to the Nazi puppet regime in Serbia and to the pan-Serb Četnik guerrilla movement, see also Štefan, *Srpska pravoslavna crkva*.

64. Velimirović, *Govori srpskom narodu*, 161–62. The procedure of canonization of Bishop Velimirović was initiated in 1985.

65. Chris Hedges, "An 'Us vs. Them' Mantra Raises the Balkan Fever," *New York Times*, January 11, 1997, A4.

66. "Predlog crkvenonacionalnog programa." The periodical, as well as the publishing house of the same name, is run by the clergy of the Šabac-Valjevo parchy.

67. Ibid., 5.

68. Jevtić, *Od Kosova do Jadovna*, 7.

69. van Dartel, "The Nations and the Churches in Yugoslavia," 284.

70. "Pismo srpskog patrijarha Pavla lordu Carringtonu," AKSA (Zagreb), no. 32 (October 1991): 10–11.

71. "Appel aux évêques serbes," *Le monde*, November 27, 1991, 2.

72. "Serbian Church Assails Belgrade," *New York Times*, May 29, 1992, A10.

73. "Deklaracija protiv genocida nad srpskim narodom," 22.

74. Ibid. In messages directed to the Orthodox East, the role of Serbia as a rampart against Roman Catholicism is emphasized.

75. Ibid.

76. Komnenić, *Kosovski polom*, 57.

77. Mirko Đorđević, "Duh trećeq milenijuma," *Republika* (Belgrade), May 1–15, 1995, 4.

78. Đorđe J. Janić, "Dan opredeljivanja—Vidovdan," *Pravoslavlje* (Belgrade), July 1, 1995, 3.

79. "Predlog srpskog crkvenonacionalnog programa," 11.

80. Popović, *Pravoslavna crkva i ekumenizam*, 184.

81. Ibid., 202.

82. Ibid., 189.

83. Ibid., 190.

84. Dostoevsky was the subject of Popović's doctoral dissertation, and in 1940 he published the book *Dostojevski o Evropi i slovenstvu* (Dostoevsky on Europe and the Slavs).

85. No. 88 (1981) of *Le messager Orthodoxe* (Paris), devoted to Justin Popović, contains articles by and about him.

86. Bremer, *Ekklesiale Struktur*, 277.

87. Although they attended, the Russians also angrily rejected the union, and arrested Metropolitan Isidore of Russia upon his return from Florence, where he had signed the bull.

88. Among them, Dimitrije Dimitrijević, Blagota Gardašević, and Čedomir Drašković.

89. *Književne novine*, September 15, 1989, 3.

90. Dušan Makavejev, "Smrtoljublje," in Čolović and Mimica, *Druga Srbija*, 110–11.

91. Poets as awakeners of tribal mysticism have played important roles in other violent nationalist movements too, but their poems, calling for readiness to rise to arms against evil enemies, are not necessarily gloomy or frightening. In his work on Italian Fascism, Giuseppe Antonio Borgese singled out a "delightful" short poem by Giosuè Carducci, "the singer of the purest memories of Italy," which celebrates the virtue and modest glory of a tiny Alpine rural commune in the Middle Ages. His idyllic vision of shepherd citizens ready to become warriors in a just, defensive war, whenever "the Hun or the Slav" should menace their innocent liberty, "provided the foundation of [poet, writer, and warlord] d'Annunzio's political system, which in turn was to be the foundation of Mussolini's and Hitler's regimes." *Goliath: The March of Fascism* (New York: Viking, 1938), 158. The essential ingredient common to poems that have served various fascist adventures is fear—fear that an innocent, superior, "heavenly" people would be crushed by evil enemies.

92. Karadžić, *Pamtivek*, 59.

93. "Jutra pola nema," in Karadžić, *Pamtivek*, 11.

94. Marko Vešović, "Estetizam percepcije," in Karadžić, *Pamtivek*, 77.

95. Čolović, *Bordel ratnika*, 89.

96. Ibid., 90.

97. Belgrade: Prosveta, vols. 1 and 2, 1972; vol. 3, 1975; vol. 4, 1979.

98. Published by Harcourt Brace Jovanovich, New York, with the overall title *This Land, This Time: A Time of Death*, 1978; *Reach to Eternity*, 1980; *South to Destiny*, 1981; *Into the Battle*, 1983.

99. D. Keith Mano, *National Review*, July 25, 1980, 913. James Sloan found the novel equally disappointing: "the scenes shift mechanically, the philosophical meditations lack authority, and the characters suffer from peculiar anonymity." *New York Times Book Review*, February 3, 1980, 15.

100. Ćosić, *Deobe*, 9.

101. Ibid., 534–35.

102. Ibid., 652–53.

103. Drašković, *Nož*, 34–35.

104. Ibid., 275.

105. Ibid., 280.

106. Makavejev, "Smrtoljublje," 111. Kiš, Selenić, and Pavić are popular Serbian novelists.

107. *Ascension* (*Vaznesenje*) received a novel-of-the-year award in Belgrade in 1990.

108. Lubarda, *Preobraženje*, 15.

109. Ibid., 28.

110. Ibid., 32.

111. Ibid., 44. *Kolo* is a popular type of folk dance performed in a circle.

112. Ibid., 13.

113. Lubarda, *Gordo posrtanje*, 7.

114. Letter to Tugomir Alaupović of July 8, 1919, in *Sveske Zadužbine Ive Andrića* (Belgrade), year 2, vol. 2 (December 1983), 303.

115. Lubarda, *Srpska bespuća*, 135.

116. Branislav Lainović, quoted in Cigar, *Genocide in Bosnia*, 25.

117. *Molitva*, vol. 2, 345.

118. *Proljeće na jugu* (1982), *Ljeto na gori, 1941* (1987), and *Biskupov dnevnik '41* (1989).

119. The most powerful Yugoslav literary work dealing with the ghastly World War II pits is Ivan Goran Kovačić's poem "Jama" (The pit, 1943). The nationality and religion of executioners and victims are never mentioned in it.

120. Milena Davidović, "La fin de l'empire de la nécessité," *Les temps modernes* (Paris), summer 1994, 119–20.

121. Georgie Anne Geyer, "Why the War in Bosnia Wasn't 'Inevitable,' " *Chicago Tribune*, February 16, 1994, I17.

122. Plavšić developed a "biological" theory of the genocide in Bosnia, advancing the idea that Muslims had a defective gene and that the "cleansing" of Muslims and Croats was a "natural phenomenon." Refuting the notion that atrocities are committed by the uneducated, Neil Kressel offers up the examples of Radovan Karadžić and Cambodia's Pol Pot, who got his inspiration for an idyllic agricultural society at the "playing fields" of the Sorbonne. See Kressel, *Mass Hate*.

123. Quoted in Čolović, *Bordel ratnika*, 5–6.

124. Russia's interest in the Adriatic ports started with Peter the Great and remained strong in the second half of the twentieth century. During

his visit to Yugoslavia in late 1976, Leonid I. Brezhnev apparently requested from Tito the use of the port of Kotor as a Soviet naval base. See Drew Middleton, "Yugoslavs Report That Tito Rebuffed Brezhnev on Air and Naval Rights and a Role in the Warsaw Pact," *New York Times,* January 9, 1977, 8.

125. The Montenegrin writer Jevrem Brković, who bravely opposed the participation of his homeland in the aggressions against Croatia and Bosnia-Herzegovina, asserts that "the so-called Montenegrin Serbdom started with the rule of Petrović-Njegoš." Brković, *Glosarij,* 120.

126. See Philip J. Cohen, "The Complicity of Serbian Intellectuals in Genocide in the 1990s," in Cushman and Meštrović, *This Time We Knew,* 39–64.

127. The responsibility of the elites for the eruption of the latest Balkan war is not exceptional at all. Erich Fromm points out that "major wars in modern times and most wars between the states of antiquity were not caused by dammed-up aggression, but by instrumental aggression of the military and political elites." *The Anatomy of Human Destructiveness,* 215.

NOTES TO CHAPTER 6

1. Emmert, "Kosovo," 77–78.
2. Laffan, *The Guardians,* 3.
3. Ibid., 263.
4. Ibid., 260.
5. Ibid., 2.
6. Emmert, "Kosovo," 78.
7. Ibid.
8. Edward Crankshaw, *The Fall of the House of Habsburg* (New York: Penguin, 1963), 377. Arthur Ponsonby explains that suddenness: "It was extremely difficult to make the Serbian cause popular" following the murder in Sarajevo. "The Serbian case, therefore, had to be written up, and 'poor little Serbia' had to be presented as an innocent small nationality subjected to the offensive brutality of the Austrians." *Falsehood in War-Time* (New York: Dutton, 1928), 43. However, the tremendous success of the "write-up" requires additional explanation.
9. Ivan Meštrović, at the time a utopian believer in the Yugoslav idea, worked on the project for the Vidovdan Temple from 1907 to 1911. In that period he produced a number of fine sculptures for the projected temple,

but the realization of the uninspired eclectic design of the temple itself was never attempted.

10. Second College Edition (New York, 1970). In fact, the number of sovereign states in the Balkans was reduced from eight to six after the First World War, since Serbia, Montenegro, and Balkan areas of the Austro-Hungarian monarchy became parts of Yugoslavia. Such a gross mistake in a renowned dictionary is ultimately due to the fact that myths are often given more credibility than reality.

11. An exception can be found in a number of Italian dictionaries that define balkanization as the spreading of conditions that are believed to prevail in Balkan countries, without reference to political fragmentation. For example, "balkanize—to reduce a country to chaotic conditions regarded as typical of Balkan countries." *Dizionario Garzanti della lingua italiana* (Milan, 1965). Geographic proximity may have made the Italians more aware of the fact that violence and disorder are an endemic feature of a large part of the Balkans (as they are of a part of Italy) regardless of the way the territory is divided.

12. Norway became independent of Sweden in 1905, Finland of Russia in 1917, and Iceland of Denmark in 1944.

13. The Benelux countries are another European proof that small countries are not necessarily a threat to peace.

14. Benjamin Schwartz, "The Diversity Myth: America's Leading Export," *Atlantic Monthly*, May 1995, 58.

15. F. Engels, "The Danish-Prussian Armistice," in *Karl Marx, Frederick Engels: Collected Works*, vol. 7 (New York: International Publishers, 1977), 423. First published in the *Neue Rheinische Zeitung*, no. 99 (September 10, 1848). Engels's contempt for Scandinavians matches the present widespread contempt for the Balkan peoples: "Scandinavianism is enthusiasm for the brutal, sordid, piratical, Old Norse national traits, for that deep-rooted inner life which is unable to express its exuberant ideas and sentiments in words, but can express them only in deeds, namely in rudeness toward women, perpetual drunkenness and wild berserk frenzy alternating with tearful sentimentality" (422).

16. Ramet, "The Albanians of Kosovo," 354–55. The desire to secure Kosovo as an integral part of Serbia was the main catalyst for the rise of extreme nationalism in Serbia in the 1980s. The newly independent Republic of Macedonia is also adversely affected by the presence of a very large Albanian minority, another result of the borders drawn in 1913.

17. "The Pact of London," 439.

18. Ibid., 438. There was nothing exceptional in the Entente powers' bargaining with other nations' territories. Austria also wooed Italy by offering it Dalmatian Croatia.

19. Quoted in Sunley, "Sold on Serbia," 15.

20. Ferdinand Schevill, *The Balkan Peninsula and the Near East* (London: Bell, 1922), 507.

21. See Arnold Suppan, *Jugoslawien und Österreich 1918–1938* (Vienna: Verlag für Geschichte und Politik; Munich: Oldenbourg, 1996), 421–37.

22. Ibid., 437.

23. Pozzi, *Black Hand*, 54–55. Pozzi was for nearly thirty years a member of the French and British intelligence services in the Balkans and Central Europe.

24. Ibid., 85.

25. Charles Rivet, *Chez les Slaves libérés: En Yougoslavie* (Paris: Librairie académique, 1919), 252.

26. "Yugoslavia: History of Serbia: The Yugoslav period," *Encyclopedia Britannica*, 1996.

27. Cohen, *Serbia's Secret War*, 72.

28. Wilhelm Hoettl, *The Secret Front: The Story of Nazi Political Espionage* (New York: Praeger, 1954), 131.

29. Prince Pavle, probably the most civilized member of the Karađorđević dynasty, was an Anglophile, but he was accused of being a Nazi sympathizer and was subjected to humiliating treatment by the British in his exile because he had refused to follow the reckless advice against the signing of the pact. See Neil Balfour and Sally Mackay, *Paul of Yugoslavia: Britain's Maligned Friend* (London: Hamilton, 1980).

30. See Tomasevich, *The Chetniks*, 50.

31. Parrott, *The Tightrope*, 105, 104.

32. Winston S. Churchill, *The Second World War*, vol. 3 (Boston: Houghton Mifflin, 1950), 168.

33. William L. Shirer, *The Rise and Fall of the Third Reich* (New York: Simon and Schuster, 1960), 824.

34. *The Oxford Companion to World War II* (Oxford: Oxford University Press, 1995), 109. At the Yugoslav negotiators' insistence, the agreement to join the Tripartite Pact forbade Germany to move its troops over Yugoslav territory. This is one of the reasons "the Belgrade *coup* can be said to have come at exactly the right moment from the German point of view. Its overall effect on the Balkan campaign was to speed up considerably the

military operations and particularly the transport of troops from 'Marita' [codeword for German military campaign in Greece] back northward." Martin L. van Creveld, *Hitler's Strategy, 1940–1941: The Balkan Clue* (Cambridge: Cambridge University Press, 1973), 182; see also 151–54. About the coup, see also Jacob B. Hoptner, *Yugoslavia in Crisis, 1934–1941* (New York: Columbia University Press, 1962), 247–92.

35. "Homogena Srbija," in Čović, *Izvori velikosrpske agresije*, 147. The Bosnian Serb lawyer Stevan Moljević, one of Mihailović's top advisors, wrote the document in June 1941. The document lists all the areas that would form part of such a Serbia, comprising all of Yugoslavia with the exception of Slovenia and a drastically reduced Croatia. It is similar to most plans for a Greater Serbia, including those guiding the organizers of the 1990s wars.

36. Sunley, "Sold on Serbia," 16.

37. There is still little awareness of this event in spite of the coverage it has received. Major studies of it are Julius Epstein, *Operation Keelhaul: The Story of Forced Repatriation from 1944 to the Present* (Old Greenwich, Conn.: Devin-Adair, 1973); Nicholas Bethell, *The Last Secret* (New York: Basic Books, 1974); Nikolai Tolstoy, *The Minister and the Massacres* (London: Century Hutchinson, 1986); and Anthony Cowgill et al., *The Repatriations from Austria in 1945* (London: Sinclair-Stevenson, 1990).

38. The trials were held in Ljubljana from April 1948 to October 1949.

39. It also included imperialist efforts to bring Albania and Bulgaria under Belgrade's rule in a Balkan federation.

40. PRO/FO/R/132/8/092, December 8, 1943, quoted by Nora Beloff in *Tito's Flawed Legacy* (Boulder: Westview, 1985), 105.

41. David Hart, "What Are We Fighting For?" *Spectator,* January 16, 1993, 14. One of Hart's arguments for helping the Serbs is that "a loose Serbian hegemony in the region would make a wider conflict less likely." The second one is that "a strong Orthodox Serbia would undoubtedly act as a bulwark against any Islamic incursion into western Europe."

42. Wyatt, "The Dangers of Being Idealistic," *Spectator,* January 18, 1997, 10.

43. Finkielkraut, *Comment peut-on être Croate?* 110–11.

44. István Bibó, *A keleteurópai kisállamok nyomorúsága* (Budapest: Új Magyarország kiadása, 1946), 81.

45. The Treaty of Sèvres, drawn up in 1920 to arrange the disposition of the Ottoman Empire, provided for an autonomous Kurdistan but was never ratified; it was superseded by the Treaty of Lausanne (1923), which

made no mention of Kurdistan or of the Kurds. In fact, the Kurds were more fragmented after the war than before. In 1991 U.S. President George Bush, whose major foreign-policy principle—no new nation-states—made Serbian aggression possible, decided not to overthrow Saddam Hussein partly in order to preserve multinational Iraq (patched together, at the same time as Yugoslavia, out of the ruins of the Ottoman Empire) and prevent the formation of a Kurdish state.

46. Daniele Conversi, "Moral Relativism and Equidistance in British Attitudes to the War in the Former Yugoslavia," in Cushman and Meštrović, *This Time We Knew,* 259.

47. Here again the British case has been documented best. Concrete instances of the successes of the Serbian lobby in the political and moral vacuum of John Major's administration are presented by David Leigh and Ed Vulliamy in *Sleaze: The Corruption of Parliament* (London: Fourth Estate, 1997), 109–21.

48. Bosnia's Muslims and Christians provided many top officials in the Ottoman Empire.

49. An even more striking example of the effect of indifference is offered by the Armenians. British politicians refused to give them their own state when they cut up the Ottoman Empire after World War I, in spite of the Turkish massacres of hundreds of thousands of Armenians during that war. Joseph Stalin, on the other hand, gave the Soviet Armenians their own republic within the Soviet Union in 1936. The difference was due to the fact that Soviet Armenians were Stalin's own citizens, and he intended to increase the stability of his empire by giving them a homeland; to the British the Turkish Armenians were a faraway people whose fate did not interest them.

50. Almond, *Europe's Backyard War,* 51. Germany's *Ostpolitik* included the cultivation of good relations with Belgrade. In September 1983 an FRG president went further than any other visiting Western statesman in pleasing his Yugoslav hosts: he visited the Sarajevo museum that celebrated the 1918 assassination of the heir to the Habsburg throne.

51. As far as the latter are concerned, the extent and quality of the coverage of communist Yugoslavia by the *Frankfurter Allgemeine Zeitung* was not matched by any other newspaper.

52. Germany's intensive business ties with Eastern Europe were an important source of knowledge of that part of the world. According to OECD data about trade with former Soviet bloc countries in 1990, quoted by Lellouche (*Le nouveau monde,* 529), the FRG exported to Poland goods

worth 15.9 billion French francs; the exports by France and the United Kingdom amounted to 2.2 billion each. There was a similar disparity in the trade with other Eastern European countries, which fed fears of Germany's power.

53. Ecumenical efforts at bridging the gap between Orthodoxy and Catholicism were vigorously pursued by south Slav Catholics for a long time. Particularly active in this regard were the Croatian Jesuit Juraj Križanić (1618–83) and Bishop Josip Juraj Strossmayer (1815–1905). The latter's strong opposition to the proclamation of the dogma of papal infallibility at the First Vatican Council in 1869–70 was a manifestation of his consistent efforts to bridge the gap between the two churches. In 1851 the Slovenian Bishop Anton Martin Slomšek founded the Brotherhood of Saints Cyril and Methodius, which actively worked toward a union with Orthodox Christians. It counted seventy-five thousand members by 1863.

54. Albert Wohlstetter, "Genocide by Mediation," *New York Times,* March 3, 1994, A21.

55. The American ambassador in Belgrade at the time the war started, Warren Zimmermann, voiced such an accusation: "it was the Slovenes who started the war." "The Last Ambassador: A Memoir of the Collapse of Yugoslavia," *Foreign Affairs*, March–April 1995, 12.

56. Conversi, *German-Bashing,* offers an elaborate analysis of that myth.

57. Baker's main advisors on decisions affecting the former Yugoslavia were the acting secretary of state, Lawrence Eagleburger, and the national security advisor Brent Scowcroft, both of whom had served in Belgrade and learned Serbian. But close exposure to an area, as Professor Albert Lord proved, does not necessarily contribute to the sound knowledge of it. It is much easier, and sometimes profitable, to accept the myths dear to the dominant group than to learn the complex reality of a country too heterogeneous to survive. A poignant example of how diplomatic service in Yugoslavia could result in a monumental ignorance about that country was offered by the UN negotiator and former Norwegian foreign minister Thorvald Stoltenberg, to whom Noel Malcolm mockingly conferred "the Lenin Prize for outstanding contribution to useful idiocy." In a speech in Oslo in May 1995, the former Norwegian ambassador to Yugoslavia said, among other nonsense, that the entire population of Bosnia was Serb: "The whole lot of them are Serbs. So are the Muslims. They are in fact Serbs who converted to Islam. And a great many of those who dress like Croats, who present themselves as Croats, are in fact also Serbs."

Noel Malcolm, "The Whole Lot of Them Are Serbs," *Spectator*, June 10, 1995, 18.

58. *Der Spiegel* and the *Süddeutsche Zeitung* are two major German newspapers that have repeatedly blamed the German government for the war in the former Yugoslavia. The latter also published Peter Handke's travelogue, published in English as *A Journey to the Rivers: Justice for Serbia*, where the famous Austrian playwright portrays the Serbs as innocent victims.

59. James J. Sadkovich, "The Former Yugoslavia, the End of the Nuremberg Era, and the New Barbarism," in Cushman and Meštrović, *This Time We Knew*, 284. About the devastating consequences of bureaucratic indifference, see also Michael N. Barnett, "The Politics of Indifference at the United Nations and Genocide in Rwanda and Bosnia," in Cushman and Meštrović, *This Time We Knew*, 128–62; and Michael Hertzfeld, *The Social Production of Indifference: Exploring the Symbolic Roots of Western Bureaucracy* (Chicago: University of Chicago Press, 1993).

60. Blaine Harden, "Bosnia-Hercegovina on the Brink," *Washington Post*, January 15, 1992, A17. The Serbs in Bosnia-Herzegovina proclaimed their own republic on January 9, 1992.

61. Quoted in "Method to the Madness," *Decision Brief* (Washington: Center for Security Policy), October 2, 1992, 3.

62. Robert Kaplan, *Balkan Ghosts: A Journey through History* (New York: St. Martin's, 1993), xxii. A reviewer, Henry R. Cooper, Jr., gave the following assessment of Kaplan's work: "unintimidated by his ignorance of local languages and history, he has cobbled together *Balkan Ghosts*, a dreadful mix of unfounded generalizations, misinformation, outdated sources, personal prejudices and bad writing." *Slavic Review*, fall 1993, 592. Except for "bad writing," this characterization fits West's *Black Lamb and Grey Falcon* as well.

63. Victoria Glendinning, *Rebecca West: A Life* (New York: Knopf, 1987), 165.

64. West, *Black Lamb and Grey Falcon*, 68.

65. *Crno jagnje i sivi soko* (Belgrade: BIGZ; Sarajevo: Svjetlost, 1989).

66. Testimony before the U.S. House Armed Services Committee, May 26, 1993.

67. Quoted in Daniel Williams, "General Rose's Mission: Recoup Pre-Bosnia Bloom," *Washington Post*, February 5, 1995, A3.

68. The settlement of large numbers of Muslim refugees from eastern

Bosnia in territories that had been inhabited predominantly by Croats also contributed to the tension between the two communities.

69. Malcolm, *Bosnia*, 241.

NOTES TO THE CONCLUSION

1. See Chris Hedges, "Fierce Serb Nationalism Pervades Student Foes of Belgrade Leader," *New York Times,* December 10, 1996, A1.

2. In October he finished first in the runoff presidential election, but the election was voided, ostensibly because of the low voter turnout. In the second runoff election in December he officially won 37.24 percent of the votes.

3. *Javnost* (Pale), November 1, 1997, 36.

4. "A Call for Sacrifice: The Co-Responsibility of the West," *Foreign Affairs* 73, no. 2 (March–April 1994): 3–4.

5. Isaiah Berlin, "On Political Judgment," *New York Review of Books,* October 3, 1996, 27.

6. Charles L. Mee Jr., *Playing God: Seven Fateful Moments when Great Men Met to Change the World* (New York: Simon and Schuster, 1993), 16.

7. The Ottoman tolerance extended only to the religions "of the Book," that is, to revealed monotheistic religions such as Judaism and Christianity. It was based on the respect for their own "Book" and on the awareness of its link with its predecessors.

Selected Bibliography

Alexander, Stella. *The Triple Myth: A Life of Archbishop Alojzije Stepinac.* Boulder: East European Monographs, 1987.

Allen, Beverly. *Rape Warfare: The Hidden Genocide in Bosnia-Herzegovina and Croatia.* Minneapolis: University of Minnesota Press, 1996.

Almond, Mark. *Europe's Backyard War: The War in the Balkans.* Rev. and updated ed. London: Mandarin, 1994.

Banac, Ivo. *The National Question in Yugoslavia: Origins, History, Politics.* Ithaca: Cornell University Press, 1984.

Bećković, Matija. *Reče mi jedan čoek.* Belgrade: Prosveta, 1970.

———. *Međa Vuka Manitoga.* Belgrade: Srpska književna zadruga, 1976.

Behschnitt, Wolf Dietrich. *Nationalismus bei Serben und Kroaten 1830–1914.* Munich: Oldenbourg, 1980.

Bennett, Christopher. *Yugoslavia's Bloody Collapse: Causes, Course and Consequences.* New York: New York University Press, 1995.

Berdyaev, Nicholas. *Dostoevsky.* New York: Meridian, 1957.

Blaskovich, Jerry. *Anatomy of Deceit: An American Physician's First-Hand Account of the Realities of the War in Croatia.* New York: Dunhill, 1997.

Boehm, Christopher. *Montenegrin Social Organization and Values: Political Ethnography of a Refuge Area Tribal Adaptation.* New York: AMS Press, 1983.

———. *Blood Revenge: The Anthropology of Feuding in Montenegro and Other Tribal Societies.* Lawrence: University of Kansas Press, 1984.

Bojović, Boško I. "Historiographie dynastique et idéologie politique en Serbie au Bas Moyen Age." *Südost-Forschungen* 51 (1992): 29–49.

Bonazza, Sergio. "Bartholomäus Kopitar: Versuch einer kritischen Würdigung." *Die Welt der Slaven* (Munich) 40 (1995): 285–303.

Bracewell, Catherine Wendy. *The Uskoks of Senj: Piracy, Banditry, and Holy War in the Sixteenth-Century Adriatic.* Ithaca: Cornell University Press, 1992.

Braun, Maximilian. *Kosovo: Die Schlacht auf dem Amselfelde in geschicht-licher und epischer Überlieferung.* Leipzig: Markert und Petters, 1937.

———. *Das serbokroatische Heldenlied.* Göttingen: Vandenhoeck und Ruprecht, 1961.

Bremer, Thomas. *Ekklesiale Struktur und Ekklesiologie in der Serbischen Orthodoxen Kirche im 19. und 20. Jahrhundert.* Würzburg: Augustinus, 1992.

Brkić, Jovan. *Moral Concepts in Traditional Serbian Epic Poetry.* 'S-Gravenhage: Mouton, 1961.

Brković, Jevrem. *Glosarij.* Zagreb: Aurora, 1996.

Brodsky, Joseph. *Less Than One.* New York: Farrar, Straus, and Giroux, 1986.

Bulatović, Radomir. *Koncentracioni logor Jasenovac s posebnim osvrtom na Donju Gradinu.* Sarajevo: Svjetlost, 1990.

Čajkanović, Veselin. *O srpskom vrhovnom bogu.* Belgrade: Serbian Royal Academy, 1941.

The Cambridge Medieval History. Vol. 4, *The Eastern Roman Empire (717–1453).* Cambridge: Cambridge University Press, 1927.

Cerović, Rajko. *Svjetlosti i sjenke jedne tradicije.* Nikšić: UR, 1986.

Cerović, Stanko. *Njegoševe tajne staze.* Podgorica: Montenegropublic, 1996.

Cigar, Norman. *Genocide in Bosnia: The Policy of "Ethnic Cleansing."* College Station: Texas A&M University Press, 1995.

Ćirković, Sima. *Kosovska bitka kao istorijski problem.* Novi Sad: Vojvodinian Academy of Sciences and Arts, 1992.

Cohen, Leonard J. 1993. *Broken Bonds: The Disintegration of Yugoslavia.* Boulder: Westview, 1993.

Cohen, Philip J. *Serbia's Secret War: Propaganda and the Deceit of History.* College Station: Texas A&M University Press, 1996.

Čolović, Ivan. *Bordel ratnika: Folklor, politika i rat.* Belgrade: Biblioteka XX vek, 1993.

Čolović, Ivan, and Aljoša Mimica, eds. *Druga Srbija.* Belgrade: Plato, Beogradski krug, Borba, 1992.

Conversi, Daniele. *German-Bashing and the Breakup of Yugoslavia.* Seattle: HMJ School of International Studies of the University of Washington, Donald W. Treadgold Papers in Russian, East European, and Central Asian Studies, no. 16, 1998.

Ćosić, Dobrica. *Deobe.* Belgrade: Prosveta, 1963.

———. *Srpsko pitanje—Demokratsko pitanje.* Belgrade: Politika, Stručna knjiga, 1992.

Čović, Bože, ed. *Izvori velikosrpske agresije: Rasprave, dokumenti, kartografski prikazi*. Zagreb: A. Cesarec, Školska knjiga, 1991.

Crnjanski, Miloš. *Sabrane pesme*. Belgrade: Srpska književna zadruga, 1978.

Cushman, Thomas, and Stjepan G. Meštrović, eds. *This Time We Knew: Western Responses to Genocide in Bosnia*. New York: New York University Press, 1996.

Cvijić, Jovan. *La péninsule balkanique: Géographie humaine*. Paris: A. Colin, 1918.

Dedijer, Vladimir. *The Road to Sarajevo*. London: MacGibbon and Kee, 1967.

———. *Veliki buntovnik Milovan Đilas: Prilozi za biografiju*. Belgrade: Prosveta, 1991.

"Deklaracija protiv genocida nad srpskim narodom: Oglašavanje o Vaskrsu." *Vreme* (Belgrade), April 26, 1997: 22.

Despalatovic, Elinor Murray. *Ljudevit Gaj and the Illyrian Movement*. Boulder: East European Monographs, 1975.

Đilas, Aleksa, ed. *Srpsko pitanje*. Belgrade: Politika, 1991.

Djilas, Milovan. *Land without Justice*. New York: Harcourt, Brace and Company, 1958.

———. *Njegoš: Poet, Prince, Bishop*. Trans. Michael B. Petrovich. New York: Harcourt, Brace and World, 1966.

———. *Wartime*. New York: Harcourt Brace Jovanovich, 1977.

Đorđević, Tihomir R. *Iz Srbije kneza Miloša: Kulturne prilike od 1815 do 1839 godine*. Belgrade: Geca Kon, 1922.

———. *Naš narodni život*. Belgrade: Srpska književna zadruga, 1923.

Drašković, Vuk. *Nož*. Belgrade: Zapis, 1982.

———. *Molitva*. 2 vols. Belgrade: Nova knjiga, 1985.

———. *Noć đenerala*. Belgrade: Srpska reč, 1994.

Ducellier, Alain. *Le drame de Byzance: Idéal et échec d'une société chrétienne*. Paris: Hachette, 1976.

Đukić, Slavoljub. *Čovek u svom vremenu: Razgovori sa Dobricom Ćosićem*. Belgrade: Višnjić, 1989.

Đuretić, Veselin, ed. *Kosovska bitka 1389. godine i njene posledice*. Belgrade: Serbian Academy of Sciences and Arts, Special Editions, vol. 44, 1991.

Đurić, Vojislav. Foreword to Dositej Obradović, *Izabrani spisi*. Novi Sad: Matica srpska, 1989.

———, ed. *Kosovski boj u srpskoj književnosti*. Belgrade: Srpska književna zadruga; Novi Sad: Matica srpska; Priština: Jedinstvo, 1990.

Dvorniković, Vladimir. *Karakterologija Jugoslovena*. Belgrade: Geca Kon, 1939.

Elias, Norbert. *The Germans: Power Struggles and the Development of Habitus in the Nineteenth and Twentieth Centuries*. Trans. Eric Dunning and Stephen Mennell. New York: Columbia University Press, 1996.

Emmert, Thomas A. "Kosovo: Development and Impact of a National Ethic." In *Nation and Ideology: Essays in Honor of Wayne S. Vucinich*, ed. Ivo Banac et al. Boulder: East European Monographs, 1981.

————. *Serbian Golgotha: Kosovo, 1389*. Boulder: East European Monographs, 1990.

Fine, John V. A. Jr. *The Late Medieval Balkans: A Critical Survey from the Late Twelfth Century to the Ottoman Conquest*. Ann Arbor: University of Michigan Press, 1987.

Finkielkraut, Alain. *Comment peut-on être Croate?* Paris: Gallimard, 1992.

Fromm, Erich. *The Anatomy of Human Destructiveness*. New York: Holt, Rinehart and Winston, 1973.

Garde, Paul. *Vie et mort de la Yougoslavie*. Paris: Fayard, 1992.

Gesemann, Gerhard. *Heroische Lebensform: Zur Literatur und Wesenskunde der balkanischen Patriarchalität*. Berlin: Wiking, 1943.

Gow, James. *Legitimacy and the Military: The Yugoslav Crisis*. New York: St. Martin's, 1992.

Graubard, Stephen R., ed. *Eastern Europe... Central Europe... Europe*. Boulder: Westview, 1991.

Grmek, Mirko, Marc Gjidara, and Neven Simac, eds. *Le nettoyage ethnique: Documents historiques sur une idéologie serbe*. Paris: Fayard, 1993.

Gutman, Roy. *A Witness to Genocide*. New York: Macmillan, 1993.

Hadrovics, László. *Le peuple serbe et son église sous la domination turque*. Paris: Presses universitaires de France, 1947.

Hall, Brian. *The Impossible Country: A Journey through the Last Days of Yugoslavia*. Boston: Godine, 1994.

————. "Rebecca West's War." *New Yorker*, April 15, 1996, 74–83.

Hehn, Paul N. "The Origins of Modern Pan-Serbism: The 1844 Načertanije of Ilija Garašanin: An Analysis and Translation." *East European Quarterly* 9, no. 2 (1975): 153–71.

Jelavich, Charles. *South Slav Nationalisms: Textbooks and Yugoslav Union before 1914*. Columbus: Ohio University Press, 1990.

Jevtić, Atanasije. *Od Kosova do Jadovna*. Belgrade: Jevtić, 1984.

————. *Velikomučenički Jasenovac: Ustaška tvornica smrti*. Valjevo: Glas crkve; Belgrade: Sfairos, 1990.

————. *Sveti Sava i Kosovski zavet*. Belgrade: Srpska književna zadruga, 1992.

Judah, Tim. *The Serbs: History, Myth, and the Destruction of Yugoslavia*. New Haven: Yale University Press, 1997.

Karadžić, Radovan. *Pamtivek*. Sarajevo: Svjetlost, 1971.

————. *Crna bajka*. Sarajevo: Svjetlost, 1990.

Karadžić, Vuk Stefanović. *Srpske narodne pjesme*. 4 vols. Vienna, 1841–62.

————. *Kovčežić za istoriju, jezik i običaje Srba sva tri zakona*. Vienna, 1849.

Kaser, Karl. *Hirten, Kämpfer, Stammeshelden: Ursprünge und Gegenwart des balkanischen Patriarchats*. Vienna: Böhlau, 1992.

————. *Familie und Verwandschaft auf dem Balkan: Analyse einer untergehenden Kultur*. Vienna: Böhlau, 1995.

Kočović, Bogoljub. *Žrtve drugog svetskog rata u Jugoslaviji*. London: Naše delo, 1985.

Koljević, Svetozar. *The Epic in the Making*. Oxford: Clarendon, 1980.

Komnenić, Milan. *Kosovski polom*. Šabac: Glas crkve, 1988.

Konstantinović, Radomir. *Filosofija palanke*. Belgrade: Nolit, 1981.

Kressel, Neil J. *Mass Hate: The Global Rise of Genocide and Terror*. New York: Plenum, 1996.

Laffan, Robert G. D. *The Guardians of the Gate: Historical Lectures on the Serbs*. Oxford: Clarendon, 1918.

Laqueur, Walter. *Black Hundred: The Rise of the Extreme Right in Russia*. New York: HarperCollins, 1993.

Le Goff, Jacques. *History and Memory*. Trans. Steven Rendall and Elisabeth Claman. New York: Columbia University Press, 1992.

Lellouche, Pierre. *Le nouveau monde*. Paris: Grasset, 1992.

Libal, Wolfgang. *Die Serben: Blüte, Wahn, und Katastrophe*. Munich: Europaverlag, 1996.

Low, David H., trans. *The Ballads of Marko Kraljević*. 1922. Reprint, New York: Greenwood, 1968.

Lubarda, Vojislav. *Gordo posrtanje*. Rijeka: Keršovani, 1970.

————. *Preobraženje*. Zagreb: Naprijed, 1979.

————. *Pokajanje*. 2 vols. Belgrade: Književne novine, 1987.

————. *Vaznesenje*. Gornji Milanovac: Dečje novine, 1989.

————. *Srpska bespuća: Književnopolitički ogledi*. Belgrade: Književne novine, 1993.

Magaš, Branka. *The Destruction of Yugoslavia: Tracing the Break-Up, 1980–92*. London: Verso, 1993.

Malcolm, Noel. *De Dominis (1560–1624): Venetian, Anglican, Ecumenist and Relapsed Heretic.* London: Strickland and Scott, 1984.

———. *Bosnia: A Short History.* New York: New York University Press, 1994.

———. *Kosovo: A Short History.* New York: New York University Press, 1998.

Mango, Cyril. *Byzantium: The Empire of New Rome.* London: Weidenfeld and Nicolson, 1980.

Medaković, V. M. G. *Život i običai Crnogoraca.* Novi Sad, 1860.

Meier, Viktor. *Wie Jugoslawien verspielt wurde.* Munich: Beck, 1995.

Memorandum (of Serbian Academy of Sciences and Arts). In Čović, *Izvori velikosrpske agresije.*

Meštrović, Stjepan C., ed. *Genocide after Emotion: The Postemotional Balkan War.* London: Routledge, 1996.

Mićunović, Veljko. *Moscow Diary.* Garden City, N.J.: Doubleday, 1980.

Mihailović, Konstantin. *Janičarove uspomene ili turska hronika.* Trans. Đorđe Živanović. Belgrade: Prosveta, 1966.

Milazzo, Matteo J. *The Chetnik Movement and the Yugoslav Resistance.* Baltimore: Johns Hopkins University Press, 1975.

Minčeta, Luka, and Marinko Vučinić, eds. *Srbi i demokratija.* Belgrade: Vidici-Dosije, 1992.

Moszyński, Leszek. *Die vorchristliche Religion der Slaven im Lichte der slavischen Sprachwissenschaft.* Cologne: Böhlau, 1992.

Myers, Paul F., and Arthur Campbell. *The Population of Yugoslavia.* Washington, D.C.: U.S. Government Printing Office, 1954.

Nikolić, Radojko. *Kamena knjiga predaka.* Belgrade: Zadruga, 1979.

Njegoš, Petar II Petrović. *Gorski vijenac: Istoričesko sobitije pri svršetku XVII vijeka.* Vienna, 1847.

Noyes, George R., and Leonard Bacon, trans. *Heroic Ballads of Servia.* Boston: Sherman, French and Company, 1913.

Obradović, Dositej. *Pismo Haralampiju; Život i priključenija.* Belgrade: Prosveta, 1968.

———. *Izabrani spisi.* Novi Sad: Matica srpska, 1989.

"The Pact of London." *American Journal of International Law, Supplement,* vol. 13 (1919): 436–40.

Parrott, Cecil. *The Tightrope.* London: Faber and Faber, 1975.

Pavić, Milorad. *Dictionary of the Khazars: A Lexicon Novel in 100,000 Words.* New York: Knopf, 1988.

Peršen, Mirko. *Ustaški logori.* Zagreb: Globus, 1990.

Petrovich, Michael B. *A History of Modern Serbia, 1804–1976.* 2 vols. New York: Harcourt, Brace, Jovanovich, 1976.

Pilar, Ivo [Südland, pseud.]. *Die südslawische Frage und der Weltkrieg.* Vienna: Manz, 1918.

Popov, Nebojša. "Le populisme serbe." *Les Temps Modernes* 49, no. 573 (1994): 22–62; no. 574 (1994): 22–84.

Popović, Justin. *Pravoslavna crkva i ekumenizam.* Salonika: Hilandar Monastery Edition, 1974.

———. *Dostojevski o Evropi i slovenstvu.* 1940. Reprint, Belgrade: Ćelije Monastery, 1981.

———. *Filosofske urvine.* 1957. Reprint, Belgrade: Ćelije Monastery, 1987.

Popović, Miodrag. *Vidovdan i časni krst: Ogled iz književne arheologije.* 2d ed. Belgrade: Slovo ljubve, 1977.

Popović-Obradović, Olga. "Zablude o 'zlatnom dobu.'" *Republika* (Belgrade), May 1–15, 1995: 14–16.

Potthoff, Wilfried, ed. *Vuk Karadžić im europäischen Kontext.* Heidelberg: Winter, 1990.

Pozzi, Henri. *Black Hand over Europe.* Zagreb: CIC, 1994. (Reprint of Francis J. Mott's 1935 translation of *La guerre revient.*)

"Predlog srpskog crkvenonacionalnog programa." *Glas crkve* (Šabac) 17, no. 3 (1989): 3–11.

Pribićević [Pribitchévitch], Svetozar. *La dictature du roi Alexandre.* Paris: Bossuet, 1933.

Radulović, Jovan. *Golubnjača.* Belgrade: BIGZ, 1981.

Ramet, Sabrina P. "The Catholic Church in Yugoslavia, 1945–1989." In *Catholicism and Politics in Communist Societies.* Vol. 2. Durham: Duke University Press, 1990.

———. "The Albanians of Kosovo: The Potential for Destabilization." *Brown Journal of World Affairs* 3, issue 1 (1996): 353–72.

———. *Balkan Babel: The Disintegration of Yugoslavia from the Death of Tito to Ethnic War.* 2d ed. Boulder: Westview, 1996.

Ranke, Leopold. *A History of Servia and the Servian Revolution.* 1848. Reprint, New York: Da Capo Press, 1973.

Rendić Miočević, Ivo. *Zlo velike jetre: Povijest i nepovijest Crnogoraca, Hrvata, Muslimana i Srba.* Split: Književni krug, 1996.

Rieff, David. *Slaughterhouse: Bosnia and the Failure of the West.* New York: Simon and Schuster, 1995.

Rizvić, Muhsin. *Kroz "Gorski vijenac": Interpretacija i tekstualno-komparativna studija o strukturi.* Sarajevo: Svjetlost, 1985.

Rohde, David. *Endgame: The Betrayal and Fall of Srebrenica: Europe's Worst Massacre since World War Two.* New York: Farrar, Strauss, and Giroux, 1997.

Sells, Michael A. *The Bridge Betrayed: Religion and Genocide in Bosnia.* Berkeley: University of California Press, 1996.

Šipovac, Neđo. *Proljeće na jugu.* Sarajevo: Svjetlost, 1982.

————. *Ljeto na gori, 1941.* Sarajevo: Masleša, 1987.

————. *Biskupov dnevnik –41.* Sarajevo: Masleša, 1989.

Soloviev, Vladimir. *Russia and the Universal Church.* Trans. Herbert Rees. London: Bles, 1948.

Srejović, Dragoslav, ed. *Bitka na Kosovu 1389. godine.* Belgrade: Serbian Academy of Sciences and Arts; Historical Museum of Serbia; BIGZ, 1989.

Stanojević, Stanoje. *Istorija srpskoga naroda.* 3d ed. Belgrade: Napredak, 1926.

————. *Sveti Sava.* 1935. Reprint, Niš: Gradina, 1991.

Štefan, Ljubica. *Srpska pravoslavna crkva i fašizam.* Zagreb: Globus, 1996.

Stiglmayer, Alexandra, ed. *Mass Rape: The War against Women in Bosnia-Herzegovina.* Trans. Marion Faber. Lincoln: University of Nebraska Press, 1994.

Sunley, Jonathan. "Sold on Serbia: Anatomy of a Strange British Attraction." *Bosnia Report* (London), no. 16 (1996): 15–17.

Terzić, Velimir. *Jugoslavija u aprilskom ratu 1941.* Titograd: Grafički zavod, 1963.

Thompson, Mark. *A Paper House: The Ending of Yugoslavia.* New York: Pantheon, 1992.

————. *Forging War: The Media in Serbia, Croatia and Bosnia-Hercegovina.* London: Article 19, 1994.

Tomasevich, Jozo. *War and Revolution in Yugoslavia, 1941–1945: The Chetniks.* Stanford: Stanford University Press, 1975.

Tomasic, Dinko A. *Personality and Culture in Eastern European Politics.* New York: G. W. Stewart, 1948.

Trifunović, Đorđe. *Srpski srednjovekovni spisi o knezu Lazaru i kosovskom boju.* Kruševac: Bagdala, 1968.

Tuchman, Barbara W. *A Distant Mirror: The Calamitous Fourteenth Century.* New York: Knopf, 1978.

Van Dartel, Geert. *Ćirilometodska ideja i svetosavlje.* Zagreb: Kršćanska sadašnjost, 1984.

————. "The Nations and the Churches in Yugoslavia." *Religion, State and Society* 20, nos. 3–4 (1992): 275–88.

Velimirović, Nikolaj. *Religija Njegoševa*. 5th ed. Belgrade: Cvijanović, 1921.

————. *Nacionalizam svetoga Save*. Belgrade: Association of the Serbian Orthodox Clergy of the Belgrade-Karlovci Eparchy, 1935.

————. *Govori srpskom narodu—kroz tamnički prozor*. Himmelsthür: Serbian Orthodox Eparchy for Western Europe, 1985.

————. *Kosovo i Vidovdan*. 3d ed., Šabac: Glas crkve and Hilandar Monastery, 1988.

Vulliamy, Ed. *Seasons in Hell: Understanding Bosnia's War*. New York: St. Martin's, 1994.

West, Rebecca. *Black Lamb and Grey Falcon: A Journey through Yugoslavia*. New York: Viking, 1964.

Wyatt, Petronella. "The Dangers of Being Idealistic about the Balkans." *Spectator*, January 18, 1997, 10.

Yakunin, Gleb. "The Moscow Patriarchate and Stalin's Cult of Personality." *Glasnost* (Moscow), March–May 1989, 8–15.

Žanić, Ivo. *Prevarena povijest: Guslarska estrada, kult hajduka i rat u Hrvatskoj i Bosni i Hercegovini 1990–1995. godine*. Zagreb: Durieux, 1998.

Žerjavić, Vladimir. *Population Losses in Yugoslavia, 1941–1945*. Trans. Lidija Šimunić Mesić. Zagreb: Hrvatski institut za povijest; Dom i svijet, 1997.

Index